Cetywayo And His White Neighbours

Or, Remarks On Recent Events In Zululand, Natal, And The Transvaal

by

H. Rider Haggard

Double 9
BOOKS

Cetywayo And His White Neighbours
Or, Remarks On Recent Events
In Zululand, Natal, And The Transvaal
by H. Rider Haggard

ISBN: 978-93-57486-22-4

Published by

DOUBLE 9 BOOKS
2/13-B, Ansari Road
Daryaganj, New Delhi – 110002
info@double9books.com
www.double9books.com
Tel. 011-40042856

ABOUT THE AUTHOR

H. Rider Haggard was born on 22 June, 1856 in Braden ham, situated in the English area of Norfolk. His father, Sir William Meybohm Rider Haggard, was a lawyer, while his mother, Ella Dove ton Haggard, was an author herself. The couple had ten children, out of which Henry was conceived as the eighth. Sir Henry Rider Haggard was an English author who was known for his African thriller novel, 'Lord Solomon's Mines'. His father was a Norfolk advocate but he was denied an honourable men's schooling compared to his siblings due to his physical bluntness. At 19 years old, he started his vocation at the command of his father as an unpaid guide to Lieutenant-Governor of the Colony of Natal. Rider Haggard was married to a Norfolk beneficiary Marianna Louisa Margitson. They had four children named Jack, who died at the age of 10 due to measles, and three girls named Angela, Dorothy, and Lilias. Rider Haggard died at the age of 68 in London. His remains were cremated at St Mary's Church, Ditchingham. A rail route point of the Canadian National Railway in British Columbia has been named after him.

CONTENTS

INTRODUCTION

The writer on Colonial Affairs is naturally, to some extent, discouraged by the knowledge that the subject is an unattractive one to a large proportion of the reading public. It is difficult to get up anything beyond a transient interest in the affairs of our Colonial dependencies; indeed, I believe that the mind of the British public was more profoundly moved by the exodus of Jumbo, than it would be were one of them to become the scene of some startling catastrophe. This is the more curious, inasmuch as, putting aside all sentimental considerations, which indeed seem to be out of harmony with the age we live in: the trade done, even with such comparatively insignificant colonies as our South African possessions, amounts to a value of many millions of pounds sterling per annum. Now, as the preachers of the new gospel that hails from Birmingham and Northampton have frequently told us, trade is the life-blood of England, and must be fostered at any price. It is therefore surprising that, looking on them in the light of a commercial speculation, in which aspect (saith the preacher) they are alone worthy of notice, a keener interest is not taken in the well-being and development of the Colonies. We have only to reflect to see how great are the advantages that the Mother Country derives from the possession of her Colonial Empire; including, as they do, a home for her surplus children, a vast and varied market for her productions, and a wealth of old-fashioned loyalty and deep attachment to the Old Country—"home," as it is always called—which, even if it is out of date, might prove useful on emergency. It seems therefore, almost a pity that some Right Honourable Gentlemen and their followers should adopt the tone they do with reference to the Colonies. After all, there is an odd shuffling of the cards going on now in England; and great as she is, her future looks by no means sunny. Events in these latter days develop themselves very quickly; and though the idea may, at the present moment, seem absurd, surely it is possible that, what between the rapid spread of Radical ideas, the enmity of

Ireland, the importation of foreign produce, and the competition of foreign trade, to say nothing of all the unforeseen accidents and risks of the future, the Englishmen of, say, two generations hence, may not find their country in her present proud position. Perhaps, and stranger things have happened in the history of the world, she may by that time be under the protection of those very Colonies for which their forefathers had such small affection.

The position of South Africa with reference to the Mother Country is somewhat different to that of her sister Colonies, in that she is regarded, not so much with apathy tinged with dislike, as with downright disgust. This feeling has its foundation in the many troubles and expenses in which this country has been recently involved, through local complications in the Cape, Zululand, and the Transvaal: and indeed is little to be wondered at. But, whilst a large portion of the press has united with a powerful party of politicians in directing a continuous stream of abuse on to the heads of the white inhabitants of South Africa, whom they do not scruple to accuse of having created the recent disturbances in order to reap a money profit from them: it does not appear to have struck anybody that the real root of this crop of troubles might, after all, be growing nearer home. The truth of the matter is, that native and other problems in South Africa have, till quite lately, been left to take their chance, and solve themselves as best they might; except when they have, in a casual manner, been made the *corpus vile* of some political experiment. It was during this long period of inaction, when each difficulty—such as the native question in Natal—was staved off to be dealt with by the next Government, that the seed was sown of which we are at present reaping the fruit. In addition to this, matters have recently been complicated by the elevation of South African affairs to the dignity of an English party question. Thus, the Transvaal Annexation was made use of as a war-cry in the last general election, a Boer rebellion was thereby encouraged, which resulted in a complete reversal of our previous policy.

Now, if there is any country dependent on England that requires the application to the conduct of its affairs of a firm, considered, and consistent policy, that country is South Africa. Boers and Natives are quite incapable of realising the political necessities of any of our parties, or of understanding why their true interests should be sacrificed in order to minister to those necessities. It is our wavering and uncertain policy, as applied to peoples, who look upon every hesitating step as a sign of fear and failing dominion, that, in conjunction with previous postponement and neglect, has really caused our troubles in South Africa. For so long as the affairs of that country are influenced by amateurs and sentimentalists, who have no real interest in it, and whose knowledge of its circumstances and conditions of life is gleaned from a few blue-books, superficially got up to enable the reader to indite theoretical articles to the "Nineteenth Century," or deliver inaccurate speeches in the House of Commons— for so long will those troubles continue.

If I may venture to make a suggestion, the affairs of South Africa should be controlled by a Board or Council, like that which formerly governed India, composed of moderate members of both parties, with an admixture of men possessing practical knowledge of the country. I do not know if any such arrangement would be possible under our constitution, but the present system of government, by which the control of savage races fluctuates in obedience of every variation of English party politics, is most mischievous in its results.

The public, however, is somewhat tired of South Africa, and the reader may, perhaps, wonder why he should be troubled with more literature on the subject. I can assure him that these pages are not written in order to give me an opportunity of airing my individual experiences or ideas. Their object is shortly—(1.) To give a true history of the events attendant on the Annexation of the Transvaal, which act has so frequently been assigned to the most unworthy motives, and has never yet been fairly described by any one who was in a position to know the facts; (2.) To throw as much publicity as possible on the present disgraceful state of Zululand, resulting from our recent settlement in that country; (3.) To show all interested in the Kafir races what has been the character of our recent surrender in the Transvaal, and what its effect will be on our abandoned native subjects living in that country.

It may, perhaps, seem an odd statement, considering that I have lived in various parts of South Africa for about six years, and have, perhaps, enjoyed exceptional advantage in forming my opinions, when I say that my chief fear in publishing the present volume, is lest my knowledge of my subject in all its bearings should not be really equal to the task. It is, I know, the fashion to treat South African difficulties as being simple of solution. Thus it only took Sir Garnet Wolseley a few weeks to understand the whole position of Zulu affairs, and to execute his memorable settlement of that country: whilst eminent writers appear to be able, in scampering from Durban *via* Kimberley to Cape Town in a post-cart, to form decided opinions upon every important question in South Africa. The power of thus rapidly assimilating intricate knowledge, and of seeing straight through a wall whilst ordinary individuals are still criticising the bricks, is no doubt one of the peculiar privileges of genius—which is, perhaps fortunately for South Africa—rare. To the common run of mind, however, the difficulty of forming a sound and accurate judgment on the interlacing problems that disclose themselves to the student of the politics of South-Eastern Africa, is exceedingly great and the work of years.

But although it is by no means perfect, I think that my knowledge of these problems and of their imminent issues is sufficiently intimate to justify me in making a prophecy—namely, that unless the native and other questions of South-Eastern Africa are treated with more honest intelligence, and on a more settled plan than it has hitherto been thought necessary to apply to them, the British taxpayer will find that he has *by no means* heard the last of that country and its wars.

There is one more point to which, although it hardly comes within the scope of this volume, I have made some allusion, and which I venture to suggest deserves the consideration of thinking Englishmen. I refer to the question of the desirability of allowing the Dutch in South Africa, who are already numerically the strongest, to continue to advance with such rapid strides towards political supremacy. That the object of this party is to reduce Englishmen and English ideas to a subordinate position in the State, if not actually to rid itself of our rule and establish a republic, there is no manner of doubt. Indeed, there exists a powerful organisation, the Africander Bond, which has its headquarters in the Cape, and openly devotes its energies to forwarding these ends, by offering a sturdy opposition to the introduction of English emigrants and the use of the English language, whilst striving in every way to excite class prejudices and embitter the already strained relations between Englishman and Boer. In considering this question, it is as well not to lose sight of the fact that the Dutch are as a body, at heart hostile to our rule, chiefly because they cannot tolerate our lenient behaviour to the native races. Should they by any chance cease to be the subjects of England, they will, I believe, become her open enemies. This of itself would be comparatively unimportant, were it not for the fact that, in the event of the blocking of the Suez Canal, it would be, to say the least, inconvenient that the Cape should be in the hands of a hostile population.

In conclusion, I wish to state that this book is not written for any party purpose. I have tried to describe a state of affairs which has for the most part come under my own observation, and events in which I have been interested, and at times engaged. That the naked truths of such a business as the Transvaal surrender, or of the present condition of Zululand, are unpleasant reading for an Englishman, there is no doubt; but, so far as these pages are concerned, they owe none of their ugliness to undue colouring or political bias.

Windham Club, St. James' Square, June 1882.

CETYWAYO AND THE ZULU SETTLEMENT

Claims of affairs of Zululand to attention — Proposed visit of Cetywayo to England — Chaka — His method of government — His death — Dingaan — Panda — Battle of the Tugela — John Dunn — Nomination of Cetywayo — His coronation — His lady advocates — Their attacks on officials — Was Cetywayo bloodthirsty? — Cause of the Zulu war — Zulu military system — States of feeling amongst the Zulus previous to the war — Cetywayo's position — His enemies — His intentions on the Transvaal — Their frustration by Sir T. Shepstone — Cetywayo's interview with Mr. Fynney — His opinion of the Boers — The annexation in connection with the Zulu war — The Natal colonists and the Zulu war — Sir Bartle Frere — The Zulu war — Cetywayo's half-heartedness — Sir Garnet Wolseley's settlement — Careless selection of chiefs — The Sitimela plot — Chief John Dunn — Appointment of Mr. Osborn as British Resident — His difficult position — Folly and cruelty of our settlement — Disappointment of the Zulus — Object and result of settlement — Slaughter in Zululand — Cetywayo's son — Necessity of proper settlement of Zululand — Should Cetywayo be restored?

Zululand and the Zulu settlement still continue to receive some attention from the home public, partly because those responsible for the conduct of affairs are not quite at ease about it, and partly because of the agitation in this country for the restoration of Cetywayo.

There is no doubt that the present state of affairs in Zululand is a subject worthy of close consideration, not only by those officially connected with them, but by the public at large. Nobody, either at home or in the colonies, wishes to see another Zulu war, or anything approaching to it. Unless, however, the affairs of Zululand receive a little more attention, and are superintended with a little more humanity and intelligence than they are at present, the public will sooner or later be startled by some fresh catastrophe. Then will follow the usual outcry, and the disturbance will be attributed to every cause under the sun except the right one—want of common precautions.

The Zulu question is a very large one, and I only propose discussing so much of it as necessary to the proper consideration of the proposed restoration of Cetywayo to his throne.

The king is now coming to England,[*] where he will doubtless make a very good impression, since his appearance is dignified, and his manners, as is common among Zulus of high rank, are those of a gentleman. It is probable that his visit will lead to a popular agitation in his favour, and very possibly to an attempt on the part of the English Government to reinstate him in his kingdom. Already Lady Florence Dixie waves his banner, and informs the public through the columns of the newspapers how good, how big, and how beautiful he is, and "F. W. G. X." describes in enthusiastic terms his pearl-like teeth. But as there are interests involved in the question of his reinstatement which are, I think, more important than Cetywayo's personal proportions of mind or body, and as the results of such a step would necessarily be very marked and far-reaching, it is as well to try and understand the matter in all its bearing before anything is done.

[*] *Since the above was written the Government have at the last moment decided to postpone Cetywayo's visit to this country, chiefly on account of the political capital which was being made out of the event by agitators in Zululand.*

The project of bringing the king to England does not, however, appear to have been abandoned.

There has been a great deal of special pleading about Cetywayo. Some writers, swayed by sentiment, and that spirit of partisanship that the sight of royalty in distress always excites, whitewash him in such a persistent manner that their readers are left under the impression that the ex-king is a model of injured innocence and virtue. Others again, for political reasons, paint him very black, and predict that his restoration would result in the destruction, or at the least, disorganisation, of our South African empire. The truth in this, as in the majority of political controversies, lies somewhere between these two extremes, though it is difficult to say exactly where.

To understand the position of Cetywayo both with reference to his subjects and the English Government, it will be necessary to touch, though briefly, on the history of Zululand since it became a nation, and also on the principal events of the ex-king's reign.

Chaka, Cetywayo's great uncle, was the first Zulu king, and doubtless one of the most remarkable men that has ever filled a throne since the days of the Pharaohs. When he came to his chieftainship, about 1813, the Zulu people consisted of a single small tribe; when his throne became vacant in 1828, their name had become a living terror, and they were the greatest Black power in South Africa. The invincible armies of this African Attila had swept north and south, east and west, had slaughtered more than a million human beings, and added vast tracts of country to his dominions. Wherever his warriors went, the blood of men, women, and children was poured out without stay or stint; indeed he reigned like a visible Death, the presiding genius of a saturnalia of slaughter.

His methods of government and warfare were peculiar and somewhat drastic, but most effective. As he conquered a tribe, he enrolled its remnants in his army, so that they might in their turn help to conquer others. He armed his regiments with the short stabbing assegai, instead of the throwing assegai which they had been accustomed to use, and kept them subject to an iron discipline. If a man was observed to show the slightest hesitation about coming to close quarters with the enemy, he was executed as soon as the fight was over. If a regiment had the misfortune to be defeated, whether by its own fault or not, it would on its return to headquarters find that a goodly proportion of the wives and children belonging to it had been beaten to death by Chaka's orders, and that he was waiting their arrival to complete his vengeance by dashing out their brains. The result was, that though Chaka's armies were occasionally annihilated, they were rarely defeated, and they never ran away. I will not enter in the history of his numerous cruelties, and indeed they are not edifying. Amongst other things, like Nero, he killed his own mother, and then caused several persons to be executed because they did not show sufficient sorrow at her death.

At length, in 1828, he too suffered the fate he had meted out to so many, and was killed by his brothers, Dingaan and Umhlangan, by the hands of one Umbopa. He was murdered in his hut, and as his life passed out of him he is reported to have addressed these words to his brothers, who were watching his end: "What! do you stab me, my brothers, dogs of mine own house, whom I have fed? You hope to be kings; but though you do kill me, think not that your line shall reign for long. I tell you that I hear the sound of the feet of the great white people, and that this land shall be trodden by them." He then expired, but his last words have always been looked upon as a prophecy by the Zulus, and indeed they have been partly fulfilled.

Having in his turn killed Umhlangan, his brother by blood and in crime, Dingaan took possession of the throne. He was less pronounced than Chaka in his foreign policy, though he seems to have kept up the family reputation as regards domestic affairs. It was he who, influenced, perhaps, by Chaka's dying prophecy about white men, massacred Retief, the Boer leader, and his fifty followers, in the most treacherous manner, and then falling on the emigrant Boers in Natal, murdered men, women, and children to the number of nearly six hundred. There seems, however, to have been but little love lost between any of the sons of Usengangacona (the father of Chaka, Dingaan, Umhlangan, and Panda), for in due course Panda, his brother, conspired with the Boers against Dingaan, and overthrew him with their assistance. Dingaan fled, and was shortly afterwards murdered in Swaziland, and Panda ascended the throne in 1840.

Panda was a man of different character to the remainder of his race, and seems to have been well content to reign in peace, only killing enough people to keep up his authority. Two of his sons, Umbelazi and Cetywayo, of whom Umbelazi was the elder and Panda's favourite, began, as their father grew old, to quarrel about the succession to the crown. On the question being referred to Panda, he is reported to have remarked that when two young cocks quarrelled the best thing they could do was to fight it out. Acting on this hint, each prince collected his forces, Panda sending down one of his favourite regiments to help Umbelazi. The fight took place in 1856 on the banks of the Tugela. A friend of the writer, happening to be on the Natal side of the river the day before the battle, and knowing it was going to take place, swam his horse across in the darkness, taking his chance of the alligators, and hid in some bush on a hillock commanding the battlefield. It was a hazardous proceeding, but the sight repaid the risk, though he describes it as very awful, more especially when the regiment of veterans sent by Panda joined in the fray. It came up at the charge, between two and three thousand strong, and was met near his hiding-place by one of Cetywayo's young regiments. The noise of the clash of their shields was like the roar of the sea, but the old regiment, after a struggle in which men fell thick and fast, annihilated the other, and passed on with thinned ranks. Another of Cetywayo's regiments took the place of the one that had been destroyed, and this time the combat was fierce and long, till victory again declared for the veterans' spears. But they had brought it dear, and were in no position to continue their charge; so the leaders of that brave battalion formed its remnants into a ring, and, like the Scotch at Flodden—

> "The stubborn spearmen still made good
> The dark, impenetrable wood;
> Each stepping where his comrade stood
> The instant that he fell,"

till there were none left to fall. The ground around them was piled with dead.

But this gallant charge availed Umbelazi but little, and by degrees Cetywayo's forces pressed his men back to the banks of the Tugela, and finally into it. Thousands fell upon the field and thousands perished in the river. When my friend swam back that night, he had nothing to fear from the alligators: they were too well fed. Umbelazi died on the battlefield of a broken heart, at least it is said that no wound could be found on his person. He probably expired in a fit brought on by anxiety of mind and fatigue. A curious story is told of Cetywayo with reference to his brother's death. After the battle was over a Zulu from one of his own regiments presented himself before him with many salutations, saying, "O prince! now canst thou sleep in peace, for Umbelazi is dead." "How knowest thou that he is dead?" said Cetywayo. "Because I slew him with my own hand," replied the Zulu. "Thou dog!" said the prince, "thou hast dared to lift thy hand against the blood royal, and now thou makest it a matter of boasting. Wast thou not afraid? By Chaka's head thou shalt have thy reward. Lead him away." And the Zulu, who was but lying after all, having possessed himself of the bracelets off the dead prince's body, was instantly executed. The probability is that Cetywayo acted thus more from motives of policy than from affection to his brother, whom indeed he hoped to destroy. It did not do to make too light of the death of an important prince: Umbelazi's fate to-day might be Cetywayo's fate to-morrow. This story bears a really remarkable resemblance to that of the young man who slew Saul, the Lord's anointed, and suffered death on account thereof at the hands of David.

This battle is also memorable as being the occasion of the first public appearance of Mr. John Dunn, now the most important chief in Zululand, and, be it understood, the unknown quantity in all future transactions in that country. At that time Dunn was a retainer of Umbelazi's, and fought on his side in the Tugela battle. After the fight, however, he went over to Cetywayo and became his man. From that time till the outbreak of the Zulu war he remained in Zululand as adviser to Cetywayo, agent for the Natal Government, and purveyor of firearms to the nation at large. As soon as Cetywayo got into trouble with the Imperial Government, Dunn, like a prudent man, deserted him and came over to us. In reward Sir Garnet Wolseley advanced him to the most important chieftainship in Zululand, which he hopes to make a stepping-stone to the vacant throne. His advice was largely followed by Sir Garnet in the bestowal of the other chieftainships, and was naturally not quite disinterested. He has already publicly announced his intention of resisting the return of the king, his old master, by force of arms, should the Government attempt to reinstate him.

A period of sixteen years elapsed before Cetywayo reaped the fruits of the battle of the Tugela by succeeding to the throne on the death of his father, Panda, the only Zulu monarch who has as yet come to his end by natural causes.

In 1861, however, Cetywayo was, at the instance of the Natal Government, formally nominated heir to the throne by Mr. Shepstone, it being thought better that a fixed succession should be established with the concurrence of the Natal Government than that matters should be left to take their chance on Panda's death. Mr. Shepstone accomplished his mission successfully, though at great personal risk. For some unknown reason, Cetywayo, who was blown up with pride, was at first adverse to being thus nominated, and came down to the royal kraal with three thousand armed followers, meaning, it would see, to kill Mr. Shepstone, whom he had never before met. Panda, the old king, had an inkling of what was to happen, but was powerless to control his son, so he confined himself to addressing the assembled multitude in what I have heard Sir Theophilus Shepstone say was the most eloquent and touching speech he ever listened to, the subject being the duties of hospitality. He did not at the time know how nearly the speech concerned him, or that its object was to preserve his life.

This, however, soon became manifest when, exception being taken to some breech of etiquette by one of his servants, he was surrounded by a mob of shouting savages, whose evident object was to put an end to him and those with him. For two hours he remained sitting there, expecting that every moment would be his last, but showing not the slightest emotion, till at length he got an opportunity of speaking, when he rose and said, "I know that you mean to kill me; it is an easy thing to do; but I tell you Zulus, that for every drop of my blood that falls to the ground, a hundred men will come out of the sea yonder, from the country of which Natal is one of the cattle-kraals, and will bitterly avenge me." As he spoke he turned and pointed towards the ocean, and so intense was the excitement that animated it, that the whole great multitude turned with him and stared towards the horizon, as though they expected to see the long lines of avengers creeping across the plains. Silence followed his speech; his imperturbability and his well-timed address had saved his life. From that day his name was a power in the land.[*]

> [*] A very good description of this scene was published in the London Quarterly Review in 1878. The following is an extract: "In the centre of those infuriated savages he (Mr. Shepstone) sat for more than two hours outwardly calm, giving confidence to his solitary European companion by his own quietness, only once saying, 'Why, Jem, you're afraid,' and imposing restraint on his native attendants. Then, when they had shouted, as Cetywayo himself said in our hearing, 'till their throats were so sore that they could shout no more,' they departed. But Sompseu (Mr. Shepstone) had conquered. Cetywayo, in describing the scene to us and our companion on a visit to him a short time afterwards, said, 'Sompseu is a great man: no man but he could have come through that day alive.' Similar testimony we have had from some of the Zulu assailants, from the native attendants, and the companion above mentioned. Next morning Cetywayo humbly begged an interview, which was not granted but on terms of unqualified submission. From that day Cetywayo has submitted to British control in the measure in which it has been exercised, and has been profuse in his expressions of respect and submission to Mr. T. Shepstone; but in his heart, as occasional

acts and speeches show, he writhes under the restraint, and bitterly hates the man who imposed it."

It was on this occasion that a curious incident occurred which afterwards became of importance. Among the Zulus there exists a certain salute, "Bayete," which it is the peculiar and exclusive privilege of Zulu royalty to receive. The word means, or is supposed to mean, "Let us bring tribute." On Mr. Shepstone's visit the point was raised by the Zulu lawyers as to what salute he should receive. It was not consistent with their ideas that the nominator of their future king should be greeted with any salute inferior to the Bayete, and this, as plain Mr. Shepstone, it was impossible to give him. The difficulty was obvious, but the Zulu mind proved equal to it. He was solemnly announced to be a Zulu king, and to stand in the place of the great founder of their nation, Chaka. Who was so fit to proclaim the successor to the throne as the great predecessor of the prince proclaimed? To us this seems a strange, not to say ludicrous, way of settling a difficulty, but there was nothing in it repugnant to Zulu ideas. Odd as it was, it invested Mr. Shepstone with all the attributes of a Zulu king, such as the power to make laws, order executions, &c., and those attributes in the eyes of Zulus he still retains.

In 1873 messengers came down from Zululand to the Natal Government, bringing with them the "king's head," that is, a complimentary present of oxen, announcing the death of Panda. "The nation," they said, "was wandering; it wanders and wanders, and wanders again;" the spirit of the king had departed from them; his words had ceased, and "none but children were left." The message ended with a request that Mr. Shepstone, as Cetywayo's "father," should come and instal him on the throne. A month or two afterwards there came another message, again requesting his attendance; and on the request being refused by the Lieutenant-Governor of Natal, there came a third message, to which the Natal Government returned a favourable answer.

Accordingly Mr. Shepstone proceeded to Zululand, and on the 3rd September 1873 proclaimed Cetywayo king with all due pomp and ceremony. It was on this occasion that, in the presence of, and with the enthusiastic assent of, both king and people, Mr. Shepstone, "standing in the place of Cetywayo's father, and so representing the nation," enunciated the four following articles, with a view to putting an end to the continual slaughter that darkens the history of Zululand: —

1. That the indiscriminate shedding of blood shall cease in the land.

2. That no Zulu shall be condemned without open trial, and the public examination of witnesses for and against, and that he shall have a right to appeal to the king.

3. That no Zulu's life shall be taken without the previous knowledge and consent of the king, after such trial has taken place, and the right of appeal has been allowed to be exercised.

4. That for minor crimes the loss of property, all or a portion, shall be substituted for the punishment of death.

Nobody will deny that these were admirable regulations, and that they were received as such at the time by the Zulu king and people. But there is no doubt that their ready acceptance by the king was a sacrifice to his desire to please "his father Sompseu" (Mr. Shepstone) and the Natal Government, with both of which he was particularly anxious to be on good terms. He has never adhered to these coronation regulations, or promises, as they have been called, and the probability is that he never intended to adhere to them. However this may be, I must say that personally I have been unable to share the views of those who see in the breach of these so-called promises a justification of the Zulu war. After all, what do they amount to, and what guarantee was there for their fulfilment? They merely represent a very laudable attempt on the part of the Natal Government to keep a restraining hand on Zulu cruelty, and to draw the bonds of friendship as tight as the idiosyncrasies of a savage state would allow. The Government of Natal had no right to dictate the terms to a Zulu king on which he was to hold his throne. The Zulu nation was an independent nation, and had never been conquered or annexed by Natal. If the Government of that colony was able by friendly negotiation to put a stop to Zulu slaughter, it was a matter for congratulation on humanitarian grounds; but it is difficult to follow the argument that because it was not able, or was only partially able, to do so, therefore England was justified in making war on the Zulus. On the other hand, it is perfectly ludicrous to observe the way in which Cetywayo's advocates overshoot the mark in arguing this and similar points; especially his lady advocates, whose writings upon these subjects bear about the same resemblance to the truth that the speech to the jury by the counsel for the defence in a hopeless murder case does to the summing up of the judge. Having demonstrated that the engagements entered into by Cetywayo meant nothing, they will proceed to show that, even if they did, cold-blooded murder, when perpetrated by a black paragon like Cetywayo, does not amount to a great offence. In the mouths of these gentle apologists for slaughter, massacre masquerades under the name of "executions," and is excused on the plea of being, "after all," only the enforcement of "an old custom." Again, the employment of such phrases, in a solemn answer to a remonstrance from the Lieutenant-Governor of Natal, as "I do kill; but do not consider that I have done anything yet in the way of killing. . . . I have not yet begun; I have yet to kill," are shown to mean nothing at all, and to be "nothing more than the mere irritation of the moment."[*] Perhaps those of Cetywayo's subjects who suffered on account of this mere momentary irritation took a more serious view of it. It is but fair to the particular authority from whom I quote (Miss Colenso's "History of the Zulu War,") to state that she considers this reply from the "usually courteous and respectful king" as "no doubt petulant and wanting in due respect." Considering that the message in question (which can be read in the footnote) was a point-blank defiance of Sir Henry Bulwer, admitting that there had been slaughter, but that it was nothing compared to what was coming, most people will not think Miss Colenso's description of it too strong.

[*] *The following is the text of the message: —*

"Did I ever tell Mr. Shepstone I would not kill? Did he tell the white people that I made such an arrangement? Because if he did he has deceived them. I do kill; but do not consider that I have done anything yet in the way of killing. Why do the white people start at nothing? I have not yet begun; I have yet to kill; it is the custom of our nation, and I shall not depart from it. Why does the Governor of Natal speak to me about my laws? Do I go to Natal and dictate to him about his laws? I shall not agree to any laws or rules from Natal, and by doing so throw the large kraal which I govern into the water. My people will not listen unless they are killed; and while wishing to be friends with the English, I do not agree to give my

*people over to be governed by laws sent to me by them. Have
I not asked the English to allow me to wash my spears since
the death of my father 'Umpandi,' and they have kept playing
with me all this time, treating me like a child? Go back and
tell the English that I shall now act on my own account, and
if they wish me to agree to their laws, I shall leave and become
a wanderer; but before I go it will be seen, as I shall not go
without having acted. Go back and tell the white men this, and
let them hear it well. The Governor of Natal and I are equal;
he is Governor of Natal, and I am Governor here."*

To admit that the Zulu king has the right to kill as many of his
subjects as he chooses, so long as they will tolerate being killed, is
one thing, but it is certainly surprising to find educated Europeans
adopting a line of defence of these proceedings on his behalf that
amounts to a virtual expression of approval, or at least of easy
toleration. Has philanthropy a deadening effect on the moral sense,
that the people who constitute themselves champions for the
unfortunate Zulu king and the oppressed Boers cannot get on to their
hobbies without becoming blind to the difference between right and
wrong? Really an examination of the utterances of these champions
of oppressed innocence would almost lead one to that conclusion. On
the one hand they suppress and explain away facts, and on the other
supply their want of argument by reckless accusations and vicious
attacks on the probity of such of their fellow-Englishmen, especially
if in office, as have had the misfortune to pursue a course of action
or to express opinions not pleasing to them or their proteges. For
instance, an innocent and unenlightened reader of the very interesting
work from which I have just quoted probably lays it down with the
conviction that both Sir Bartle Frere and Sir Theophilus Shepstone
are very wicked men and full of bad motives, and will wonder how
a civilised Government could employ such monsters of bloodthirsty
duplicity. As he proceeds he will also find that there is not much
to be said for the characters of either Sir Garnet Wolseley or Lord
Chelmsford; whilst as regards such small fry as Mr. John Shepstone,
the present Secretary of Native Affairs in Natal, after passing through
Miss Colenso's mill their reputations come out literally in rags and
tatters. He will be shocked to find that not only did one and all of
these gentlemen make gross errors of judgment, but, trusted and

distinguished servants of their country as they are, they were one and all actuated by dark personal motives that will not bear examination.

Heaven help the members of the Shepstone family when they fall into the hands of the gentler but more enthusiastic sex, for Miss Colenso is not their only foe. In a recent publication called a "Defence of Zululand and its Kings," Lady Florence Dixie gibbets Mr. Henrique Shepstone, and points him out to be execrated by a Cetywayo-worshipping public, because the ex-king is to be sent to England in his charge; when, according to Lady Dixie, he will certainly be scoundrel enough to misinterpret all that Cetywayo says for his own ends, and will thereby inflict a "cruel wrong" upon him, and render his visit to England "perfectly meaningless." Perhaps it has never occurred to Lady Dixie that this is a very serious charge to bring against an honourable man, whose reputation is probably as dear to him as the advancement of Cetywayo's cause is to her. It is all very well to be enthusiastic, but ladies should remember that there are other people in the world to be considered beside Cetywayo.

As regards the question of Cetywayo's bloodthirstiness, which is so strenuously denied by his apologists, I cannot say that a careful study of the blue books bearing on the subject brings me to the same conclusion. It is true that there is not much information on the point, for the obvious reason that the history of slaughters in Zululand in the vast majority of cases only reached Natal in the form of rumours, which nobody thought it worth while to report. There were no newspaper correspondents in Zululand. There is not, however, any doubt that Cetywayo was in the habit of killing large numbers of people; indeed it was a matter of the commonest notoriety; nor, as will be seen from the message I have transcribed, did he himself deny it, when, being angry, he spoke the truth. At the same time that this message was sent, we find Mr. Osborn, then resident magistrate at Newcastle in Natal, who is certainly not given to exaggeration, writing to the Secretary for Native Affairs thus:—"From all I have been able to learn, Cetywayo's conduct has been, and continues to be, disgraceful. He is putting people to death in a shameful manner, especially girls. The dead bodies are placed by his order in the principal paths, especially where the paths intersect each other (cross roads). A few of the parents of the young people so killed buried the bodies, and thus brought Cetywayo's wrath on themselves, resulting not only on their own death, but destruction of the whole family. . . . It is really terrible that such horrible savagery could take place on our own borders. . . . Uhamu reproved Cetywayo the other day, reminded him of his promises to Mr. Shepstone, and begged him to spare the people. This advice, as could be expected, was not relished."

Again, Mr. Fynney, in his report of his visit to Zululand in 1877, states that though the king and his "indunas" (councillors) denied that men were killed without trial, the people told a very different tale. Thus he says, "In every instance, where I had so far gained the confidence of the Zulus as to cause them to speak freely, was I assured of the truthfulness of the statement that the king, Cetywayo, caused his people to be put to death in great numbers; and when I remarked that of course he did so after a fair and proper trial, in some cases my remark was greeted with a suppressed laugh or a smile. Some remarked, 'Yes, a trial of bullets;' others, 'Yes, we get a trial, but that means surrounding the kraal at daybreak and shooting us down like cattle.' One asked me what the Government in Natal intended doing, or what was thought in Natal about the killing, saying, 'It was not in the night that Sompseu spoke, but in the sunshine; the king was not alone, but his people were around him, and the ears of all Zululand heard these words, and the hearts of all Zulus were joyful, and in gladness they lifted up their hands saying: The mouth of our white father has spoken good words; he has cautioned his child in the presence of his people, and a good sun has risen this day over Zululand! How is it now? Has the king listened? Does he hold fast those words? No! not one. The promises he made are all broken. What does Sompseu say to this? You should dine at my kraal yonder for a few days, and see the izizi (cattle and other property of people who have been killed) pass, and you would then see with your own eyes how a case is tried.'" Farther on Mr. Fynney says, "When a charge is made against a Zulu, the question is generally asked, 'Has he any cattle?' and if answered in the affirmative, there is little chance of escape. Instances of killing occurred while I was in Zululand, and to my knowledge no trial was allowed. An armed party was despatched on the morning I left Ondine, and, as I was informed, to kill."

There is no reason to suppose that Mr. Fynney was in any way prejudiced in making these remarks; on the contrary, he was simply carrying out an official mission, and reporting for the general information of the Governments of Natal and the Transvaal. It is, however, noticeable that neither these nor similar passages are ever alluded to by Cetywayo's advocates, whose object seems to be rather to suppress the truth than to put it fairly before the public, if by such suppression they think they can advance the cause of the ex-king.

The whole matter of Cetywayo's private policy, however, appears to me to be very much beside the question. Whether or no he slaughtered his oppressed subjects in bygone years, which there is no doubt he did, is not our affair, since we were not then, as we are now, responsible for the good government of Zululand; and seeing the amount of slaughter that goes on under our protectorate, it ill becomes us to rake up these things against Cetywayo. What we have to consider is his foreign policy, not the domestic details of his government.[*]

[*] *A gentleman, who has recently returned from travelling in Zululand, relates the following story as nearly as possible in the words in which it was told to him by a well-known hunter in Zululand, Piet Hogg by name, now residing near Dundee on the Zulu border. The story is a curious one as illustrative of Zulu character, and scarcely represents Cetywayo in as amiable a light as one might wish. Piet Hogg and my informant were one day talking about the king when the former said, "I was hunting and trading in Zululand, and was at a military kraal occupied by Cetywayo, where I saw a Basuto who had been engaged by the king to instruct his people in building houses, that were to be square instead of circular (as are all Zulu buildings), for which his pay was to be thirty head of cattle. The Basuto came to Cetywayo in my presence, and said that the square buildings were made; he now wished to have his thirty head of cattle and to depart. Cetywayo having obtained what he required, began to think the man overpaid, so said, 'I have observed that you like − − (a Zulu woman belonging to the kraal); suppose you take her instead of the thirty head of cattle.' Now this was a very bad bargain for the Basuto, as the woman was not*

worth more, in Zulu estimation, than ten head of cattle; but the Basuto, knowing with whom he had to deal, thought it might be better to comply with the suggestion rather than insist upon his rights, and asked to be allowed till the next morning to consider the proposal. After he had been dismissed on this understanding, Cetywayo sent for the woman, and accused her of misconduct with the Basuto, the punishment of which, if proved, would be death. She denied this vehemently, with protestations and tears. He insisted, but, looking up at a tree almost denuded of leaves which grew close by, said, significantly, 'Take care that not a leaf remains on that tree by the morning.' The woman understood the metaphor, and in an hour or two, aided by other strapping Zulu females, attacked the unfortunate Basuto and killed him with clubs. But Cetywayo having thus, like the monkey in the fable, employed a cat's paw to do his dirty work, began to think the Basuto's untimely death might have an ugly appearance in my eyes, so gave orders in my presence that, as a punishment, six of the women who had killed the Basuto should also be put to death. This was too much for me, knowing as I did, all that had passed. I reproached Cetywayo for his cruelty, and declared I would leave Zululand without trading there, and without making him the present he expected. I also said I should take care the great English 'Inkose' (the Governor of Natal) should hear of his conduct and the reason of my return. Cetywayo was then on friendly terms with the English, and being impressed by my threats, he reconsidered his orders, and spared the lives of the women."

I do not propose to follow out all the details of the boundary dispute between Cetywayo and the Transvaal, or to comment on the different opinions held on the point by the various authorities, English and Zulu. The question has been, for the moment, settled by the Transvaal Convention, and is besides a most uninteresting one to the general reader.

Nor shall I enter into a discussion concerning the outrages on which Sir Bartle Frere based his ultimatum previous to the Zulu war. They were after all insignificant, although sufficient to serve as a *casus belli* to a statesman determined to fight. The Zulu war was, in the opinion of Sir B. Frere, necessary in self-defence, which is the first principle of existence. If it admits of justification, it is on the ground that the Zulu army was a menace to the white population of South Africa, and that it was therefore necessary to destroy it, lest at some future time it should destroy the whites. It is ridiculous to say that the capture of two Zulu women in Natal and their subsequent murder, or the expulsion on political grounds of a few missionaries, justified us in breaking up a kingdom and slaughtering ten thousand men. Sir Bartle Frere declared war upon the Zulus because he was afraid, and had good reason to be afraid, that if he did not, Cetywayo would before long sweep either the Transvaal or Natal; whilst, on the other hand, the Zulus fought us because our policy was too philanthropic to allow them to fight anybody else. This statement may appear strange, but a little examination into Zulu character and circumstances will, I think, show it to be correct.

It must be remembered that for some years before Panda's death the Zulus had not been engaged in any foreign war. When Cetywayo ascended the throne, it was the general hope and expectation of the army, and therefore of the nation, that this period of inaction would come to an end, and that the new king would inaugurate an active foreign policy. They did not greatly care in what direction the activity developed itself, provided it did develop. It must also be borne in mind that every able-bodied man in the Zulu country was a member of a regiment, even the lads being attached to regiments as carriers, and the women being similarly enrolled, though they did not fight. The Zulu military system was the universal-service system of Germany brought to an absolute perfection, obtained by subordinating all the ties and duties of civil life to military ends. Thus, for instance, marriage could not be contracted at will, but only by the permission of the king, which was generally delayed until a regiment was well advanced in years, when a number of girls were handed over to it to take to wife. This regulation came into force because it was found that men without home ties were more ferocious and made better soldiers, and the result of these harsh rules was that the Zulu warrior, living as he did under the shadow of a savage discipline, for any breach of which there was but one punishment, death, can hardly be said to have led a life of domestic comfort, such as men of all times and nations have thought their common right. But even a Zulu must have some object in life, some shrine at which to worship, some mistress of his affections. Home he had none, religion he had none, mistress he had none, but in their stead he had his career as a warrior, and his hope of honour and riches to be gained by the assegai. His home was on the war-track with his regiment, his religion the fierce denunciation of the isanusi,[*] and his affections were fixed on the sudden rush of battle, the red slaughter, and the spoils of the slain. "War," says Sir T. Shepstone, in a very remarkable despatch written about a year before the outbreak of the Zulu war, "is the universal cry among the soldiers, who are anxious to live up to their traditions, ... and the idea is gaining ground among the people that their nation has outlived the object of its existence." Again he says, "The engine (the Zulu military organisation) has not ceased to exist or to generate its forces, although the reason or excuse for its existence has died away: these forces have continued to accumulate and are daily accumulating without safety-valve or outlet."

> [*] Witch-doctor. These persons are largely employed in Zululand to smell out witches who are supposed to have bewitched others, and are of course very useful as political agents. Any person denounced by them is at once executed. A friend of the writer's was once present at a political smelling-out on a large scale, and describes it as a very curious and unpleasant scene. The men, of whom there were some thousands, were seated in a circle, as pale with terror as Zulus can be. Within the circle were several witch doctors; one of whom amidst his or her incantations would now and again step forward and touch some unfortunate man with a forked stick. The victim was instantly led away a few paces and his neck twisted. The circle awaited each denunciation in breathless expectation, for not a man among

them knew whose turn it might be next. On another occasion, an unfortunate wretch who had been similarly condemned by an isanusi rushed up to the same gentleman's waggon and besought shelter. He was hidden under some blankets, but presently his pursuers arrived, and insisted upon his being handed over. All possible resistance was made, until the executioners announced that they would search the waggon and kill him there. It was then covenanted that he should have a start in the race for life. He was, however, overtaken and killed. These instances will show how dark and terrible is the Zulu superstition connected with witchcraft, and what a formidable weapon it becomes in the hands of the king or chief.

Desirable as such a state of feeling may be in an army just leaving for the battlefield, it is obvious that for some fifty thousand men, comprising the whole manhood of the nation, to be continually on the boil with sanguinary animosity against the human race in general, is an awkward element to fit into the peaceable government of a state.

Yet this was doubtless the state of affairs with which Cetywayo had to contend during the latter years of his reign. He found himself surrounded by a great army, in a high state of efficiency and warlike preparation, proclaiming itself wearied with camp life, and clamouring to be led against an enemy, that it might justify its traditions and find employment for its spears. Often and often he must have been sorely puzzled to find excuses wherewithal to put it off. Indeed his position was both awkward and dangerous: on the one hand was Scylla in the shape of the English Government, and on the other the stormy and uncertain Charybdis of his clamouring regiments. Slowly the idea must have began to dawn upon him that unless he found employment for the army, which, besides being disgusted with his inactivity, was somewhat wearied with his cruelties, for domestic slaughter had ceased to divert and had begun to irritate: the army, or some enterprising members of it, might put it beyond his power ever to find employment for it at all, and bring one of his brothers to rule in his stead.

And yet who was he to fight, if fight he must? There were three possible enemies—1. The Swazis; 2. The Transvaal Boers; 3. The English.

Although the English may have held a place on Cetywayo's list as possible foes, there is no ground for supposing that, until shortly before the war, he had any wish to fight with us. Indeed, whereas their hatred of the Boers was pronounced, and openly expressed, both the Zulu king and people always professed great respect for Englishmen, and even a certain amount of liking and regard.

Therefore, when Cetywayo had to settle on an enemy to attack, it was not the English that he chose, but the Swazis, whose territory adjoined his own, lying along the borders of the Transvaal towards Delagoa Bay. The Swazis are themselves Zulus, and Cetywayo claimed certain sovereign rights over them, which, however, they refused to recognise. They are a powerful tribe, and can turn out about 10,000 fighting men, quite enough for Cetywayo's young warriors to try their mettle on. Still the king does not appear to have wished to undertake the war without first obtaining the approval of the Natal Government, to whom he applied several times for permission "to wash his spears," saying that he was but half a king until he had done so. The Natal Government, however, invariably replied that he was on no account to do anything of the sort. This shows the inconveniences of possessing a complimentary feudal hold over a savage potentate, the shadow of power without the reality. The Governor of Natal could not in decency sanction such a proceeding as a war of extermination against the Swazis, but if it had occurred without his sanction, the Swazis would have suffered no doubt, but the Zulu spears would have been satisfactorily washed, and there would have been no Zulu war. As it is, Englishmen have been killed instead of Swazis.

Thwarted in his designs on the Swazis, Cetywayo next turned his attention to the Transvaal Boers. The Zulus and the Boers had never been good friends since the days of the massacre of Retief, and of late years their mutual animosity had been greatly increased owing to their quarrels about the boundary question previously alluded to. This animosity reached blood-heat when the Boer Government, acting with the arrogance it always displayed towards natives, began to lay its commands upon Cetywayo about his relations with the Amaswazi, the alleged trespassing on Boer territory, and other matters. The arrogance was all the more offensive because it was impotent. The Boers were not in a position to undertake the chastisement of the Zulus. But the king and council of Zululand now determined to try conclusions with the Transvaal on the first convenient opportunity, and this time without consulting the Government of Natal. The opportunity soon occurred. Secocoeni, the powerful chief of the Bapedi, one of the tribes whose territories border on the Transvaal, came to a difference with the Boers over another border question. There is good ground for supposing that Cetywayo incited him to withstand the Boer demands; it is certain that during the course of the war that followed he assisted him with advice, and more substantially still, with Zulu volunteers.

To be brief, the Secocoeni war resulted in the discomfiture of the Transvaal forces. Another result of this struggle was to throw the whole state into the most utter confusion, of which the Dutch burghers, always glad of an opportunity to defy the law, took advantage to refuse to pay taxes. National bankruptcy ensued, and confusion grew worse confounded.

Cetywayo took note of all this, and saw that now was his opportunity to attack. The Boers had suffered both in morale and prestige from their defeat by Secocoeni, who was still in arms against them; whilst the natives were proportionately elated by their success over the dreaded white men. There was, he knew well, but little chance of a rapid concentration to resist a sudden raid, especially when made by such a powerful army, or rather chain of armies, as he could set in motion. Everything favoured the undertaking; indeed, humanly speaking, it is difficult to see what could have saved the greater part of the population of the Transvaal from sudden extinction, if a kind Providence had not just then put it into the head of Lord Carnarvon to send out Sir T. Shepstone as Special Commissioner to their country. When Cetywayo heard that his father Sompseu (Sir T. Shepstone) was going up to the Transvaal, he held his hand, sent out spies, and awaited the course of events. The following incident will show with what interest he was watching what took place. At the Vaal River a party of Boers met the Special Commissioner and fired salutes to welcome him. It was immediately reported to Cetywayo by his spies that the Boers had fired over Sir T. Shepstone's waggon. Shortly afterwards a message arrived at Pretoria from Cetywayo to inquire into the truth of the story, coolly announcing his intention of sweeping the Transvaal if it were true that "his father" had been fired at. In a conversation with Mr. Fynney after the Annexation Cetywayo alludes to his intentions in these words:—

"I heard that the Boers were not treating him (Sompseu) properly, and that they intended to put him in a corner. If they had done so I should not have waited for anything more. *Had but one shot been fired*, I should have said, 'What more do I wait for? they have touched my father.' I should have poured my men over the land, and I can tell you, son of Mr. Fynney, the land would have burned with fire." This will show how eagerly Cetywayo was searching for an excuse to commence his attack on the Transvaal. When the hope of finding a pretext in the supposed firing at Sir T. Shepstone or any incident of a similar nature faded away, he appears to have determined to carry out his plans without any immediate pretext, and to make a *casus belli* of his previous differences with the Government of the Republic. Accordingly he massed his impis (army corps) at different points along the Transvaal border, where they awaited the signal to advance and sweep the country. Information of Cetywayo's doings and of his secret plans reached Pretoria shortly before the Annexation, and confirmed the mind of the Special Commissioner as to the absolute necessity of that measure to save the citizens of the Republic from coming to a violent end, and South Africa from being plunged into a native war of unexampled magnitude. The day before the Annexation took place, when it was quite certain that it would take place, a message was sent to Cetywayo by Sir T. Shepstone telling him of what was about to happen, and telling him too in the sternest and most straightforward language, that the Transvaal had become the Queen's land like Natal, and that he must no more think of attacking it than he would of attacking Natal. Cetywayo on receiving the message at once disbanded his armies and sent them to their kraals. "Kabuna," he said to the messenger, "my impis were gathered; now at my father's (Sir T. Shepstone's) bidding I send them back to their homes."

This fact, namely, that at the bidding of his old mentor Sir T. Shepstone, Cetywayo abandoned his long-cherished plans, and his undoubted opportunity of paying off old scores with the Boers in a most effectual manner, and gave up a policy that had so many charms for him, must be held by every unprejudiced man to speak volumes in his favour. It must be remembered that it was not merely to oblige his "father Sompseu" that he did this, but to meet the wishes of the English Government, and the act shows how anxious he was to retain the friendship and fall in with the views of that Government. Evidently Cetywayo had no animosity against us in April 1877.

In his interview with Mr. Fynney, Cetywayo speaks out quite frankly as to what his intentions had been; he says, "I know all about the soldiers being on their way up, but I would have asked Sompseu to allow the soldiers to stand on one side for just a little while, only a little, and see what my men could do. It would have been unnecessary for the Queen's people to trouble. My men were all ready, and how big must that stone have been, with my father Sompseu digging at one side and myself at the other, that would not have toppled over? Even though the size of that mountain (pointing to a mountain range), we could put it on its back. Again I say I am glad to know the Transvaal is English ground; perhaps now there may be rest."

This and other passages show beyond all doubt from what an awful catastrophe the Transvaal was saved by the Annexation. That Cetywayo personally detested the Boers is made clear by his words to Mr. Fynney. "'The Boers,' he says, 'are a nation of liars; they are a bad people, bad altogether. I do not want them near my people; they lie and claim what is not theirs, and ill-use my people. Where is Thomas?' (President Burgers). I informed him that Mr. Burgers had left the Transvaal. 'Then let them pack up and follow Thomas,' said he. 'Let them go. The Queen does not want such people as those about her land. What can the Queen make of them or do with them? Their evil ways puzzled both Thomas and Rudolph, Landdrost of Utrecht; they will not be quiet.'"

It is very clear that if Cetywayo had been left to work his will, a great many of the Boers would have found it necessary to "pack up and follow Thomas," whilst many more would have never needed to pack again.

I am aware that attempts have been made to put another explanation on Cetywayo's warlike preparations against the Boers. It has been said that the Zulu army was called up by Sir T. Shepstone to coerce the Transvaal. It is satisfactory to be able, from intimate personal knowledge, to give unqualified denial to that statement, which is a pure invention, as indeed is easily proved by clear evidence, which

I have entered into in another part of this book. Cetywayo played for his own hand all along, and received neither commands nor hints from the Special Commissioner to get his army together. Indeed, when Sir T. Shepstone discovered what was going on, he suffered great anxiety lest some catastrophe should occur before he was in a position to prevent it. Nothing short of the Annexation could have saved the Transvaal at that moment, and the conduct of the Boers after the danger had been taken on to the shoulders of the Imperial Government is a startling instance of national ingratitude.

Here again the Zulu king was brought face to face with the ubiquitous British Government, and that too at a particularly aggravating moment. He was about to commence his attack when he was met with a polite, "Hands off; this is British territory." No wonder that we find him in despair renewing his prayer that Sompseu will allow him to make "one little raid only, one small swoop," and saying that "it is the custom of our country, when a new king is placed over the nation, to wash their spears, and it has been done in the case of all former kings of Zululand. I am no king, but sit in a heap. I cannot be a king till I have washed my assegais." All of which is doubtless very savage and very wrong, but such is the depravity of human nature, that there is something taking about it for all that.

It was at this period of the history of South Africa that many people think we made our crowning mistake. We annexed the Transvaal, say they, six months too soon. As things have turned out, it would have been wiser to have left Zulus and Transvaal Boers to try conclusions, and done our best to guard our own frontiers. There is no doubt that such a consummation of affairs would have cleared the political atmosphere wonderfully; the Zulus would have got enough fighting to last them some time, and the remainder of the Boers would have entreated our protection and become contented British subjects; there would have been no Isandhlwana and no Majuba Hill. But to these I say who could foresee the future, and who, in the then state of kindly feeling towards the Boers, could wish to leave them, and all the English mixed up with them, to undergo, unprepared as they were, the terrible experience of a Zulu invasion? Besides, what guarantee was there that the slaughter would stop in the Transvaal, or that the combat would not have developed into a war of races throughout South Africa? Even looking at the matter in the light of after events, it is difficult to regret that humanity was on this occasion allowed to take precedence of a more cold-blooded policy. If the opponents of the Annexation, or even the members of the Transvaal Independence Committee, knew what a Zulu invasion meant, they would scarcely have been so bitter about that act.

From the time of the Annexation it was a mere matter of opinion as to which direction the Zulu explosion would take. The safety-valves were loaded whilst the pressure daily increased, and all acquainted with the people knew that it must come sooner or later.

Shortly after the Transvaal became British territory the old Zulu boundary question came to the fore again and was made more complicated than ever by Sir T. Shepstone, who had hitherto favoured the Zulu claims, taking the Boer side of the controversy, after examination of the locality and of persons acquainted with the details of the matter. There was nothing wonderful in this change of opinion, though of course it was attributed to various motives by advocates of the Zulu claims, and there is no doubt that Cetywayo himself did not at all like it, and, excited thereto by vexation and the outcry of his regiments, adopted a very different and aggressive tone in his communications with the English authorities. Indeed his irritation against the Boers and everybody connected with them was very great. Probably if he had been left alone he would in time have carried out his old programme, and attacked the Transvaal. But, fortunately for the Transvaal, which, like sailors and drunken men, always seems to have had a special Providence taking care of it: at this juncture Sir Bartle Frere appeared upon the scene, and after a few preliminaries and the presentation of a strong ultimatum, which was quite impracticable so far as Cetywayo was concerned, since it demanded what it was almost impossible for him to concede—the disbandment of his army—invaded Zululand.

It is generally supposed that the Natal colonists had a great deal to do with making the Zulu war, but this is not the case. It is quite true that they were rejoiced at the prospect of the break-up of Cetywayo's power, because they were very much afraid of him and of his "celibate man-slaying machine," which, under all the circumstances, is not wonderful. But the war was a distinctly Imperial war, made by an Imperial officer, without consultation with Colonial authorities, on Imperial grounds, viz., because Cetywayo menaced Her Majesty's power in South Africa. Of course, if there had been no colonies there would have been no war, but in that way only are they responsible for it. Natal, however, has not grudged to pay 250,000 pounds towards its expenses, which is a great deal more than it can afford, and, considering that the foolish settlement made by Sir Garnet Wolseley is almost sure to involve the colony in trouble, quite as much as should be asked.

The fact of the matter was, that Sir Bartle Frere was a statesman who had the courage of his convictions; he saw that a Zulu disturbance of one kind or another was inevitable, so he boldly took the initiative. If things had gone right with him, as he supposed they would, praise would have been lavished on him by the Home authorities, and he would have been made a peer, and perhaps Governor-General of India to boot; but he reckoned without his Lord Chelmsford, and the element of success which was necessary to gild his policy in the eyes of the home public was conspicuous by its absence. As it was, no language was considered to be too bad to apply to this "imperious proconsul" who had taken upon himself to declare a war. If it is any consolation to him, he has at any rate the gratitude of the South African Colonies, not so much for what he has done, for that is being carefully nullified by the subsequent action of the Home Government, but because, believing his policy to be right, he had the boldness to carry it out at the risk of his official reputation. Sir Bartle Frere took a larger view of the duties of the governor of a great dependency than to constitute himself the flickering shadow of the Secretary of State in Downing Street, who, knowing little of the real interests of the colony, is himself only the reflection of those that hold the balance of power, to whom the subject is one of entire indifference, provided that there is nothing to pay.

The details of the Zulu war are matters of melancholy history, which it is useless to recapitulate here. With the exception of the affair at Rorke's Drift, there is nothing to be proud of in connection with it, and a great deal to be ashamed of, more especially its final settlement. There is, however, one point that I wish to submit to the consideration of my readers, and that is, that Cetywayo was never thoroughly in earnest about the war. If he had been in earnest, if he had been determined to put out his full strength, he would certainly have swept Natal from end to end after his victory at Isandhlwana. There was no force to prevent his doing so: on the contrary, it is probable that if he had advanced a strong army over the border, a great number of the Natal natives would have declared in his favour through fear of his vengeance, or at the least would have remained neutral. He had ample time at his disposal to have executed the manoeuvre twice over before the arrival of the reinforcements, of which the results must have been very dreadful, and yet he never destroyed a single family. The reason he has himself given for this conduct is that he did not wish to irritate the white man; that he had not made the war, and was only anxious to defend his country.

When the fighting came to an end after the battle of Ulundi, there were two apparent courses open to us to take. One was to take over the country and rule it for the benefit of the Zulus, and the other to enforce the demands in Sir Bartle Frere's ultimatum, and, taking such guarantees as circumstances would admit of, leave Cetywayo on the throne. Instead of acting on either of these plans, however, Sir Garnet Wolseley proceeded, in the face of an extraordinary consensus of adverse opinion, which he treated with calm contempt, to execute what has proved to be a very cruel settlement. Sir Garnet Wolseley has the reputation of being an extremely able man, and it is only fair to him to suppose that he was not the sole parent of this political monster, by which all the blood and treasure expended on the Zulu war were made of no account, but that it was partially dictated to him by authorities at home, who were anxious to gratify English opinion, and partly ignorant, partly careless of the consequences. At the same time, it is clear that he is responsible for the details of the scheme, since immediately after the capture of Cetywayo he writes a despatch about them which was considered so important, that a member of his staff was sent to England in charge of it. In this document he informs the Secretary of State that Cetywayo's rule was resolutely built up "without any of the ordinary and lawful foundations of authority, and by the mere vigour and vitality of an individual character." It is difficult to understand what Sir Garnet means in this passage. If the fact of being the rightful and generally accepted occupant of the throne is not an "ordinary and lawful foundation of authority," what is? As regards Cetywayo having built up his rule by the "mere vigour and vitality of an individual character," he is surely in error. Cetywayo's position was not different to that of his immediate predecessors. If

Sir Garnet had applied the remark to Chaka, the first king, to the vigour and vitality of whose individual character Zululand owes its existence as a nation, it would have been more appropriate. The despatch goes on to announce that he has made up his mind to divide the country into thirteen portions, in order to prevent the "possibility of any reunion of its inhabitants under one rule," and ends in these words: "I have laboured with the great aim of establishing for Her Majesty's subjects in South Africa, both white and coloured, as well as for this spirited people against whom unhappily we have been involved in war, the enduring foundations of peace, happiness and prosperity." The spirited people were no doubt vastly thankful, but the white man, reading such a passage as this, and knowing the facts of the case, will only recognise Sir Garnet Wolseley's admirable talent for ironical writing.

Sir Garnet entered into an agreement with each of his kinglets, who, amongst other things, promised that they would not make war without the sanction of the British Government. He also issued a paper of instructions to the gentleman who was first appointed British Resident (who, by the way, very soon threw up his post in despair). From this document we learn that all the ex-king's brothers are to "be under the eye of the chief John Dunn," but it is chiefly remarkable for the hostility it evinces to all missionary enterprise. The Resident is instructed to "be careful to hold yourself entirely aloof from all missionary or proselytising enterprises," and that "grants of land by former kings to missionaries cannot be recognised by the British Government," although Sir Garnet will allow missionaries to live in the country if the chief of the district does not object. These instructions created some adverse comment in England, with the result that, in the supplementary instructions issued on the occasion of Mr. Osborn's appointment as Resident, they were somewhat modified. In the despatch to the Secretary of State in which he announces the new appointment, Sir Garnet says that Mr. Osborn is to be the "councillor, guide, and friend" of the native chiefs, and that to his "moral influence" "we should look I think for the spread of civilisation and the propagation of the Gospel." What a conglomeration of duties, — at once "prophet, priest, and king!" Poor Mr. Osborn!

Of the chiefs appointed under this unfortunate settlement, some were so carelessly chosen that they have no authority whatsoever over the districts to which they were appointed, their nominal subjects preferring to remain under the leadership of their hereditary chief. Several of Sir Garnet's little kings cannot turn out an hundred men, whilst the hereditary chief, who has no official authority, can bring up three or four thousand. Thus, for instance, a territory was given to a chief called Infaneulela. The retainers of this gentleman live in a kraal of five or six huts on the battlefield of Ulundi. A chief called Dilligane, to whom the district should have been given, is practically head man of the district, and takes every possible opportunity of defying the nominee chief, Infaneulela, who is not acknowledged by the people. Another case is that of Umgitchwa, to whom a territory was given. In this instance there are two brothers, Umgitchwa and Somhlolo, born of different mothers. Umgitchwa is the elder, but Somhlolo is the son of a daughter of the king, and therefore, according to Zulu custom, entitled to succeed to the chieftainship. Somhlolo was disinherited by Sir Garnet on account of his youth (he is about twenty-five and has many wives). But an ancient custom is not to be thus abrogated by a stroke of the pen, and Somhlolo is practically chief of the district. Fighting is imminent between the two brothers.

A third case is that of Hlubi, who, though being a good, well-meaning man, is a Basuto, and being a foreigner, has no influence over the Zulus under him.

A fourth instance is that of Umlandela, an old and infirm Zulu, who was made chief over a large proportion of the Umtetwa tribe on the coast of Zululand. His appointment was a fatal mistake, and has already led to much bloodshed under the following curious circumstances, which are not without interest, as showing the intricacy of Zulu plots.

The Umtetwas were in the days of Chaka a very powerful tribe, but suffered the same fate at his hands as did every other that ventured to cross spears with him. They were partially annihilated, and whilst some of the survivors, of whom the Umtetwas in Zululand are the descendants, were embodied in the Zulu regiments, others were scattered far and wide. Branches of this important tribe exist as far off as the Cape Colony. Dingiswayo, who was the chief of the Umtetwas when Chaka conquered the tribe, fled after his defeat into Basutoland, and is supposed to have died there. After the Zulu war Sir G. Wolseley divided the Umtetwa into two districts, appointing an

Umtetwa chief named Somkeli ruler over one, and Umlandela over the other.

Umlandela, being a Zulu and worn with age, has never had any authority over his nominal subjects, and has been anxious to rid himself of the danger and responsibility of his chieftainship by transferring it on to the shoulders of Mr. John Dunn, whose territory adjoins his own, and who would be, needless to say, nothing loth to avail himself of the opportunity of increasing his taxable area. Whilst this intrigue was in progress all Zululand was convulsed with the news of our defeat by the Boers and the consequent surrender of the Transvaal. It was commonly rumoured that our forces were utterly destroyed, and that the Boers were now the dominant Power. Following on the heels of this intelligence was a rumour to the effect that Cetywayo was coming back. These two reports, both of which had a foundation of truth, had a very bad effect on the vulgar mind in Zululand, and resulted in the setting in motion of a variety of plots, of which the following was the most important.

The Umtetwa tribe is among those who are not anxious for the return of Cetywayo, but see in the present state of affairs an opportunity of regaining the power they possessed before the days of Chaka. If they were to have a king over Zululand they determined that it should be an Umtetwa king, and Somkeli, one of the chiefs appointed by Sir Garnet, was the man who aimed at the throne. He was not, however, anxious to put out his hand at first further than he could draw it back, so he adopted a very ingenious expedient. It will be remembered that the old Chief Dingiswayo fled to Basutoland, where he is reported to have married. It occurred to Somkeli that if he could produce a descendant or a pseudo-descendant of Dingiswayo he would have no difficulty in beginning operations by dispossessing Umlandela of his territory in favour of the supposed lawful heir. In fact he wanted a cat to pull the chestnuts out of the fire for him, who could easily be got rid of afterwards. Accordingly one Sitimela was produced who is supposed to be an escaped convict from Natal, who gave out that he was a grandson of Dingiswayo by a Basuto woman, and a great medicine-man, able to kill everybody by a glance of his eye.

To this impostor adherents flocked from all parts of Zululand, and Umlandela flying for his life into John Dunn's territory, Sitimela seized upon the chieftainship. The Resident thereupon ordered him to appear before him, but he, as might be expected, refused to come. As it was positively necessary to put an end to the plot by some means, since its further development would have endangered and perhaps destroyed the weak-knee'd Zulu settlement, Mr. Osborn determined to proceed to the scene of action. Mahomet would not go to the mountain, so the mountain had to go to Mahomet. On arrival he pitched his tents half way between the camps of Sitimela and John Dunn, who had Umlandela under his charge, and summoned Somkeli, the author of the plot, to appear before him. Ten days elapsed before the summons was obeyed. During this time, and indeed until they finally escaped, the Resident and his companion could not even venture to the spring, which was close at hand, to wash, for fear of being assassinated. All day long they could see lines of armed men swarming over the hills round them, and hear them yelling their war-songs. At length Somkeli appeared, accompanied by over a thousand armed warriors. He was ordered to withdraw his forces from Sitimela's army and go home. He went home, but did not withdraw his forces. The next day Sitimela himself appeared before the Resident. He was ordered to come with ten men: he came with two thousand all armed, wild with excitement and "moutied" (medicined). To make this medicine they had killed and pounded up a little cripple boy and several of Umlandela's wives. It afterwards transpired that the only reason Sitimela did not then and there kill the Resident was that he (Mr. Osborn) had with him several chiefs who were secretly favourable to Sitimela's cause, and if he had killed him he would, according to Zulu custom, have had to kill them too. Mr. Osborn ordered Sitimela to disperse his forces or take the consequences, and waited a few days for him to do so; but seeing no signs of his compliance, he then ordered the neighbouring chiefs to fall on him, and at length withdrew from his encampment, —none too soon. That very night a party of Sitimela's men came down to kill him, and finding the tent in which he and his companions had slept standing, stabbed at its supposed occupants through the canvas.

Sitimela was defeated by the forces ordered out by the Resident with a loss of about 500 men. It is, however, worthy of note, and shows how widespread was the conspiracy, that out of all the thousands promised, Mr. Osborn was only able to call out two thousand men.

The appointment, however, that has occasioned the most criticism is that of John Dunn, who got the Benjamin share of Zululand in preference to his brother chiefs. The converting of an Englishman into a Zulu chief is such a very odd proceeding that it is difficult to know what to think of it. John Dunn is an ambitious man, and most probably has designs on the throne; he is also a man who understands the value of money, of which he makes a great deal out of his chieftainship. At the same time, it is clear that, so far as it goes, his rule is better than that of the other chiefs; he has a uniform tax fixed, and has even done something in the way of starting schools and making roads. From all that I have been able to gather, his popularity and influence with the Zulus are overrated, though he has lived amongst them so many years, and taken so many of their women to wife. His appointment was a hazardous experiment, and in the long run is likely to prove a mischievous one, since any attempted amendment of the settlement will be violently resisted by him on the ground of vested interests. Also, if white men are set over Zulus at all, they should be *gentlemen* in the position of government officers, not successful adventurers.

Perhaps the only wise thing done in connection with the settlement was the appointment of Mr. Osborn, C.M.G., as British Resident. It is not easy to find a man fitted for that difficult and dangerous position, for the proper filling of which many qualifications are required. Possessed of an intimate knowledge of the Zulus, their language, and their mode of thought and life, and being besides a very able and energetic officer, Mr. Osborn would have saved the settlement from breaking down if anybody could have saved it. As it is, by the exercise of ceaseless energy and at great personal risk, he has preserved it from total collapse. Of the dangers and anxieties to which he is exposed, the account I have given of the Sitimela incident is a sufficient example. He is, in fact, nothing but a shadow, for he has no force at his command to ensure obedience to his decisions, or to prevent civil war; and in Zululand, oddly enough, force is a remedy. Should one chief threaten the peace of the country, he can only deal with him by calling on another chief for aid, a position that is neither dignified nor right. What is worst of all is that the Zulus are beginning to discover what a shadow he is, and with this weakened position he has to pit his single brains against all the thousand and one plots which are being woven throughout Zululand. The whole country teems with plots. Mnyamane, the late Prime Minister, and one of the ablest, and perhaps the most influential man in Zululand, is plotting for the return of Cetywayo. Bishop Colenso, again, is as usual working his own wires, and creating agitations to forward his ends, whatever they may be at the moment. John Dunn, on the other hand, is plotting to succeed Cetywayo, and so on *ad infinitum*. Such is the state of affairs with which our unfortunate Resident has to contend. Invested with large imaginary powers, he has in reality nothing but his personal influence and his own wits to help him. He has no white man to assist him, but living alone in a broken-down tent and some mud huts built by his son's hands (for the Government have never kept their promise to put him up a house), in the midst of thousands of restless and scheming savages, amidst plots against the peace and against his authority, he has to do the best he can to carry out an impracticable settlement, and to maintain the character of English justice and the honour of the English name. Were Mr. Osborn to throw up his post or to be assassinated, the authorities would find it difficult to keep the whole settlement from collapsing like a card castle.

Nobody who understood Zulu character and aspirations could ever have executed such a settlement as Sir Garnet Wolseley's, unless he did it in obedience to some motive or instructions that it was not advisable to publish. It is true that Sir Garnet's experience of the Zulus was extremely small, and that he put aside the advice of those who did know them with that contempt with which he is wont to treat colonists and their opinions. Sir Garnet Wolseley does not like colonial people, possibly because they have signally failed to appreciate heaven-born genius in his person, or his slap-dash drumhead sort of way of settling the fate of countries, and are, indeed, so rude as to openly say, that, in their opinion, he did more mischief in Africa in a few months, than it would take an ordinary official a lifetime to accomplish.

However this may be, stop his ears as much as he might, Sir Garnet cannot have been entirely blind to the import of what he was doing, and the only explanation of his action is that he entered on it more with the idea of flattering and gratifying English public opinion, than of doing his best for the Zulus or the white Colonists on their borders. A great outcry had been raised at home, where, in common with most South African affairs, the matter was not thoroughly understood, against the supposed intended annexation of Zululand for the benefit of "greedy colonists." It was argued that colonists were anxious for the annexation in order that they might get the land to speculate with, and doubtless this was, in individual instances, true. I fully agree with those who think that it would be unwise to throw open Zululand to the European settler, not on account of the Zulus, who would benefit by the change, but because the result would be a state of affairs similar to that in Natal, where there are a few white men surrounded by an ever-growing mass of Kafirs. But there is a vast difference between Annexation proper and the Protectorate it was our duty to establish over the natives. Such an arrangement would have presented few difficulties, and have brought with it many advantages. White men could have been forbidden to settle in the country. A small hut-tax, such as the Zulus would have cheerfully paid, would have brought in forty or fifty thousand a year, an ample sum to defray the expenses of the Resident and sub-Residents: the maintenance of an adequate native force to keep order: and even the execution of necessary public works. It is impossible to overrate the advantages that must have resulted both to the Zulus and their white neighbours from the adoption of this obvious plan, among them being lasting peace and security to life and property; or to understand the folly and cruelty that dictated the present arrangement, or rather want of arrangement. Not for many years has England missed such an opportunity of doing good, not only at no cost, but with positive advantage to herself. Did we owe nothing to this people whose kingdom we had broken up, and whom we had been shooting down by thousands? They may well ask, as they do continually, what they have done that we should treat them as we have and are doing?

It cannot be too clearly understood, that, when the Zulus laid down their arms they did so, hoping and believing that they would be taken over by the English Government, which, having been fairly beaten by it, they now looked on as their head or king, and be ruled like their brethren in Natal. They expected to have to pay taxes and to have white magistrates placed over them, and they or the bulk of them looked forward to the change with pleasure. It must be remembered that when once they have found their master, there exists no more law-abiding people in the world than the Zulus, provided they are ruled firmly, and above all justly. Believing that such a rule would fall to their lot they surrendered when they did. How great, then, must their surprise have been when they found, that without their wishes being consulted in the matter, their own hereditary king was to be sent away, and thirteen little kings set up in his place, with, strangest of all, a white man as chief little king, whilst the British Government contented itself with placing a Resident in the country, to watch the troubles that must ensue.

Such a settlement as this could only have one object and one result, neither of which is at all creditable to the English people. The Zulus were parcelled out among thirteen chiefs, in order that their strength might be kept down by internecine war and mutual distrust and jealousy: and, as though it were intended to render this result more certain, territories were chucked about in the careless way I have described, whilst central authority was abolished, and the vacant throne is dangled before all eyes labelled "the prize of the strongest." Of course Sir Garnet's paper agreements with the chiefs were for the most part disregarded from the first. For instance, every chief has his army and uses it too. In Zululand bloodshed is now a thing of every-day occurrence, and the whole country is torn by fear, uncertainly, and consequent want.[*] The settlement is bearing its legitimate fruit; some thousands of Zulus have already been killed in direct consequence of it, and more will doubtless follow. And this is the outcome of all the blood and treasure spent over the Zulu war! Well, we have settled Zululand on the most approved principles, and thank Heaven, British influence has not been extended!

[*] A severe famine is said to be imminent in Zululand.

To show that I am not singular in my opinion as to the present state of Zululand, I may be allowed to quote a few short extracts taken at random, from half-a-dozen numbers of the "Natal Mercury." Talking of the Zulu settlement terms as dictated by Sir G. Wolseley, the leading article of the issue 21st November 1881 says:—"It will at once be apparent that these terms have in several cases been flagrantly violated, especially as regards clauses of 2, 3, 4, and 6. This last will assuredly be broken again and yet again, so long as the British Resident occupies the position of an official mollusc. The chiefs themselves perceive and admit the evils that must arise out of the absence of any effective central authority. These evils are so obvious, they were so generally recognised at the outset as being inherent in the scheme, that we might almost suppose their occurrence had been deliberately anticipated as a desired outcome of the settlement. The morality of such a line of policy would be precisely on a par with that which is involved in the proposal to reinstate Cetywayo as a means of dealing with the Boers. The creation of thirteen kinglets in order that they might destroy each other, is as humane and high-minded an effort of statesmanship as would be the restoration of a banished king in order that he might eat up a people to whom the same power has just given back their independence. To the simple colonial mind such deep designs of Machiavellian statecraft are as hateful as they are inhuman and dishonest."

A correspondent of the "Mercury" in Zululand writes under date of 13th October:—

"I send a line at the last moment to say that things are going from bad to worse at railway speed. Up to the arrival of Sir Evelyn Wood, the chiefs did not fully realise that they were really independent at all. Now they do, and if I mistake not, like a beggar on horseback will ride to the devil sharp. Oham has begun by killing a large number of the Amagalusi people. My information is derived from native sources, and may be somewhat exaggerated. It is that the killed at Isandhlwana were few compared with those killed by Uhamu a few days ago. Usibebu also and Undabuka are, I am told, on the point of coming to blows; and if they do that it will be worse still, for Undabuka will find supporters throughout the length and breadth of Zululand. Undabuka, the full brother of the ex-king, is the protege of the Bishop of Natal. The Bishop, I find, has again sent one of his agents (Amajuba by name) calling for another deputation. The deputation is now on its way to Natal, and that, I understand, against the express refusal of the Resident to allow it." In the issue of 14th November is published a letter from Mr. Nunn, a gentleman well known in Zululand, from which, as it is too long to quote in its entirety, I give a few extracts:—
"*Oham's Camp, Oct.15.*—The Zulus cannot comprehend the Transvaal affair, and it has been industriously circulated among them that the English have been beaten and forced to give back the Transvaal. They do not understand gracious acts of restoration after we have been beaten. Four times this year has Umnyamana called his army together and menaced Oham, who has several times had to have parties of his followers sleeping around his kraal in the hills adjacent, so as to give

him timely notice to fly. When Oham left his kraal for the purpose of attending the meeting at Inslasatye, the same day the whole of the Maquilisini Tribe came on to the hills adjacent to Oham's kraal, the 'Injamin,' and threatened that district. This has been the case on two or three former occasions, and simultaneously Umnyamana's tribe and Undabuka's followers always flew to arms, thus threatening on all sides. . . . Trading is and has been for months entirely suspended in this district. The fields are unplanted, no ploughs or Kafir-picks at work—all are in a state of excitement, not knowing the moment a collision may take place. Hunger will stare many in the face next year, and all the men yelling to their chiefs to be let loose and put an end to this state of uncertainty."

Mr. Nunn encloses an account by an eye-witness of a battle which took place on the 2d October 1881 between Oham's army and the Maquilisini Tribe. The following is an extract:—"On the 2nd there was a heavy mist, and on moving forward the mounted party found themselves in the midst of the enemy (the Maquilisini), and on hearing a cry to stab the horses, they rode through them with no casualty (except one horse slightly wounded with a bullet). The army, moving in a half circle, now became generally engaged in a hand-to-hand fight, and our men were checked and annoyed by a number of the enemy armed with guns, who were in a stone-kraal and kept up a constant fire. Amatonga, now at the head of the mounted party, charged and drove the enemy out of the kraal, from which they three several times charged the enemy on the flank, assisted by a small infantry party, and cut paths through their ranks. The fight, which had now lasted nearly an hour, commenced to flag, and Oham's army making a sudden rush entirely routed the enemy, and the carnage lasted to the Bevan river, the boundary of the Transvaal. No women or children were killed, but out of an army of about 1500 of the enemy but few escaped" (sic) . . . . "The men, as they were being killed, repeatedly exclaimed, 'We are dying through Umnyamana and Umlabaku.'"

In the "Natal Mercury" of the 13th March occurs the following:—

"*Zulu Country.*—As to the state of the country it is something we cannot describe; everything is upside down, and the chiefs appointed by the government are mere nobodies, and have not any power over their own people. Even the Resident is in a false position, and seems perfectly powerless to act either way. We had one row, just arriving at a kraal in time to save it from being eaten up. Witchcraft and killing, one of the pretences on which the English made war, are of every-day occurrence, and fifty times worse than they were before the war. Oham and Tibysio (?) keep their men continually in the field, consequently those districts are at present in a state of famine."

Sir Garnet Wolseley executed the Zulu settlement on the 1st September 1879. The above extracts will suffice to show the state of the country after it has been working for little more than two years. They will also, I believe, suffice to convince any just and impartial mind that I do not exaggerate when I say that it is an abomination and a disgrace to England. The language may be strong, but when one hears of 1500 unfortunates (nearly twice as many as we lost at Isandhlwana) being slaughtered in a single intertribal broil, it is time to use strong language. It is not as though this were an unexpected or an unavoidable development of events, every man who knew the Zulus predicted the misery that must result from such a settlement, but those who directed their destinies turned a deaf ear to all warnings. They did not wish to hear.

And now we are told that civil war is imminent between the Cetywayo or anti-settlement party, and what I must, for want of a better name, call the John Dunn party, or those who have acquired interests under the settlement, and who for various reasons wish to see Cetywayo's face no more. If this occurs, and it will occur unless the Government makes up its mind to do something before long, the slaughter, not only of men but also of women and children, will be enormous; fugitives will pour into Natal, followed perhaps by their pursuers, and for aught we know the war may spread into our own dominions. We are a philanthropic people, very, when Bulgarians are concerned, or when the subject is one that piques the morbid curiosity, or is the rage of the moment, and the subject of addresses from great and eloquent speakers. But we can sit still, and let such massacres as these take place, when we have but to hold up our hand to stop them. When occasionally the veil is lifted a little, and the public hears of "fresh fighting in Zululand;" a question is asked in the House; Mr. Courtney, as usual, has no information, but generally discredits the report, and it is put aside as "probably not true." I am well aware that of the few who read these words, many will discredit them, or say that they are written for some object, or for party purposes. But it is not the case; they are written in the interest of the truth, and in the somewhat faint hope that they may awaken a portion of the public, however small, to a knowledge of our responsibilities to the unfortunate Zulus. For try to get rid of it as we may, those responsibilities rest upon our shoulders. When we conquered the Zulu nation and sent away the Zulu king, we undertook, morally at any rate, to provide for the future good government of the country; otherwise, the Zulu war was unjust indeed. If we continue to fail, as we have hitherto, to carry out our responsibilities as a humane and Christian nation ought to do, our lapse from what is right will certainly recoil upon our own heads, and, in the stern lessons of future troubles and disasters, we shall learn that Providence with the nation, as with the individual, makes a neglected duty its own avenger. We have sown the wind, let us be careful lest we reap the whirlwind.

It is very clear that things cannot remain in their present condition. If they do, it is probable that the Resident will sooner or later be assassinated; not from any personal motives, but as a political necessity, and some second Chaka will rise up and found a new Zulu dynasty, sweeping away our artificial chiefs and divisions like cobwebs. This idea seems to have penetrated into Lord Kimberley's official mind, since in his despatch of instructions to Sir H. Bulwer, written in February last, he says, "Probably if the chiefs are left to themselves after a period more or less prolonged of war and anarchy, some man will raise himself to the position of supreme chief." The prospect of war and anarchy in Zululand does not, however, trouble Lord Kimberley at all; in fact, the whole despatch is typical to a degree of the Liberal Colonial policy. Lord Kimberley admits that what little quiet the country has enjoyed under the settlement, "was due to a mistaken belief on the part of the Zulus that the British Government was ruling them, or would rule them through the Resident." He evidently clearly sees all the evils and bloodshed that are resulting and that must result from the present state of affairs; indeed he recapitulates them, and then ends up by even refusing to allow such slight measures of relief as the appointment of sub-Residents to be carried out, although begged for by the chiefs, on the ground that it might extend British influence. Of the interests of the Zulus himself he is quite careless. The whole despatch can be summed up thus: "If you can find any method to improve the state of affairs which will not subject us to the smallest cost, risk, or responsibility, you can employ it; if not, let them fight it out." Perhaps Lord Kimberley may live (officially) long enough to find out that meanness and selfishness do not always pay, and that it is not always desirable, thus to sacrifice the respect, and crush the legitimate aspirations of a generous people.

Unless something is done before long, it is possible that John Dunn may succeed after a bloody war in securing the throne; but this would not prove a permanent arrangement, since he is now getting on in life and has no son to carry on the dynasty. Another possibility, and one that is not generally known, at any rate in this country, though it is perhaps the most probable of all, is this. Cetywayo has left a son in Zululand, who is being carefully educated under the care of Mnyamane, the late King's Prime Minister. The boy is now about 16 years of age, and is reported to possess very good abilities, and is the trump card that Mnyamane will play as soon as the time is ripe. This young man is the hereditary heir to the Zulu crown, and it is more than probable that if he is proclaimed king the vast majority of the nation will rally round him and establish him firmly on his throne. There is little use in keeping Cetywayo confined whilst his son is at large. The lad should have been brought to England and educated, so that he might at some future time have assisted in the civilisation of his country: as it is, he is growing up in a bad school.

And now I come to the root of the whole matter, the question whether or no, under all these circumstances, it is right or desirable to re-establish Cetywayo on the throne of Zululand. In considering this question, I think that Cetywayo's individuality ought to be out on one side, however much we may sympathise with his position, as I confess I do to some extent myself. After all, Cetywayo is only one man, whereas the happiness, security, and perhaps the lives of many thousands are involved in the issue of the question. In coming to any conclusion in the matter it is necessary to keep in view the intentions of the Government as regards our future connection with Zululand. If the Government intends to do its duty and rule Zululand as it ought to be ruled, by the appointment of proper magistrates, the establishment of an adequate force, and the imposition of the necessary taxes; then it would be the height of folly to permit Cetywayo to return, since his presence would defeat the scheme. It must be remembered that there is as yet nothing whatsoever to prevent this plan being carried out. It would be welcomed with joy by the large majority of both Zulus and Colonists. It would also solve the problem of the increase of the native population of Natal, which is assuming the most alarming proportions, since Zululand, being very much underpopulated, it would be easy, were that country once quietly settled, to draft the majority of the Natal Zulus back into it. This is undoubtedly the best course, and indeed the only right course; but it does not at all follow that it will be taken, since governments are unfortunately more concerned at the prospect of losing votes than with the genuine interests of their dependencies. The proper settlement of Zululand would not be popular amongst a large class in this country, and therefore it is not likely to be carried out, however right and necessary it may be.

If nothing is going to be done, then it becomes a question whether or no Cetywayo should be sent back.

The large majority of the Natalians consider that his restoration would be an act of suicidal folly, and their opinion is certainly entitled to great weight, since they are after all the people principally concerned. The issue of the experiment would be a matter of comparative indifference to people living 7000 miles away, but is naturally regarded with some anxiety by those who have their homes on the borders of Zululand. It is very well to sympathise with savage royalty in distress, but it must be borne in mind that there are others to be considered besides the captive king. Many of the Zulus, for instance, are by no means anxious to see him again, since they look forward with just apprehension to the line of action he may take with those who have not shown sufficient anxiety for his return, or have in other ways incurred his resentment. One thing is clear, to send the king back to Zululand is to restore the *status in quo* as it was before the war. There can be no half measures about it, no more worthless paper stipulations; a Zulu king must either be allowed to rule in his own fashion or not at all. The war would go for nothing, and would doubtless have to be fought over again with one of Cetywayo's successors.

Also it must be remembered that it is one thing to talk of restoring Cetywayo, and another to carry his restoration into effect. It would not simply be a question of turning him down on the borders of Zululand, and letting him find his own way back to his throne, for such a proceeding would be the signal for the outbreak of civil war. It is not to be supposed that John Dunn, and those whose interests are identical with Dunn's, would allow the ex-king to reseat himself on the throne without a struggle; indeed the former has openly declared his intention of resisting the attempt by force of arms if necessary. He is by no means anxious to give up the 15,000 pounds a year his hut-tax brings in, and all the contingent profits and advantages of his chieftainship. If we wish to restore Cetywayo we must first depose Dunn; in fact, we must be ready to support his restoration by force of arms.

As regards Cetywayo himself, I cannot share the opinion of those who think that he would be personally dangerous. He has learnt his lesson, and would not be anxious to try conclusions with the English again; indeed, I believe he would prove a staunch ally. But supposing him re-established on the throne, how long would it be before a revolution, or the hand of the assassin, to say nothing of the ordinary chances of nature, put an end to him, and how do we know that his successor in power would share his views?

Cetywayo's rule, bad as it was, was perhaps preferable to the reign of terror that we have established, under the name of a settlement. But that we can still remedy if we choose to do so, whereas, if we once restore Cetywayo, all power over the Zulus passes out of our hands.

We have many interests to consider in South Africa, all of which will be more or less affected by our action in this matter. On the whole, I am of opinion that the Government that replaces Cetywayo on the throne of his fathers will undertake a very grave responsibility, and must be prepared to deal with many resulting complications, not the least of which will be the utter exasperation of the white inhabitants of Natal.

NATAL AND RESPONSIBLE GOVERNMENT

Natal – Causes of increase of the native population – Happy condition of the Natal Zulus – Polygamy – Its results on population – The impossibility of eradicating it – Relations between a Zulu and his wives – Connection between polygamy and native law – Missionary work amongst the Zulus – Its failure – Reasons of its failure – Early days of Natal – Growth of the native question – Coming struggle between white and black over the land question – Difficulty of civilising the Zulu – Natal as a black settlement – The constitution of Natal – Request for responsible government – Its refusal – The request renewed and granted – Terms and reason of Lord Kimberley's offer – Infatuation of responsible government party in Natal – Systematic abuse of colonists in England – Colonial speculators – Grievances against the Imperial Government – Sir Henry Bulwer – Uncertain future of Natal – Its available force – Exterior dangers – The defence question shirked by the "party of progress" – The confederation question – The difficulty of obtaining desirable immigrants – The only real key to the Natal native question – Folly of accepting self-government till it is solved.

Natal has an area of about 18,000 square miles, and its present population is, roughly, 25,000 whites and 400,000 natives of the Zulu race. When, in 1843, it first became a British colony, the number of natives living within its borders was very small, and they were for the most part wanderers, fragmentary remnants of the tribes that Chaka had destroyed. I shall probably be under, rather than over the mark, if I say, that the Zulu population of the colony has multiplied itself by ten during the last thirty years. Two causes have combined to bring about this extraordinary increase; firstly, wholesale immigration from the surrounding territories; and secondly, the practice of polygamy.

This immigration has been due to a great want of foresight, or want of knowledge, on the part of the Home authorities, who have allowed it to go on without check or hindrance till it has, in conjunction with its twin evil polygamy, produced the state of affairs it is my object to describe. Ever since its first establishment as a colony Natal has been turned into a city of refuge for the native inhabitants of Zululand, the Transvaal, Swaziland, and elsewhere. If news came to a Zulu chief that his king purposed to eat him up, he at once fled across the Tugela with his wives and followers and settled in Natal. If the Boers or Swazis destroyed a tribe, the remnant found its way to Natal.

That country, indeed, is to the South African native a modern Isles of the Blest. Once across the border line, and, whatever his crime, he is in a position to defy his worst enemy, and can rest secure in the protection of the Home and local Governments, and of the enactments specially passed to protect him and his privileges. The Government allots him land, or if it does not he squats on private land: bringing with him his own peculiar and barbarous customs. In all the world I do not know a race more favoured by circumstances than the Natal Zulus. They live on the produce of the fields that their wives cultivate, or rather scratch, doing little or no work, and having no occasion to do any. They are very rich, and their taxes are a mere trifle, fifteen shillings per annum for each hut. They bear no share of the curse that comes to all other men as a birthright; they need not labour. Protected by a powerful Government, they do not fear attack from without, or internal disorder. What all men desire, riches and women, are theirs in abundance, and even their children, the objects of so much expense and sore perplexity to civilised parents, are to them a source of wealth. Their needs are few; a straw hut, corn for food, and the bright sun. They are not even troubled with the thought of a future life, but, like the animals, live through their healthy, happy days, and at last, in extreme old age, meet a death which for them has no terrors, because it simply means extinction. When compared to that of civilised races, or even of their own brethren in the interior, their lot is indeed a happy one.

But the stream of immigration, continuous though it has been, would not by itself have sufficed to bring up the native population to its present enormous total, without the assistance of the polygamous customs of the immigrants.

I believe that inquirers have ascertained, that, as a general rule, the practice of polygamy has not the effect of bringing about an abnormal growth of population. However this may be elsewhere, in Natal, owing in great measure to the healthy customs of the Zulu race,[*] the rate of increase is unprecedented. Many writers and other authorities consider polygamy as an institution, to be at once wicked and disgusting. As to its morality, it is a point upon which it is difficult to express any opinion, nor, indeed, does the question enter into the scope of what I have to say; but it must be remembered that in the case of the Zulu his whole law and existence is mixed up with the institution, and that it is necessary to him to repair the gaps made in his ranks by war. Violent anti-polygamists in this country always make a strong point of the cruelty it is supposed to involve to the women, and talk about the "violation of their holiest feelings." As a matter of fact, sad as it may appear, the Zulu women are much attached to the custom, nor would they, as a general rule, consent to marry a man who only purposed taking one wife. There are various reasons for this: for instance, the first wife is a person of importance, and takes precedence of all the others, a fact as much appreciated by the Zulu woman as by the London lady. Again, the more wives there are, the more wealth it brings into the family, since in the ordinary course of nature more wives mean more female children, who, when they come to a marriageable age, mean in their turn at least ten cows each (the Government price for a wife). The amount thus obtained is placed to the credit of the estate of the mother of the girl married, and for this reason all Zulu women are extremely anxious to have children, especially female children. Finally, the liking of Zulu women for the custom is bred in them. It has been going on for countless generations, and it is probable that it will go on for so long as the race endures. Nations do not change such habits unless the change is forced on them, with the alternative of extermination.

[*] *As soon as a Zulu woman is discovered to be pregnant, her husband ceases to cohabit with her, nor does he live with her again until the child is weaned, eighteen months, and sometimes two years, after its birth.*

Polygamy will never be eradicated by moral persuasion, because, even if a native could be brought to think it wrong, which is in itself impossible, its abolition would affect his interests irredeemably. A Zulu's wives are also his servants; they plough his land and husband his grain, in addition to bearing his children. Had he but one wife most of her time would be taken up with the latter occupation, and then the mealie-planting and gathering would necessarily fall to the lot of the husband, a state of affairs he would never consent to.

Again, if monogamy were established, girls would lose their value, and a great source of wealth would be destroyed. It must, however, be understood that Zulu girls are not exactly sold; the cows received by the parents are by a legal fiction supposed to be a gift presented, not a price paid. Should the wife subsequently run away, they are, I believe, returnable.

On these subjects, as is not to be wondered at when so many interests are concerned, the Zulu law is a little intricate. The cleverest counsel in the Temple could not give an opinion on such a case as the following: —

A. has four wives and children by Nos. 1 and 3. On his death his brother, B., a rich man, takes over his wives and property, and has children by each of the four women. He has also children by other wives. On his death, in extreme old age, how should the property be divided amongst the descendants of the various marriages?

It is clear that if such a case as this is to be dealt with at all it must be under native law, and this is one of the great dangers of polygamy. Once rooted in a state it necessitates a double system of laws, since civilised law is quite unable to cope with the cases daily arising from its practice. It is sometimes argued that the law employed is a matter of indifference, provided that substantial justice is done, according to the ideas of people concerned, and this is doubtless very true if it is accepted as a fact that the Zulu population of Natal is always to remain in its present condition of barbarism. To continue to administer their law is to give it the sanction of the white man's authority, and every day that it is so administered makes it more impossible to do away with it. I say "more impossible" advisedly, because I believe its abrogation is already impossible. There is no satisfactory way out of the difficulty, because it has its roots in, and draws its existence from, the principle of polygamy, which I believe will last while the people last.

Some rely on the Missionary to effect this stupendous change, and turn a polygamous people into monogamists. But it is a well-known fact that the missionaries produce no more permanent effect on the Zulu mind than a child does on the granite rock which he chips at with a chisel. How many real Christians are there in Zululand and Natal, and of that select and saintly band how many practise monogamy? But very few, and among those few there is a large proportion of bad characters, men who have adopted Christianity as a last resource. I mean no disrespect to the missionaries, many of whom are good men, doing their best under the most unpromising conditions, though some are simply traders and political agitators. But the fact remains the same. Christianity makes no appreciable progress amongst the Zulu natives, whilst, on the other hand, no one having any experience in the country will, if he can avoid it, have a so-called Christian Kafir in his house, because the term is but too frequently synonymous with that of drunkard and thief. I do not wish it to be understood that it is the fact of his Christianity that so degrades the Zulu, because I do not think it has anything to do with it. It is only that the novice, standing on the threshold of civilisation, as a rule finds the vices of the white man more congenial than his virtues.

The Zulus are as difficult to convince of the truths of Christianity as were the Jews, whom they so much resemble in their customs. They have a natural disinclination to believe that which they cannot see, and, being constitutionally very clever and casuistical, are prepared to argue each individual point with an ability very trying to missionaries. It was one of these Zulus, known as the Intelligent Zulu, but in reality no more intelligent than his fellows, whose shrewd remarks first caused doubts to arise in the mind of Bishop Colenso, and through him in those of thousands of others.

Another difficulty in the way of the Missionary is, that he is obliged to insist on the putting away of surplus wives, and thus to place himself out of court at the outset. It is quite conceivable that in the opinion of wild and savage men, it is preferable to let the new teaching alone, rather than to adopt it at the cost of such a radical change in their domestic arrangements. As a case in point I may quote that of Hlubi, the Basutu appointed chief of one of the divisions of Zululand, by Sir G. Wolseley. Hlubi is at heart a Christian, and a good man, and anxious to be baptized. The missionaries, however, refuse to baptize him, because he has two wives. Hlubi therefore remains a heathen, saying, not unnaturally, that he feels it would be impossible for him to put away a woman with whom he has lived for so many years.

Whilst polygamy endures Christianity will advance with but small strides. It seems to me that we are beginning at the wrong end. We must civilise first and Christianise afterwards. As well try to sow corn among rocks and look to gather a full crop, as expect the words of Grace and Divine love to bear fruit in the hearts of a people whose forefathers have for countless generations been men of blood, whose prized traditions are one long story of slaughter, and who, if they are now at peace are, as it were, only gathering strength for a surer spring. First, the soil must be prepared before the seed is sown.

To do this there is but one way. Abolish native customs and laws, especially polygamy, and bring our Zulu subjects within the pale of our own law. Deprive them of their troops of servants in the shape of wives, and thus force them to betake themselves to honest labour like the rest of mankind.

There is only one objection in the way of the realisation of this scheme, which would, doubtless, bring about, in the course of a generation, a much better state of things, and gather many thousand converts into the fold of the Church; and that is, the opportunity has, so far as Natal is concerned, been missed—the time has gone by when it could have been carried out. To young countries, as to young men, there come sometimes opportunities of controlling their future destinies which, if not seized at the moment, pass away for ever, or only to return after long and troubled years. Natal has had her chance, and it has gone away from her, though through no fault of her own. If, when the colony was first settled, the few natives who then lived there had been forced to conform to the usages of civilised life or to quit its borders; if refugees had been refused admission save on the same terms, it would not occupy the very serious position it does at the present moment.

To understand the situation into which Natal has drifted with reference to its native inhabitants, it is necessary to premise that that country has hitherto had practically no control over its own affairs, more especially as regards native legislation.

In its early days it was a happy, quiet place, a favoured clime, where the traveller or settler could find good shooting, cheap labour, and cheap living. No enemy threatened its rest, and the natives were respectful and peaceful in their behaviour. But it was in those days that the native difficulty, that Upas tree that now overshadows and poisons the whole land, took root; for slowly, from all parts, all through that quiet time, by ones, by tens, by hundreds, refugees were flowing in, and asking and receiving land to settle on from the Government.

It is not, however, to be supposed that the local officials did not perceive the gathering danger, since it has again and again been pointed out to different Secretaries of State, and again and again been ignored by them, or put off for the consideration of their successors. Hand-to-mouth legislation has always been the characteristic of our rule in South Africa. On one occasion Sir Theophilus, then Mr. Shepstone, went so far as to offer to personally draw off a large portion of the native population, and settle them on some vacant territory bordering on the Cape Colony, but the suggestion was not acceded to, for fear lest the execution of the scheme should excite disturbances amongst the natives of the Cape. Thus year after year has passed away—plan after plan has been put aside,—and nothing has been done.

In the colony a great deal of abuse is poured out on the head of Sir T. Shepstone, to whom the present native situation is unjustly attributed by a certain party of politicians. Sir T. Shepstone was for very many years Secretary for Native Affairs in Natal, but until he came to England, shortly before the termination of his official career, he was personally unknown to the Colonial Office, and had no influence there. It was totally out of his power to control the policy of the Home Government with reference to the Natal natives; he could only take things as he found them, and make the best of such materials as came to his hand. As he could not keep the natives out of the colony or prevent polygamy, he did what he could towards making them loyal and contented subjects. How well he succeeded, and with what consummate tact and knowledge he must have exercised his authority, is shown by the fact that in all these years there has been but one native disturbance, namely that of Langalibalele, and by the further fact that the loyalty of the Natal Zulus stood the strain of the Zulu war. Also, there never has been, and probably never will be, another white man so universally beloved and reverenced by the natives throughout the length and breadth of South Africa.

But Sir T. Shepstone's influence for good will pass away, as all purely personal influence must, and meanwhile, what is the situation? On the one hand, there is a very slowly increasing, scattered, and mixed population of about 25,000 whites, capable, at the outside, of putting a force of 4000 men in the field. On the other, there is a warlike native population, united by the ties of race and common interests, numbering at the present moment between 400,000 and

500,000, and increasing by leaps and bounds: capable of putting quite 80,000 warriors into the field, and possessing, besides, numerous strongholds called locations. At present these two rival populations live side by side in peace and amity, though at heart neither loves the other. The two races are so totally distinct that it is quite impossible for them to have much community of feeling; they can never mingle; their ideas are different, their objects are different, and in Natal their very law is different. Kafirs respect and like individual Englishmen, but I doubt whether they are particularly fond of us as a race, though they much prefer us to any other white men, and are devoted to our rule, so long as it is necessary to them. The average white man, on the other hand, detests the Kafir, and looks on him as a lazy good-for-nothing, who ought to work for him and will not work for him, whilst he is quite incapable of appreciating his many good points. It is an odd trait about Zulus that only gentlemen, in the true sense of the word, can win their regard, or get anything out of them.

It is obvious that, sooner or later, these two races must come into contact, the question being how long the present calm will last. To this question I will venture to suggest an answer,—I believe the right one. It will last until the native gets so cramped for room that he has no place left to settle on, except the white man's lands. The white man will then try to turn him off, whereupon the native will fall back on the primary resource of killing him, and possessing himself of the land by force. This plan, simultaneously carried out on a large scale, would place the colony at the mercy of its native inhabitants.

Nor is the time so very far distant when Englishmen and Zulus will stand face to face over this land question. In the early days of the colony, locations were established in the mountainous districts, because they were comparatively worthless, and the natives were settled in them by tribes. Of what goes on in these locations very little is known, except that they are crowded, and that the inhabitants are as entirely wedded to their savage customs as their forefathers were before them. As there is no more room in the locations, many thousands of Kafirs have settled upon private lands, sometimes with and sometimes without the leave of the owners. But, for many reasons, this is a state of affairs that cannot go on for ever. In a few years, the private lands will be filled up, as well as the locations, and what then?

Zulus are a people who require a very large quantity of land, since they possess great numbers of cattle which must have grazing room. Also their cultivation being of the most primitive order, and consisting as it does of picking out the very richest patches of land, and cropping them till they are exhausted, all ordinary land being rejected as too much trouble to work, the possession, or the right of usor, of several hundred acres is necessary to the support of a single family. Nor, if we may judge from precedent, and its well-marked characteristics, is it to be supposed that this race will at the pinch suit itself to circumstances, take up less land, and work harder. Zulus would rather fight to the last than discard a cherished and an ancient custom. Savages they are, and savages they will remain, and in the struggle between them and civilisation it is possible that they may be conquered, but I do not believe that they will be converted. The Zulu Kafir is incompatible with civilisation.

It will be seen, from what I have said, that Natal might more properly be called a Black settlement than an English colony. Looking at it from the former point of view, it is a very interesting experiment. For the first time probably since their race came into existence, Zulu natives have got a chance given them of increasing and multiplying without being periodically decimated by the accidents of war, whilst at the same time enjoying the protection of a strong and a just government. It remains to be seen what use they will make of their opportunity. That they will avail themselves of it for the purposes of civilising themselves I do not believe; but it seems to me possible that they will learn from the white man the advantages of combination, and aim at developing themselves into a powerful and united black nation.

It is in the face of this state of things that Lord Kimberley now proposes to grant responsible government to the white inhabitants of Natal, should they be willing to accept it, providing that it is to carry with it the responsibility of ruling the natives, and further, of defending the colony from the attacks of its neighbours, whether white or coloured.

Natal has hitherto been ruled under a hybrid constitution, which, whilst allowing the Legislative Assembly of the colony to pass laws, &c., reserves all real authority to the Crown. There has, however, been for some years past a growing agitation amongst a proportion of its inhabitants, instituted with the object of inducing the Home Government to concede practical independence to the colony, Her Majesty having on several occasions been petitioned on the subject by the Legislative Council. On the 13th February 1880, Sir G. Wolseley, who was at the time Governor of Natal, wrote what I can only call, a very intemperate despatch to the Secretary of State, commenting on the prayer for responsible government, which he strongly condemned. He also took the opportunity to make a series of somewhat vicious attacks on the colonists in general, whose object in asking for independence was, he implied, to bring the black man in relations of "appropriate servitude to his white superior." It would appear, however, from words used by him towards the end of his despatch, that the real reason of his violence was, that he feared, that one of the first acts of the Natal Parliament would be to put an end to his settlement in Zululand, which was and is the laughing-stock of the colony. He was probably right in this supposition. The various charges he brings against the colonists are admirably and conclusively refuted in a minute adopted by the Legislative Council of Natal, dated 20th December 1880.

In a despatch, dated 15th March 1881, Lord Kimberley refuses to accede to the request for the grant of Responsible Government.

On the 28th of December, the Legislative Council again petitioned the Crown on the subject, and forward to Lord Kimberley a report of a Select committee appointed to consider the matter, in which the following words occur:—

"Your committee hold that while the colony may well be held responsible for its defence from such aggression as may be caused by the acts or policy of a responsible government, it cannot justly be saddled with the obligation to meet acts of aggression from bordering territories that have arisen out of the circumstances or measures over which such government have had no control; although, as a matter of fact, the brunt of defence (must be borne?) in the first instance by the colonists. The Council, therefore, neither exercises, nor desires to exercise, any control over territories adjacent to or bordering on the colony; for the preservation of its own internal peace and order the colony is prepared to provide. The duty of protecting the colony from external foes, whether by sea or land, devolves on the Empire as a whole, otherwise to be a section of that Empire constitutes no real privilege."

To this report, somewhat to the surprise of the Natalians, Lord Kimberley returned, in a despatch addressed to Sir H. Bulwer, on the occasion of his departure to take up the Governorship of Natal, and dated 2d February 1882, a most favourable reply. In fact, he is so obliging as to far exceed the wishes of the Natalians, as expressed in the passage just quoted, and to tell them that Her Majesty's Government is not only ready to give them responsible government, but that it will expect them to defend their own frontiers, independently of any assistance from the Imperial Government. He further informs them that the Imperial troops will be withdrawn, and that the only responsibility Her Majesty's Government will retain with reference to the colony will be that of its defence against aggression by foreign powers.

This sudden change of face on the part of the Imperial Government, which had up till now flatly refused to grant *any measure* of self-government to Natal, may at first seem rather odd, but on examination it will be found to be quite in accordance with the recently developed South African policy of Mr. Gladstone's Government. There is little doubt that it is an article of faith among the Liberal party that the less the mother-country has to do with her colonies, and more especially her South African colonies, the better. A grand step was made in the direction of the abandonment of our South African Empire when we surrendered the Transvaal to the Boers, and it is clear that if our troops can be withdrawn from Natal and all responsibility for the safety of that colony put an end to, the triumph of self-effacement will be still more complete. But there is another and more immediate reason for Lord Kimberley's generous offer. He knows, no one better, that the policy pursued in South Africa, both as regards the Transvaal and Zululand, must produce its legitimate fruit—bloodshed—before very long. He, or rather his Government, is consequently anxious to cut the connection before anything of the sort occurs, when they will be able to attribute the trouble, whatever it is, to the ill-advised action of the Colonial Legislature.

What is still more strange, however, is that the colonists, having regard to the position they occupy with reference to the Kafirs that surround them, to whom they bear the same relative proportion that the oases do in the desert, or the islands of an archipelago to the ocean that washes their shores, should wish for such a dangerous boon as that of self-government, if indeed they really do wish it. When I lived in Natal, I often heard the subject discussed, and watched the Legislative Council pass its periodical resolutions about it, but I confess I always looked on the matter as being more or less of a farce. There exists, however, in Natal a knot of politicians who are doubtless desirous of the change, partly because they think that it would be really beneficial, and partly because they are possessed by a laudable ambition to fill the high positions of Prime Minister, Treasurer, &c., in the future Parliament. But these gentlemen for the most part live in towns, where they are comparatively safe should a native rising occur. I have not noticed the same enthusiasm for responsible government among those Natalians who live up country in the neighbourhood of the locations.

Still there does exist a considerable party who are in favour of the change, a party that has recently sprung into existence. Many things have occurred within the last few years to irritate and even exasperate people in Natal with the Imperial Government, and generally with the treatment that they have received at our hands. For instance, colonists are proverbially sensitive, and it is therefore rather hard that every newspaper correspondent or itinerant bookmaker who comes to their shores, should at once proceed to print endless letters and books abusing them without mercy. The fact of the matter is that these gentlemen come, and put up at the hotels and pot-shops, where they meet all the loafers and bad characters in the country, whom they take to be specimens of the best class of colonists, whom they describe accordingly as the "riddlings of society." Into the quiet, respectable, and happy homes that really give the tone to the colony they do not enter.

It is also a favourite accusation to bring against the people of Natal that they make the South African wars in order to make money out of them. For instance, in a leading article of one of the principal English journals, it was stated not long ago, that the murmurs of the colonists at being forced to eat the bread of humiliation in the Transvaal matter, arose from no patriotic feeling, but from sorrow at the early termination of a war out of which they hoped to suck no small advantage. This statement is quite untrue.

No doubt a great deal of money has been made out of the wars by a few colonial speculators, some of it, maybe, dishonestly; but this is not an unusual occurrence in a foreign war. Was no money made dishonestly by English speculators and contractors in the Crimean War? Cannot Manchester boast manufacturers ready to supply our enemies,—for cash payments,—with guns to shoot us with, or any other material of war?

It is not to be supposed that because a few speculators made fortunes out of the Commissariat that the whole colony participated in the spoils of the various wars. On the contrary, the majority of its inhabitants have suffered very largely. Not only have they run considerable personal risk, but since, and owing to, the Zulu and Boer wars the cost of living has almost, if not quite doubled, which, needless to say, has not been the case with their incomes. It is therefore particularly cruel that Natal should be gibbeted as the abode of scoundrels of the worst sort, men prepared to bring about bloodshed in order to profit by it. Sir Garnet Wolseley, however, found in this report of colonial dishonesty a convenient point of vantage from which to attack the colonists generally, and in his despatch about responsible government we may be sure he did not spare them. The Legislative Council thus comments on his remarks: "To colonists a war means the spreading among them of distress, alarm, and confusion, peril to life and property in outlying districts, the arrest of progress, and general disorganisation. . . . The Council regard with pain and indignation the uncalled-for and cruel stigma thus cast upon the colonists by Sir Garnet Wolseley."

At first sight these accusations may not appear to have much to do with the question of whether or no the colonists should accept responsible government, but in reality they have, inasmuch as they create a feeling of soreness that inclines the Natalians to get rid of Imperial interference and the attendant criticism at any price.

More substantial grievances against the English Government are the present condition of the native problem, which the colonists justly attribute to Imperial mismanagement, and that triumph of genius, Sir Garnet Wolseley's settlement in Zululand. They see these evils, which they know were preventable, growing more formidable day by day, and they imagine, or some of them do, that if they had free institutions it would still be in their power to stop that growth.

The whole question has now been referred to the colony, which is to elect a fresh Legislative Assembly on the issue of responsible government. The struggle between "the party of progress," i.e., the responsible government section, and the reactionists, or those who are prepared to dispense with "freedom," provided they can be sure of safety, is being carried on keenly, and at present it is doubtful which side will have a majority. I do not, however, believe that the majority of any Council returned will consent to accept Lord Kimberley's proposal as it stands; to walk into a parlour in which the spider is so very obvious, and to deliberately undertake the guardianship of all the Imperial interests in South-Eastern Africa. If they do, they will, in my opinion, deserve all they will get.[*]

[*] Since this chapter was written the Natal constituencies have, as I thought probable, declared against the acceptance of Lord Kimberley's offer in its present form, by returning a majority of anti-responsible Government men. It is, however, probable that the new Legislative Council will try to re-open negotiations on a different, or, at any rate, a modified basis.

The Natalians are fortunate at the present crisis in having, by dint of vigorous agitation against the appointment of Mr. Sendall, a gentleman selected by Lord Kimberley to govern them, obtained the reappointment of their former Governor, Sir Henry Bulwer. Sir Henry, during his first tenure of office, lost credit with the South African colonists on account of his lukewarmness with reference to the Zulu war, but the course of events has gone far towards justifying his views. He is one of the most hard-working and careful Governors that Natal has ever had, and, perhaps, the most judicious. Of a temperate and a cautious mind, he may be more safely trusted to pilot a country so surrounded with difficulties and dangers as Natal is, than most men, and it is to be hoped that the application to the questions of the day, of the strong common sense that he possesses in such an eminent degree, may have a cooling effect on the hot heads and excited imaginations of the "party of progress."

In considering the pros and cons of the responsible government question, it must be steadily kept in sight that Natal is not likely to be a country with a peaceful future. To begin with, she has her native inhabitants to deal with. To-day they number, say 450,000, fifteen or twenty years hence they will number a million, or perhaps more. These men are no longer the docile overgrown children they were twenty years ago. The lessons of our performances in the Zulu and Boer wars, more especially the latter, have not been lost upon them, and they are beginning to think that the white man, instead of being the unconquerable demigod they thought him, is somewhat of a humbug. Pharaoh, we know, grew afraid of the Israelites; Natal, with a much weaker power at command than that of Pharaoh, has got to cope with a still more dangerous element, and one that cannot be induced to depart into the wilderness.

And after all what does the power of Natal amount to? Let us be liberal, and say six thousand men, it is the outside. In the event of a native rising, or any other serious war, I believe that of this number, at least two thousand would make themselves scarce. There exists in all colonies a floating element of individuals who have drifted there for the purpose of making money, but who have no real affection for the (temporary) country of their adoption. Their capital is, as a rule, small and easily realised, and the very last thing that they would think of doing, would be to engage in a deadly life or death struggle, on behalf of a land that they only look on as a milch cow, out of which their object is to draw as much as possible. On the contrary, they would promptly seek another cow, leaving the old one to the tender mercies of the butcher.

Their defection would leave some 4000 men to cope with the difficulty, whatever it was, of which number at least 1000 would be ineffective from age and various other causes, whilst of the remainder, quite 1000 would be obliged to remain where they were to protect women and children in outlying districts. This would leave a total effective force of 2000 men, or, deducting 500 for garrison purposes, of 1500 ready to take the field. But it would take some time to collect, arm, and equip even this number, and in the meanwhile, in the case of a sudden and preconcerted native rising, half the inhabitants of the colony would be murdered in detail.

But Natalians have got other dangers to fear besides those arising from the presence of this vast mass of barbarism in their midst. After a period of anarchy a new king may possess himself of the throne of Zululand, and it is even possible that he might, under circumstances that will arise hereafter, lead his armies into Natal, and create a difficulty with which the 1500 available white men would find it difficult to cope. Or the Boers of the Orange Free State and Transvaal may get tired of paying customs dues at Durban, and march 5000 men down to take possession of the port! Perhaps Natal might provide herself with an effective force by enrolling an army of 10,000 or 20,000 Kafirs, but it seems to me that the proceeding would be both uncertain and expensive, and, should the army take it into its head to mutiny, very dangerous to boot.

It is a noticeable fact that those who so ardently advocate the acceptance of Lord Kimberley's offer, in all their speeches, addresses, and articles, almost entirely shirk this question of defence, which is, after all, the root of the matter. I have formed my estimate of the number of men forthcoming in time of danger, on the supposition that a burgher law was in force in Natal, that is, that every man remaining in the country should be obliged to take a part in its defence. But they do not even hint at a burgher law—in fact, they repudiate the idea, because they know that it would not be tolerated. The universal service system is not the Natalian's idea of happiness. They simply avoid the question, calling it the "defence bugbear," and assume that it will all be arranged in some unforeseen way.

The only suggestion that I have yet seen as regards the arrangements for the future defence of the colony should it become independent, is a somewhat ominous one, namely:—that Natal should enter into a close alliance, offensive and defensive, with the Transvaal and the Orange Free State. But, as the advocates of "freedom" would soon find, the Orange Free State (for even if willing to help them, the Transvaal will for some years have enough to do with its own affairs) will not come forward for nothing. There would first have to be a few business formalities with reference to the customs dues collected in Durban, on goods passing through to the interior, which yield the bulk of the Natal revenue: and possibly, some concessions to Boer public opinion as regards the English mode of dealing with the Natal natives. I incline to the opinion that in relying on the assistance of the Boers in time of trouble the inhabitants of Natal would be leaning on a broken reed. They are more likely to find them in arms against them than fighting on their side.

The party of progress also talks much about the prospects of confederation with the Cape, if once they get responsible government. Most people, however, will think that the fact of their being independent, and therefore responsible for their own defence, will hardly prove an inducement to the Cape to offer to share those responsibilities. The only confederation possible to Natal as a self-governing community will be a Boer confederation, to which it may be admitted—on certain terms. Another cry is that the moment responsible government is established immigrants will flow into the country, and thus restore the balance of races. I take the liberty to doubt the truth of this supposition. The intending emigrant from Europe does not, it is true, understand the ins and outs of the Natal native question, but he does now that it is a place where there are wars and rumours of wars, and where he might possibly be killed, and the result is that he wisely goes to some other colony, that has equal advantages to offer and no Kafirs. To suppose that the emigrant would go to Natal when he came to understand that it was an independent settlement of a few white men, living in the midst of a mass of warlike Kafirs, when Australia, New Zealand, Canada, and the United States, are all holding out their arms to him, is to suppose him a bigger fool than he is. At the best of times Natal is not likely to attract many desirable emigrants: under a responsible government I do not believe that it will attract any.

It seems to me, that there is only one condition of affairs under which it would be at all possible for the Natalians to assume the responsibilities of self-government with any safety, and that is when the great bulk of the native population has been removed back to whence it came—Zululand. Causes of a diametrically opposite nature to those that have been at work among the natives of Natal, have been in operation amongst their brethren in Zululand. In Natal, peace, polygamy, plenty and immigration have bred up an enormous native population. In Zululand, war, private slaughter by the king's order, and the severe restrictions put upon marriage, have kept down the increase of the race; also an enormous number of individuals have fled from the one country into the other. I do not suppose that the population of Zululand amounts, at the present moment, to much more than half that of Natal.

In this state of affairs lies the only real key to the Natal native difficulty. Let Zululand be converted into a black colony under English control, and its present inhabitants be established in suitable locations; then let all the natives of Natal, with the exception of those who choose to become monogamists and be subject to civilised law, be moved into Zululand, and also established in locations. There would be plenty of room for them all. Of course there would be difficulties in the way of the realisation of this scheme, but I do not think that they would prove insuperable. It is probable, however, that it would require a show of force before the Natal natives would consent to budge. Indeed, it is absurd to suppose, that anything would induce them to leave peaceful Natal, and plunge into the seething cauldron of bloodshed, extortion, and political plots that we have cooked up in Zululand under the name of a settlement. Proper provisions must first be made for the government of the country, and security to life and property made certain. Till this is done, no natives in their senses will return to Zululand.

Till this is done, too, or till some other plan is discovered by means of which the native difficulty can be effectively dealt with, the Natalians will indeed be foolish if they discard the protection of England, and accept the fatal boon of self-government. If they do, their future career may be brilliant; but I believe that it will be brief.

It is no answer to urge that at present the natives seem quite quiet, and that there is no indication of disturbance.

History tells us that before the destruction of doomed Pompeii, Vesuvius was very still; only day by day the dark cloud hanging over the mountain's summit grew denser and blacker. We know what happened to Pompeii.

I do not wish to suggest anything unpleasant, far from it; but sometimes, I cannot help thinking, that it is perhaps a matter worth the consideration of the Natalians, whether it might not be as well, instead of talking about responsible government: to improve upon the example of the inhabitants of Pompeii, and take to their ships *before* the volcano begins to work.

It seems to me that there is an ugly cloud gathering on the political horizon in Natal.

THE TRANSVAAL

CHAPTER I.
ITS INHABITANTS, LAWS, AND CUSTOMS

Invasion by Mosilikatze – Arrival of the emigrant Boers – Establishment of the South African republic – The Sand River convention – Growth of the territory of the republic – The native tribes surrounding it – Capabilities of the country – Its climate – Its inhabitants – The Boers – Their peculiarities and mode of life – Their abhorrence of settled government and payment of taxes – The Dutch patriotic party – Form of government previous to the annexation – Courts of law – The commando system – Revenue arrangements – Native races in the Transvaal.

The Transvaal is a country without a history. Its very existence was hardly known of until about fifty years ago. Of its past we know nothing. The generations who peopled its great plains have passed utterly out of the memory and even the traditions of man, leaving no monument to mark that they have existed, not even a tomb.

During the reign of Chaka, 1813-1828, whose history has been sketched in a previous chapter, one of his most famous generals, Mosilikatze, surnamed the Lion, seceded from him with a large number of his soldiers, and striking up in a north-westerly direction, settled in or about what is now the Morico district of the Transvaal. The country through which Mosilikatze passed was at that time thickly populated with natives of the Basutu or Macatee race, whom the Zulus look upon with great contempt. Mosilikatze expressed the feelings of his tribe in a practical manner, by massacring every living soul of them that came within his reach. That the numbers slaughtered were very great, the numerous ruins of Basutu kraals all over the country testify.

It was Chaka's intention to follow up Mosilikatze and destroy him, but he was himself assassinated before he could do so. Dingaan, his successor, however, carried out his brother's design, and despatched a large force to punish him. This army, after marching over 300 miles, burst upon Mosilikatze, drove him back with slaughter, and returned home triumphant. The invasion is important, because the Zulus claim the greater part of the Transvaal territory by virtue of it.

About the time that Mosilikatze was conquered, 1835-1840, the discontented Boers were leaving the Cape Colony exasperated at the emancipation of the slaves by the Imperial authorities. First they made their way to Natal, but being followed thither by the English flag they travelled further inland over the Vaal River and founded the town of Mooi River Dorp or Potchefstroom. Here they were joined by other malcontents from the Orange Sovereignty, which, although afterwards abandoned, was at that time a British possession. Acting upon

> The good old rule, the simple plan
> Of let him take who has the power,
> And let him keep who can,

the Boers now proceeded to possess themselves of as much territory as they wanted. Nor was this a difficult task. The country was, as I have said, peopled by Macatees, who are a poor-spirited race as compared to the Zulus, and had had what little courage they possessed crushed out of them by the rough handling they had received at the hands of Mosilikatze and Dingaan. The Boers, they argued, could not treat them worse than the Zulus had done. Occasionally a Chief, bolder than the rest, would hold out, and then such an example was made of him and his people that few cared to follow in his footsteps.

As soon as the Boers were fairly settled in their new home, they began to think about setting up a Government. First they tried a system of Commandants, with a Commandant-general, but this does not seem to have answered. Next, those of their number who lived in Lydenburg district (where the gold fields now are) set up a Republic, with a President and Volksraad, or popular assembly. This example was followed by the other white inhabitants of the country, who formed another Republic and elected another President, with Pretoria for their capital. The two republics were subsequently incorporated.

In 1852 the Imperial authorities, having regard to the expense of maintaining an effective government over an unwilling people in an undeveloped and half-conquered country, concluded a convention with the emigrant Boers "beyond the Vaal River." The following were the principal stipulations of this convention, drawn up between Major Hogg and Mr. Owen, Her Majesty's Assistant-Commissioners for the settling and adjusting of the affairs of the eastern and north-eastern boundaries of the Colony of the Cape of Good Hope on the one part, and a deputation representative of the emigrant farmers north of the Vaal River on the other. It was guaranteed "in the fullest manner on the part of the British Government to the emigrant farmers beyond the Vaal River the right to manage their own affairs, and to govern themselves according to their own laws, without any interference on the part of the British Government, and that no encroachment shall be made by the said Government on the territory beyond to the north of the Vaal River, with the further assurance that the warmest wish of the British Government is to promote peace, free trade, and friendly intercourse with the emigrant farmers now inhabiting, or who hereafter may inhabit that country, it being understood that this system of non-interference is binding on both parties."

Next were disclaimed, on behalf of the British Government, "all alliances whatever and with whomsoever of the coloured nations to the north of the Vaal River."

It was also agreed "that no slavery is or shall be permitted or practised in the country to the north of the Vaal River by the emigrant farmers."

It was further agreed "that no objection shall be made by any British authority against the emigrant Boers purchasing their supplies of ammunition in any of the British colonies and possessions of South Africa; it being mutually understood that all trade in ammunition with the native tribes is prohibited both by the British Government and the emigrant farmers on both sides of the Vaal River."

These were the terms of this famous convention, which is as slipshod in its diction as it is vague in its meaning. What, for instance, is meant by the territory to the north of the Vaal River? According to the letter of the agreement, Messrs. Hogg and Owen ceded all the territory between the Vaal and Egypt. This historical document was the Charta of the new-born South African Republic. Under its provisions, the Boers, now safe from interference on the part of the

British, established their own Government and promulgated their "Grond Wet," or Constitution.

The history of the Republic between 1852 and 1876 is not very interesting, and is besides too wearisome to enter into here. It consists of an oft-told tale of civil broils, attacks on native tribes, and encroachment on native territories. Until shortly before the Annexation, every burgher was, on coming of age, entitled to receive from the Government 6000 acres of land. As these rights were in the early days of the Republic frequently sold to speculators for such trifles as a bottle of brandy or half a dozen of beer, and as the seller still required his 6000 acres: for a Boer considers it beneath his dignity to settle on less, it is obvious that it required a very large country to satisfy all demands. To meet these demands, the territories of the Republic had to be stretched like an elastic band, and they were stretched accordingly,—at the expense of the natives. The stretching process was an ingenious one, and is very well described in a minute written by Mr. Osborn, the late Magistrate at Newcastle, dated 22d September, 1876, in these words:—

"The Boers, as they have done in other cases and are still doing, encroached by degrees on native territory, commencing by obtaining permission to graze stock upon portions of it at certain seasons of the year, followed by individual graziers obtaining from native headmen a sort of right or license to squat upon certain defined portions, ostensibly in order to keep other Boer squatters away from the same land. These licenses, temporarily intended as friendly or neighbourly acts by unauthorised headmen, after a few seasons of occupation by the Boer, are construed by him as title, and his permanent occupation ensues. Damage for trespass is levied by him from the very man from whom he obtained the right to squat, to which the natives submit out of fear of the matter reaching the ears of the paramount chief, who would in all probability severely punish them for opening the door to encroachment by the Boer. After a while, however, the matter comes to a crisis in consequence of the incessant disputes between the Boers and the natives; one or other of the disputants lays the case before the paramount chief, who, when hearing both parties, is literally frightened with violence and threats by the Boer into granting him the land. Upon this the usual plan followed by the Boer is at once to collect a few neighbouring Boers, including a field cornet, or even an acting provisional field cornet, appointed by the field cornet or provisional cornet, the latter to represent the Government, although without instructions authorising him to act in the matter. A few cattle are collected among themselves, which the party takes to the chief, and his signature is obtained to a written document alienating to the Republican Boers a large slice of all his territory. The contents of this document are, as far as I can make out, never clearly or intelligibly explained to the chief who signs and accepts of the cattle under the impression that it is all in settlement of hire for the grazing licenses granted by his headmen. This, I have no hesitation in saying, is the usual method by which the Boers obtain what they call cessions to them of territories by native chiefs. In Secocoeni's case they allege that his father Sequati cedes to them the whole of his territory (hundreds of square miles) for a hundred head of cattle."

So rapidly did this progress go on that the little Republic to the "North of the Vaal River," had at the time of the Annexation grown into a country of the size of France. Its boundaries had only been clearly defined where they abutted on neighbouring White Communities, or on the territories of great native powers, on which the Government had not dared to infringe to any marked degree, such as those of Lo Bengula's people in the north. But wheresoever on the State's borders there had been no white Power to limit its advances, or where the native tribes had found themselves too isolated or too weak to resist aggressions, there the Republic had by degrees encroached and extended the shadow, if not the substance, of its authority.

The Transvaal has a boundary line of over 1,600 miles in circumference, and of this a large portion is disputed by different native tribes. Speaking generally, the territory lies between the 22 and 28 degrees of South Latitude and the 25 and 32 degrees of East Longitude, or between the Orange Free State, Natal and Griqualand West on the south, and the Limpopo River on the north; and between the Lebombo mountains on the east, and the Kalihari desert on the west. On the north of its territory live three great tribes, the Makalaka, the Matabele (descendants of the Zulus who deserted Chaka under Mosilikatze) and the Matyana. These tribes are all warlike. On the west, following the line down to the Diamond Field territory, are the Sicheli, the Bangoaketsi, the Baralong and the Koranna tribes. Passing round by Griqualand West, the Free State, and Natal, we reach Zululand on the south-east corner; then come the Lebombo mountains on the east, separating the Transvaal from Amatonga land, and from the so-called Portuguese possessions, which are entirely in the hands of native tribes, most of them subject to the great Zulu chief, Umzeila, who has his stronghold in the north-east.

It will be observed that the country is almost surrounded by native tribes. Besides these there are about one million native inhabitants living within its borders. In one district alone, Zoutpansberg, it is computed that there are 364,250 natives, as compared to about 750 whites.

If a beautiful and fertile country were alone necessary to make a state and its inhabitants happy and prosperous, happiness and prosperity would rain upon the Transvaal and the Dutch Boers. The capabilities of this favoured land are vast and various. Within its borders are to be found highlands and lowlands, vast stretches of rolling veldt like gigantic sheep downs, hundreds of miles of swelling bushland, huge tracts of mountainous country, and even little glades spotted with timber that remind one of an English park. There is every possible variety of soil and scenery. Some districts will grow all tropical produce, whilst others are well suited for breeding sheep, cattle and horses. Most of the districts will produce wheat and all other cereals in greater perfection and abundance than any of the other South African colonies. Two crops of cereals may be obtained from the soil every year, and both the vine and tobacco are cultivated with great success. Coffee, sugar-cane and cotton have been grown with profit in the northern parts of the State. Also the undeveloped mineral wealth of the country is very great. Its known minerals are gold, copper, lead, cobalt, iron, coal, tin and plumbago: copper and iron having long been worked by the natives. Altogether there is little doubt that the Transvaal is the richest of all the South African states, and had it remained under English rule it would, with the aid of English enterprise and capital, have become a very wealthy and prosperous country. However there is little chance of that now.

Perhaps the greatest charm of the Transvaal lies in its climate, which is among the best in the world, and in all the southern districts very healthy. During the winter months, that is from April to October, little or no rain falls, and the climate is cold and bracing. In summer it is rather warm, but not overpoweringly hot, the thermometer at

Pretoria averaging from 65 to 73 degrees, and in the winter from 59 to 56 degrees. The population of the Transvaal is estimated at about 40,000 whites, mostly of Dutch origin, consisting of about thirty vast families: and one million natives. There are several towns, the largest of which are Pretoria and Potchefstroom.

Such is the country that we annexed in 1877, and were drummed out of in 1881. Now let us turn to its inhabitants. It has been the fashion to talk of the Transvaal as though nobody but Boers lived in it. In reality the inhabitants were divided into three classes: 1. Natives; 2. Boers; 3. English. I say were divided, because the English class can now hardly be said to exist, the country having been made too hot to hold it, since the war. The natives stand in the proportion of nearly twenty to one to the whites. The Boers were in their turn much more numerous than the English, but the latter owned nearly all the trading establishments in the country, and also a very large amount of property.

The Transvaal Boers have been very much praised up by members of the Government in England, and others who are anxious to advance their interests, as against English interests. Mr. Gladstone, indeed, can hardly find words strong enough to express his admiration of their leaders, those "able men," since they inflicted a national humiliation on us; and doubtless they are a people with many good points. That they are not devoid of sagacity can be seen by the way they have dealt with the English Government.

The Boers are certainly a peculiar people, though they can hardly be said to be "zealous of good works." They are very religious, but their religion takes it colour from the darkest portions of the Old Testament; lessons of mercy and gentleness are not at all to their liking, and they seldom care to read the Gospels. What they delight in are the stories of wholesale butchery by the Israelites of old; and in their own position they find a reproduction of that of the first settlers in the Holy Land. Like them they think they are entrusted by the Almighty with the task of exterminating the heathen native tribes around them, and are always ready with a scriptural precedent for slaughter and robbery. The name of the Divinity is continually on their lips, sometimes in connection with very doubtful statements. They are divided into three sects, none of which care much for the other two. These are the Doppers, who number about half the population, the Orthodox Reform, and the Liberal Reform, which is the least numerous. Of these three sects, the Doppers are by far the most uncompromising and difficult to deal with. They much resemble the puritans of Charles the First's time, of the extreme Hew-Agag-in-pieces stamp.

It is difficult to agree with those who call the Boers cowards, an accusation which the whole of their history belies. A Boer does not like fighting if he can avoid it, because he sets a high value on his own life; but if he is cornered, he will fight as well as anybody else. The Boers fought well enough, in the late war, though that, it is true, is no great criterion of courage, since they were throughout flushed with victory, and, owing to the poor shooting of the British troop, in but little personal danger. One very unpleasant characteristic they have, and that is an absence of regard for the truth, especially where land is concerned. Indeed the national characteristic is crystallised into a proverb, "I am no slave to my word." It has several times happened to me, to see one set of highly respectable witnesses in a land case, go into the box and swear distinctly that they saw a beacon placed on a certain spot, whilst an equal number on the other side will swear that they saw it placed a mile away. Filled as they are with a land hunger, to which that of the Irish peasant is a weak and colourless sentiment, there is little that they will not do to gratify their taste. It is the subject of constant litigation amongst them, and it is by no means uncommon for a Boer to spend several thousand pounds in lawsuits over a piece of land not worth as many hundreds.

Personally Boers are fine men, but as a rule ugly. Their women-folk are good-looking in early life, but get very stout as they grow older. They, in common with most of their sex, understand how to use their tongues; indeed, it is said, that it was the women who caused the rising against the English Government. None of the refinements of civilisation enter into the life of an ordinary Boer. He lives in a way that would shock an English labourer at twenty-five shillings the week, although he is very probably worthy fifteen or twenty thousand pounds. His home is but too frequently squalid and filthy to an extraordinary degree. He himself has no education, and does not care that his children should receive any. He lives by himself in the middle of a great plot of land, his nearest neighbour being perhaps ten or twelve miles away, caring but little for the news of the outside world, and nothing for its opinions, doing very little work, but growing daily richer through the increase of his flocks and herds. His expenses are almost nothing, and as he gets older, wealth increases upon him. The events in his life consist of an occasional trip on "commando," against some native tribe, attending a few political meetings, and the journeys he makes with his family to the nearest town, some four times a year, in order to be present at "Nachtmaal" or communion. Foreigners, especially Englishmen, he detests, but he is kindly and hospitable to his own people. Living isolated as he does, the lord of a little kingdom, he naturally comes to have a great idea of himself, and a corresponding contempt for all the rest of mankind. Laws and taxes are things distasteful to him, and he looks upon it as an impertinence that any court should venture to call him to account for his doings. He is rich and prosperous, and the cares of poverty, and all the other troubles that fall to the lot of civilised men, do not affect him. He has no romance in him, nor any of the higher feelings and aspirations that are found in almost every other race; in short, unlike the Zulu he despises, there is little of the gentleman in his composition, though he is at times capable of acts of kindness and even generosity. His happiness is to live alone in the great wilderness, with his children, his men-servants and his maid-servants, his flocks and his herds, the monarch of all he surveys. If civilisation presses him too closely, his remedy is a simple one. He sells his farm, packs up his goods and cash in his waggon, and starts for regions more congenially wild. Such are some of the leading characteristics of that remarkable product of South Africa, the Transvaal Boer, who resembles no other white man in the world.

Perhaps, however, the most striking of all his oddities is his abhorrence of all government, more especially if that government be carried out according to English principles. The Boers have always been more or less in rebellion; they rebelled against the rule of the Company when the Cape belonged to Holland, they rebelled against the English Government in the Cape, they were always in a state of semi-rebellion against their own government in the Transvaal, and now they have for the second time, with the most complete success, rebelled against the English Government. The fact of the matter is that the bulk of their number hate all Governments, because Governments enforce law and order, and they hate the English Government worst of all, because it enforces law and order most of all. It is not liberty they long for, but license. The "sturdy independence" of the Boer resolves itself into a determination not to have his affairs interfered with by any superior power whatsoever, and not to pay taxes if he can possibly avoid it. But he has also a specific cause of complaint against the English Government, which would alone cause him to do his utmost to get rid of it, and that is its mode of dealing with natives, which is radically opposite to his own. This is the secret of Boer patriotism. To understand it, it must be remembered that the Englishman and the Boer look at natives from a different point of view. The Englishman, though he may not be very fond of him, at any rate regards the Kafir as a fellow human being with feelings like his own. The average Boer does not. He looks upon the "black creature" as having been delivered into his hand by the "Lord" for his own purposes, that is, to shoot and enslave. He must not be blamed too harshly for this, for, besides being naturally of a somewhat hard disposition, hatred of the native is hereditary, and is partly induced by the history of many a bloody struggle. Also the native hates the Boer fully as much as the Boer hates the native, though with better reason. Now native labour is a necessity to the Boer, because he will not as a rule do hard manual labour himself, and there must be some one to plant and garner the crops, and herd the cattle. On the other hand, the natives are not anxious to serve the Boers, which means little or no pay and plenty of thick stick, and sometimes worse. The result of this state of affairs is that the Boer often has to rely on forced labour to a very great extent. But this is a thing that an English Government will not tolerate, and the consequence is that under its rule he cannot get the labour that is necessary to him.

Then there is the tax question. If he lives under the English flag the money has to be paid regularly, but under his own Government he pays or not as he likes. It was this habit of his of refusing payment of taxes that brought the Republic into difficulties in 1877, and that will ere long bring it into trouble again. He cannot understand that cash is necessary to carry on a Government, and looks upon a tax as though it were so much money stolen from him. These things are the real springs of the "sturdy independence" and the patriotism of the ordinary Transvaal farmer. Doubtless, there are some who are really patriotic; for instance, one of their leaders, Paul Kruger. But with the majority, patriotism is only another word for unbounded license and forced labour.

These remarks must not be taken to apply to the Cape Boers, who are a superior class of men, since they, living under a settled and civilised Government, have been steadily improving, whilst their cousins, living every man for his own hand, have been deteriorating. The old Voortrekkers, the fathers and grandfathers of the Transvaal Boer of to-day, were, without doubt, a very fine set of men, and occasionally you may in the Transvaal meet individuals of the same stamp whom it is a pleasure to know. But these are generally men of a certain age with some experience of the world; the younger men are very objectionable in their manners.

The real Dutch Patriotic party is not to be found in the Transvaal, but in the Cape Colony. Their object, which, as affairs now are, is well within the bounds of possibility, is by fair means or foul to swamp the English element in South Africa, and to establish a great Dutch Republic. It was this party, which consists of clever and well educated men, who raised the outcry against the Transvaal Annexation, because it meant an enormous extension of English influence, and who had the wit, by means of their emissaries and newspapers, to work upon the feeling of the ignorant Transvaal farmers until they persuaded them to rebel; and finally, to avail themselves of the yearnings of English radicalism for the disruption of the Empire and the minimisation of British authority, to get the Annexation cancelled. All through this business the Boers have more or less danced in obedience to strings pulled at Cape Town, and it is now said that one of the chief wire-pullers, Mr. Hofmeyer, is to be asked to become President of the Republic. These men are the real patriots of South Africa, and very clever ones too, not the Transvaal Boers, who vapour about their blood and their country and the accursed Englishman to order, and are in reality influenced by very small motives, such as the desire to avoid payment of taxes, or to hunt away a neighbouring Englishman, whose civilisation and refinement are as offensive as his farm is desirable. Such are the Dutch inhabitants of the Transvaal. I will now give a short sketch of their institutions as they were before the Annexation, and to which the community has reverted since its recision, with, I believe, but few alterations.

The form of government is republican, and to all intents and purposes, manhood suffrage prevails, supreme power resting in the people. The executive power of the State centres in a President elected by the people to hold office for a term of five years, every voter having a voice in his election. He is assisted in the execution of his duties by an Executive Council, consisting of the State Secretary and such other three members as are selected for that purpose by the legislative body, the Volksraad. The State Secretary holds office for four years, and is elected by the Volksraad. The members of the Executive all have seats in the Volksraad, but have no votes. The Volksraad is the legislative body of the State, and consists of forty-two members. The country is divided into twelve electoral districts, each of which has the right to return three members; the Gold Fields have also the right of electing two members, and the four principal towns, one member each. There is no power in the State competent to either prorogue or dissolve the Volksraad except that body itself, so that an appeal to the country on a given subject or policy is impossible without its concurrence. Members are elected for four years, but half retire by rotation every two years, the vacancies being filled by re-elections. Members must have been voters for three years, and be not less than thirty years of age, must belong to a Protestant Church, be resident in the country, and owners of immovable property therein. A father and son cannot sit in the same Raad, neither can seats be occupied by coloured persons, bastards, or officials.

For each electoral district there is a magistrate or Landdrost whose duties are similar to those of a Civil Commissioner. These districts are again subdivided into wards presided over by field cornets, who exercise judicial powers in minor matters, and in times of war have considerable authority. The Roman Dutch law is the common law of the country, as it is of the colonies of the Cape of Good Hope and Natal, and of the Orange Free State.

Prior to the Annexation justice was administered in a very primitive fashion. First, there was the Landdrosts' Court, from which an appeal lay to a court consisting of the Landdrost and six councillors elected by the public. This was a court of first instance as well as a court of appeal. Then there was a Supreme Court, consisting of three Landdrosts from three different districts, and a jury of twelve selected from the burghers of the State. There was no appeal from this court, but cases have sometimes been brought under the consideration of the Volksraad as the supreme power. It is easy to imagine what the administration of justice was like when the presidents of all the law courts in the country were elected by the mob, not on account of their knowledge of the law, but because they were popular. Suitors before the old Transvaal courts found the law surprisingly uncertain. A High Court of Justice was, however, established after the Annexation, and has been continued by the Volksraad, but an agitation is being got up against it, and it will possibly be abolished in favour of the old system.

In such a community as that of the Transvaal Boers, the question of public defence was evidently of the first importance. This is provided for under what is known as the Commando system. The President, with the concurrence of the Executive Council, has the right of declaring war, and of calling up a Commando, in which the burghers are placed under the field cornets and commandants. These last are chosen by the field cornets for each district, and a Commandant-general is chosen by the whole laager or force, but the President is the Commander-in-Chief of the army. All the inhabitants of the state between sixteen and sixty, with a few exceptions, are liable for service. Young men under eighteen, and men over fifty, are only called out under circumstances of emergency. Members of the Volksraad, officials, clergymen, and school-teachers are exempt from personal service, unless martial law is proclaimed, but must contribute an amount not exceeding 15 pounds towards the expense of the war. All legal proceedings in civil cases are suspended against persons on commando, no summonses can be made out, and as soon as martial law is proclaimed no legal execution can be prosecuted, the pounds are closed, and transfer dues payments are suspended, until after thirty days from the recall of the proclamation of martial law. Owners of land residing beyond the borders of the Republic are also liable, in addition to the ordinary war tax, to place a fit and proper substitute at the disposal of the Government, or otherwise to pay a fine of 15 pounds. The first levy of the burghers is, of men from eighteen to thirty-four years of age; the second, thirty-four to fifty; and the third, from sixteen to eighteen, and from fifty to sixty years. Every man is bound to provide himself with clothing, a gun, and ammunition, and there must be enough waggons and oxen found between them to suffice for their joint use. Of the booty taken, one quarter goes to Government and the rest to the burghers. The most disagreeable part of the commandeering system is, however, yet to come; personal service is not all that the resident in the Transvaal Republic has to endure. The right is vested in field cornets to commandeer articles as well as individuals, and to call upon inhabitants to furnish requisites for the commando. As may be imagined, it goes very hard on these occasions with the property of any individual whom the field cornet may not happen to like.

Each ward is expected to turn out its contingent ready and equipped for war, and this can only be done by seizing goods right and left. One unfortunate will have to find a waggon, another to deliver his favourite span of trek oxen, another his riding-horse, or some slaughter cattle, and so on. Even when the officer making the levy is desirous of doing his duty as fairly as he can, it is obvious that very great hardships must be inflicted under such a system. Requisitions are made more with regard to what is wanted, than with a view to an equitable distribution of demands; and like the Jews in the time of the Crusades, he who has got most must pay most, or take the consequences, which may be unpleasant. Articles which are not perishable, such as waggons, are supposed to be returned, but if they come back at all they are generally worthless.

In case of war, the native tribes living within the borders of the State are also expected to furnish contingents, and it is on them that most of the hard work of the campaign generally falls. They are put in the front of the battle, and have to do the hand-to-hand fighting, which, however, if of the Zulu race, they do not object to.

The revenue of the State is so arranged that the burden of it should fall as much as possible on the trading community and as little as possible on the farmer. It is chiefly derived from licenses on trades, professions, and callings, 30s. per annum quit-rent on farms, transfer dues and stamps, auction dues, court fees, and contributions from such native tribes as can be made to pay them. Since we have given up the country, the Volksraad has put a very heavy tax on all imported goods, hoping thereby to beguile the Boers into paying taxes without knowing it, and at the same time strike a blow at the trading community, which is English in its proclivities. The result has been to paralyse what little trade there was left in the country, and to cause great dissatisfaction amongst the farmers, who cannot understand why, now that the English are gone, they should have to pay twice as much for their sugar and coffee as they have been accustomed to do.

I will conclude this chapter with a few words about the natives, who swarm in and around the Transvaal. They can be roughly divided into two great races, the Amazulu and their offshoots, and the Macatee or Basutu tribes. All those of Zulu blood, including the Swazies, Mapock's Kafirs, the Matabele, the Knobnodes, and others are very warlike in disposition, and men of fine physique. The Basutus (who must not be confounded with the Cape Basutus), however, differ from these tribes in every respect, including their language, which is called Sisutu, the only mutual feeling between the two races being their common detestation of the Boers. They do not love war; in fact, they are timid and cowardly by nature, and only fight when they are obliged to. Unlike the Zulus, they are much addicted to the arts of peace, show considerable capacities for civilisation, and are even willing to become Christians. There would have been a far better field for the Missionary in the Transvaal than in Zululand and Natal. Indeed, the most successful mission station I have seen in Africa is near Middelburg, under the control of Mr. Merensky. In person the Basutus are thin and weakly when compared to the stalwart Zulu, and it is their consciousness of inferiority both to the white men, and their black brethren, that, together with their natural timidity, makes them submit as easily as they do to the yoke of the Boer.

CHAPTER II.
EVENTS PRECEDING THE ANNEXATION

Mr. Burgers elected president – His character and aspirations – His pension from the English Government – His visit to England – The railway loan – Relations of the republic with native tribes – The pass laws – Its quarrel with Cetywayo – Confiscation of native territory by the Keate award – Treaty with the Swazi king – The Secocoeni war – Capture of Johannes' stronghold by the Swazi allies – Attack on Secocoeni's mountain – Defeat and dispersion of the Boers – Elation of the natives – Von Schlickmann's volunteers – Cruelties perpetrated – Abel Erasmus – Treatment of natives by Boers – Public meeting at Potchefstroom in 1768 – The slavery question – Some evidence on the subject – Pecuniary position of the Transvaal prior to the annexation – Internal troubles – Divisions amongst the Boers – Hopeless condition of the country.

In or about the year 1872, the burghers of the Republic elected Mr. Burgers their President. This remarkable man was a native of the Cape Colony, and passed the first sixteen or seventeen years of his life, he once informed me, on a farm herding sheep. He afterwards became a clergyman noted for the eloquence of his preaching, but his ideas proving too broad for his congregation, he resigned his cure, and in an evil moment for himself took to politics.

President Burgers was a man of striking presence and striking talents, especially as regards his oratory, which was really of a very high class, and would have commanded attention in our own House of Commons. He possessed, however, a mind of that peculiarly volatile order, that is sometimes met with in conjunction with great talents, and which seems to be entirely without ballast. His intellect was of a balloon-like nature, and as incapable of being steered. He was always soaring in the clouds, and, as is natural to one in that elevated position, taking a very different and more sanguine view of affairs to that which men of a more lowly, and perhaps a more practical, turn of mind would do.

But notwithstanding his fly-away ideas, President Burgers was undoubtedly a true patriot, labouring night and day for the welfare of the state of which he had to undertake the guidance: but his patriotism was too exalted for his surroundings. He wished to elevate to the rank of a nation a people who had not got the desire to be elevated; with this view he contracted railway loans, made wars, minted gold, &c., and then suddenly discovered that the country refused to support him. In short, he was made of a very different clay to that of the people he had to do with. He dreamt of a great Dutch Republic "with eight millions of inhabitants," doing a vast trade with the interior through the Delagoa Bay Railway. They, on the other hand, cared nothing about republics or railways, but fixed their affections on forced labour and getting rid of the necessity of paying taxes—and so between them the Republic came to grief. But it must be borne in mind that President Burgers was throughout actuated by good motives; he did his best by a stubborn and stiff-necked people; and if he failed, as fail he did, it was more their fault than his. As regards the pension he received from the English Government, which has so often been brought up against him, it was after all no more than his due after five years of arduous work. If the Republic had continued to exist, it is to be presumed that they would have made some provision for their old President, more especially as he seems to have exhausted his private means in paying the debts of the country. Whatever may be said of some of the other officials of the Republic, its President was, I believe, an honest man.

In 1875, Mr. Burgers proceeded to Europe, having, he says in a posthumous document recently published, been empowered by the Volksraad "to carry out my plans for the development of the country, by opening up a direct communication for it, free from the trammels of British ports and influence." According to this document, during his absence, two powerful parties, viz., "the faction of unprincipled fortune-hunters, rascals, and runaways on the one hand, and the faction of the extreme orthodox party in a certain branch of the Dutch Reform Church on the other, began to co-operate against the Government of the Republic and me personally. . . . . . Ill as I was, and contrary to the advice of my medical men, I proceeded to Europe, in the beginning of 1875, to carry out my project, and no sooner was my back turned on the Transvaal, than the conspiring elements began to act. The new coat of arms and flag adopted in the

Raad by an almost unanimous vote were abolished. The laws for a free and secular education were tampered with, and my resistance to a reckless inspection and disposal of Government lands, still occupied by natives, was openly defied. The Raad, filled up to a large extent with men of ill repute, who, under the cloak of progress and favour to the Government view, obtained their seats, was too weak to cope with the skill of the conspirators, and granted leave to the acting President to carry out measures diametrically opposed to my policy. *Native lands* were inspected and given out to a few speculators, who held large numbers of claims to lands which were destined for citizens, and so a war was prepared for me, on my return from Europe, which I could not avert." This extract is interesting, as showing the state of feeling existing between the President and his officers previous to the outbreak of the Secocoeni war. It also shows how entirely he was out of sympathy with the citizens, seeing that as soon as his back was turned, they, with Mr. Joubert and Paul Kruger at their head, at once undid all the little good he had done.

When Mr. Burgers got to England, he found that city capitalists would have nothing whatever to say to his railway scheme. In Holland, however, he succeeded in getting 90,000 pounds of the 300,000 pounds he wished to borrow at a high rate of interest, and by passing a bond on five hundred government farms. This money was immediately invested in a railway plant, which, when it arrived at Delagoa Bay, had to be mortgaged to pay the freight on it, and that was the end of the Delagoa Bay railway scheme, except that the 90,000 pounds is, I believe, still owing to the confiding shareholders in Holland.

On his return to the Transvaal the President was well received, and for a month or so all went smoothly. But the relations of the Republic with the surrounding native tribes had by this time become so bad that an explosion was imminent somewhere. In the year 1874 the Volksraad raised the price of passes under the iniquitous pass law, by which every native travelling through the territory was made to pay from 1 pound to five pounds. In case of non-payment the native was made subject to a fine of from 1 pound to 10 pounds, and to a beating of from "ten to twenty-five lashes." He was also to go into service for three months, and have a certificate thereof, for which he must pay five shillings; the avowed object of the law being to obtain a supply of Kafir labour. This was done in spite of the earnest protest of the President, who gave the Raad distinctly to understand that by accepting this law they would, in point of fact, annul treaties concluded with the chiefs on the south-western borders. It was not clear, however, if this amended pass law ever came into force. It is to be hoped it did not, for even under the old law natives were shamefully treated by the Boers, who would pretend that they were authorised by the Government to collect the tax; the result being that the unfortunate Kafir was frequently obliged to pay twice over. Natives had such a horror of the pass laws of the country, that when travelling to the Diamond Fields to work they would frequently go round some hundreds of miles rather than pass through the Transvaal.

That the Volksraad should have thought it necessary to enact such a law in order that the farmers should obtain a supply of Kafir labour in a territory that had nearly a million of native inhabitants, who, unlike the Zulus, are willing to work if only they meet with decent treatment, is in itself an instructive commentary on the feelings existing between the Boer master and Kafir servant.

But besides the general quarrel with the Kafir race in its entirety, which the Boers always have on hand, they had just then several individual differences, in each of which there lurked the possibilities of disturbance.

To begin with, their relations with Cetywayo were by no means amicable. During Mr. Burgers' absence the Boer Government, then under the leadership of P. J. Joubert, sent Cetywayo a very stern message—a message that gives the reader the idea that Mr. Joubert was ready to enforce it with ten thousand men. After making various statements and demands with reference to the Amaswazi tribe, the disputed boundary line, &c., it ends thus:—

"Although the Government of the South African Republic has never wished, and does not now desire, that serious disaffection and animosities should exist between you and them, yet it is not the less of the greatest consequence and importance for you earnestly to weigh these matters and risks, and to satisfy them; the more so, if you on your side also wish that peace and friendship shall be maintained between you and us."

The Secretary for Native Affairs for Natal comments on this message in these words: "The tone of this message to Cetywayo is not very friendly, it has the look of an ultimatum, and if the Government of the Transvaal were in circumstances different to what it is, the message would suggest an intention to coerce if the demands it conveys are not at once complied with; but I am inclined to the opinion that no such intention exists, and that the transmission of a copy of the message to the Natal Government is intended as a notification that the Transvaal Government has proclaimed the territory hitherto in dispute between it and the Zulus to be Republican territory, and that the Republic intends to occupy it."

In the territories marked out by a decision known as the Keate Award, in which Lieutenant-Governor Keate of Natal, at the request of both parties, laid down the boundary line between the Boers and certain native tribes, the Boer Government carried it with a yet higher hand, insomuch as the natives of those districts, being comparatively unwarlike, were less likely to resist.

On the 18th August 1875, Acting President Joubert issued a proclamation by which a line was laid down far to the southward of that marked out by Mr. Keate, and consequently included more territory within the elastic boundaries of the Republic. A Government notice of the same date invites all claiming lands now declared to belong to the Republic, to send in their claims to be settled by a land commission.

On the 6th March 1876, another chief in the same neighbourhood (Montsoia) writes to the Lieutenant-Governor of Griqualand West in these terms:—

"My Friend,—I wish to acquaint you with the doings of some people connected with the Boers. A man-servant of mine has been severely injured in the head by one of the Boers' servants, which has proved fatal. Another of my people has been cruelly treated by a Boer tying a rein about his neck, and then mounting his horse and dragging him about the place. My brother Molema, who is the bearer of this, will give you full particulars."

Molema explains the assaults thus: "The assaulted man is not dead; his skull was fractured. The assault was committed by a Boer named Wessels Badenhorst, who shamefully ill-treated the man, beat him till he fainted, and, on his revival, fastened a rim around his neck, and made him run to the homestead by the side of his (Badenhorst's) horse cantering. At the homestead he tied him to the waggon-wheel, and flogged him again till Mrs. Badenhorst stopped her husband."

Though it will be seen that the Boers were on good terms neither with the Zulus nor the Keate Award natives, they still had one Kafir ally, namely, Umbandeni, the Amaswazi king. This alliance was concluded under circumstances so peculiar that they are worthy of a brief recapitulation. It appears that in the winter of the year 1875 Mr. Rudolph, the Landdrost of Utrecht, went to Swazieland, and, imitating the example of the Natal Government with Cetywayo, crowned Umbandeni king, on behalf of the Boer Government. He further made a treaty of alliance with him, and promised him a commando to help him in case of his being attacked by the Zulus. Now comes the curious part of the story. On the 18th May 1876, a message came from this same Umbandeni to Sir H. Bulwer, of which the following is an extract:—"We are sent by our king to thank the Government of Natal for the information sent to him last winter by that Government, and conveyed by Mr. Rudolph, of the intended attack on his people by the Zulus. We are further instructed by the king to thank the Natal Government for the influence it used to stop the intended raid, and for instructing a Boer commando to go to his country to render him assistance in case of need; and further for appointing Mr. Randolph at the head of the commando to place him (Umbandeni) as king over the Amaswazi, and to make a treaty with him and his people on behalf of the Natal Government. . . . . . The Transvaal Government has asked Umbandeni to acknowledge himself a subject of the Republic, but he has distinctly refused to do so." In a minute written on this subject, the Secretary for Native Affairs for Natal says, "No explanation or assurance was sufficient to convince them (Umbandeni's messengers) that they had on that occasion made themselves subjects of the South African Republic; they declared it was not their wish or intention to do so, and that they would refuse to acknowledge a position into which they had been unwittingly betrayed." I must conclude this episode by quoting the last paragraph of Sir H. Bulwer's covering despatch, because it concerns larger issues than the supposed treaty: "It will not be necessary that I should at present add any remarks to those contained in the minute for the Secretary for Native Affairs, but I would observe that the situation arising out of the relations of the Government of the South African Republic with the neighbouring states is so complicated, and presents so many elements of confusion and of danger to the peace of this portion of South Africa, that I trust some way may be found to an early settlement of questions that ought not, in my opinion, to be left alone, as so many have been left, to take the chance of the future."

And now I come to the last and most imminent native difficulty that at the time faced the Republic. On the borders of Lydenburg district there lived a powerful chief named Secocoeni. Between this chief and the Transvaal Government difficulties arose in the beginning of 1876 on the usual subject—land. The Boers declared that they had bought the land from the Swazies, who had conquered portions of the country, and that the Swazies offered to make it "clean from brambles," i.e., kill everybody living on it; but that they (the Boers) said that they were to let them be, that they might be their servants. The Basutus, on the other hand, said that no such sale ever took place, and, even if it did take place, it was invalid, because the Swazies were not in occupation of the land, and therefore could not sell it. It was a Christian Kafir called Johannes, a brother of Secocoeni, who was the immediate cause of the war. This Johannes used to live at a place called Botsobelo, the mission-station of Mr. Merensky, but moved to a stronghold on the Spekboom river, in the disputed territory. The Boers sent to him to come back, but he refused, and warned the Boers off his land. Secocoeni was then appealed to, but declared that the land belonged to his tribe, and would be occupied by Johannes. He also told the Boers "that he did not wish to fight, but that he was quite ready to do so if they preferred it." Thereupon the Transvaal Government declared war, although it does not appear that the natives committed any outrage or acts of hostility before the declaration. As regards the Boers' right to Secocoeni's country, Sir H. Barkly sums up the question thus, in a despatch addressed to President Burgers, dated 28th Nov. 1876:—"On the whole, it seems perfectly clear, and I feel bound to repeat it, that Sikukuni was neither *de jure* or *de facto* a subject of the Republic when your Honour declared war against him in June last." As soon as war had been declared, the clumsy commando system was set working, and about 2500 white men collected; the Swazies also were applied to to send a contingent, which they did, being only too glad of the opportunity of slaughter.

At first all went well, and the President, who accompanied the commando in person, succeeded in reducing a mountain stronghold, which, in his high-flown way, he called a "glorious victory" over a "Kafir Gibraltar."

On the 14th July another engagement took place, when the Boers and Swazies attacked Johannes' stronghold. The place was taken with circumstances of great barbarity by the Swazies, for when the signal was given to advance the Boers did not move. Nearly all the women were killed, and the brains of the children were dashed out against the stones; in one instance, before the captive mother's face. Johannes was badly wounded, and died two days afterwards. When he was dying he said to his brother, "I am going to die. I am thankful I do not die by the hands of these cowardly Boers, but by the hand of a black and courageous nation like myself . . ." He then took leave of his people, told his brother to read the Bible, and expired. The Swazies were so infuriated at the cowardice displayed by the Boers on this occasion that they returned home in great dudgeon.

On the 2nd of August Secocoeni's mountain, which is a very strong fortification, was attacked in two columns, or rather an attempt was made to attack it, for when it came to the pinch only about forty men, mostly English and Germans, would advance. Thereupon the whole commando retreated with great haste, the greater part of it going straight home. In vain the President entreated them to shoot him rather than desert him; they had had enough of Secocoeni and his stronghold, and home they went. The President then retreated with what few men he had left to Steelport, where he built a fort, and from thence returned to Pretoria. The news of the collapse of the commando was received throughout the Transvaal, and indeed the whole of South Africa, with the greatest dismay. For the first time in the history of that country the white man had been completely worsted by a native tribe, and that tribe wretched Basutus, people whom the Zulus call their "dogs." It was glad tidings to every native from the Zambesi to the Cape, who learnt thereby that the white man was not so invincible as he used to be. Meanwhile the inhabitants of Lydenburg were filled with alarm, and again and again petitioned the Governors of the Cape and Natal for assistance. Their fears were, however, to a great extent groundless, for, with the exception of occasional cattle-lifting, Secocoeni did not follow up his victory.

On the 4th September the President opened the special sitting of the Volksraad, and presented to that body a scheme for the establishment of a border force to take the place of the commando system, announcing that he had appointed a certain Captain Von Schlickmann to command it. He also requested the Raad to make some provision for the expenses of the expedition, which they had omitted to do in their former sitting.

Captain Von Schlickmann determined to carry on the war upon a different system. He got together a band of very rough characters on the Diamond Fields, and occupied the fort built by the President, from whence he would sally out from time to time and destroy kraals. He seems, if we may believe the reports in the blue books and the stories of eye-witnesses, to have carried on his proceedings in a somewhat savage way. The following is an extract from a private letter written by one of his volunteers:—

"About daylight we came across four Kafirs. Saw them first, and charged in front of them to cut off their retreat. Saw they were women, and called out not to fire. In spite of that, one of the poor things got her head blown off (a d——d shame). . . . Afterwards two women and a baby were brought to the camp prisoners. The same night they were taken out by our Kafirs and murdered in cold blood by the order of ——. Mr. —— and myself strongly protested against it, but without avail. I never heard such a cowardly piece of business in my life. No good will come of it, you may depend. . . . —— says he would cut all the women and children's throats he catches. Told him distinctly he was a d——d coward."

Schlickmann was, however, a mild-mannered man when compared to a certain Abel Erasmus, afterwards denounced at a public dinner by Sir Garnet Wolseley as a "fiend in human form." This gentleman, in the month of October, attacked a friendly kraal of Kafirs. The incident is described thus in a correspondent's letter:—

"The people of the kraals, taken quite by surprise, fled when they saw their foes, and most of them took shelter in the neighbouring bush. Two or three men were distinctly seen in their flight from the kraal, and one of them is known to have been wounded. According to my informant the remainder were women and children, who were pursued into the bush, and there, all shivering and shrieking, were put to death by the Boers' Kafirs, some being shot, but the majority stabbed with assegais. After the massacre he counted thirteen women and three children, but he says he did not see the body of a single man. Another Kafir said, pointing to a place in the road where the stones were thickly strewn, 'the bodies of the women and children lay like these stones.' The Boer before mentioned, who has been stationed outside, has told one of his own friends, whom he thought would not mention it, that the shrieks were fearful to hear."

Several accounts of, or allusion to, this atrocity can be found in the blue books, and I may add that it, in common with others of the same stamp, was the talk of the country at the time.

I do not relate these horrors out of any wish to rake up old stories to the prejudice of the Boers, but because I am describing the state of the country before the Annexation, in which they form an interesting and important item. Also, it is as well that people in England should know into what hands they have delivered over the native tribes who trusted in their protection. What happened in 1876 is probably happening again now, and will certainly happen again and again. The character of the Transvaal Boer and his sentiments towards the native races have not modified during the last five years, but, on the contrary, a large amount of energy, which has been accumulating during the period of British protection, will now be expended on their devoted heads.

As regards the truth of these atrocities, the majority of them are beyond the possibility of doubt; indeed, to the best of my knowledge, no serious attempt has ever been made to refute such of them as have come into public notice, except in a general way, for party purposes. As, however, they may be doubted, I will quote the following extract from a despatch written by Sir H. Barkly to Lord Carnarvon, dated 18th December 1876:—

"As Von Schlickmann has since fallen fighting bravely, it is not without reluctance that I join in affixing this dark stain on his memory, but truth compels me to add the following extract from a letter which I have since received from one whose name (which I communicate to your Lordship privately) forbids disbelief: 'There is no longer the *slightest doubt* as to the murder of the two women and the child at Steelport by the direct order of Schlickmann, and in the attack on the kraal near which these women were captured (or some attack about that period) he ordered his men to cut the throats of all the wounded! This is no mere report; it is positively true.'" He concludes by expressing a hope that the course of events will enable Her Majesty's Government to take such steps "as will terminate this wanton and useless bloodshed, and prevent the recurrence of the *scenes of injustice, cruelty, and rapine which abundant evidence is every day forthcoming to prove have rarely ceased to disgrace the Republics beyond the Vaal ever since they first sprang into existence."* [*]

[*] *The italics are my own. – Author.*

These are strong words, but none too strong for the facts of the case. Injustice, cruelty, and rapine have always been the watchwords of the Transvaal Boers. The stories of wholesale slaughter in the earlier days of the Republic are very numerous. One of the best known of those shocking occurrences took place in the Zoutpansberg war in 1865. On this occasion a large number of Kafirs took refuge in caves, where the Boers smoked them to death. Some years afterwards Dr. Wangeman, whose account is, I believe, thoroughly reliable, describes the scene of their operations in these words: —

"The roof of the first cave was black with smoke; the remains of the logs which were burnt lay at the entrance. The floor was strewn with hundreds of skulls and skeletons. In confused heaps lay karosses, kerries, assegais, pots, spoons, snuff-boxes, and the bones of men, giving one the impression that this was the grave of a whole people. Some estimate the number of those who perished here from twenty to thirty thousand. This is, I believe, too high. In the one chamber there were from two hundred to three hundred skeletons; the other chambers I did not visit."

In 1868 a public meeting was held at Potchefstroom to consider the war then going on with the Zoutpansberg natives. According to the report of the proceedings, the Rev. Mr. Ludorf said that "on a particular occasion a number of native children, who were too young to be removed, had been collected in a heap, covered with long grass, and burned alive. Other atrocities had also been committed, but these were too horrible to relate." When called upon to produce his authority for this statement, Mr. Ludorf named his authority "in a solemn declaration to the State Attorney." At this same meeting Mr. J.

G. Steyn, who had been Landdrost of Potchefstroom, said "there now was innocent blood on our hands which had not yet been avenged, and the curse of God rested on the land in consequence." Mr. Rosalt remarked that "it was a singular circumstance that in the different colonial Kafir wars, as also in the Basutu wars, one did not hear of destitute children being found by the commandoes, and asked how it was that every petty commando that took the field in this Republic invariably found numbers of destitute children. He gave it as his opinion that the present system of apprenticeship was an essential cause of our frequent hostilities with the natives." Mr. Jan Talyard said, "Children were forcibly taken from their parents, and were then called destitute and apprenticed." Mr. Daniel Van Nooren was heard to say, "If they had to clear the country, and could not have the children they found, he would shoot them." Mr. Field-Cornet Furstenburg stated "that when he was at Zoutpansberg with his burghers, the chief Katse-Kats was told to come down from the mountains; that he sent one of his subordinates as a proof of amity; that whilst a delay of five days was guaranteed by Commandant Paul Kruger, who was then in command, orders were given at the same time to attack the natives at break of day, which was accordingly done, but which resulted in total failure." Truly, this must have been an interesting meeting.

Before leaving these unsavoury subjects, I must touch on the question of slavery. It has been again and again denied, on behalf of the Transvaal Boers, that slavery existed in the Republic. Now, this is, strictly speaking, true; slavery did not exist, but apprenticeship did—the rose was called by another name, that is all. The poor destitute children who were picked up by kindhearted Boers, after the extermination of their parents, were apprenticed to farmers till they came of age. It is a remarkable fact that these children never attained their majority. You might meet oldish men in the Transvaal who were not, according to their masters' reckoning, twenty-one years of age. The assertion that slavery did not exist in the Transvaal is only made to hoodwink the English public. I have known men who have owned slaves, and who have seen whole waggon-loads of "black ivory," as they were called, sold for about 15 pounds a-piece. I have at this moment a tenant, Carolus by name, on some land I own in Natal, now a well-to-do man, who was for many years—about twenty, if I remember right—a Boer slave. During those years, he told me, he worked from morning till night, and the only reward he received was two calves. He finally escaped into Natal.

If other evidence is needed it is not difficult to find, so I will quote a little. On the 22d August 1876 we find Khama, king of the Bamangwato, one of the most worthy chiefs in South Africa, sending a message to "Victoria, the great Queen of the English people," in these words:—

"I write to you, Sir Henry, in order that your Queen may preserve for me my country, it being in her hands. The Boers are coming into it, and I do not like them. Their actions are cruel among us black people. We are like money, they sell us and our children. I ask Her Majesty to pity me, and to hear that which I write quickly. I wish to hear upon what conditions Her Majesty will receive me, and my country and my people, under her protection. I am weary with fighting. I do not like war, and I ask Her Majesty to give me peace. I am very much distressed that my people are being destroyed by war, and I wish them to obtain peace. I ask Her Majesty to defend me, as she defends all her people. There are three things which distress me very much— war, selling people, and drink. All these things I shall find in the Boers, and it is these things which destroy people to make an end of them in the country. *The custom of the Boers has always been to cause people to be sold, and to-day they are still selling people.* Last year I saw them pass with two waggons full of people whom they had bought at the river at Tanane" (Lake Ngate).

The Special Correspondence of the "Cape Argus," a highly respectable journal, writes thus on the 28th November 1876:—"The Boer from whom this information was gleaned has furnished besides some facts which may not be uninteresting, as a commentary on the repeated denials by Mr. Burgers of the existence of slavery. During the last week slaves have been offered for sale on his farm. The captives have been taken from Secocoeni's country by Mapoch's people, and are being exchanged at the rate of a child for a heifer. He also assures us that the whole of the Highveld is bring replenished with Kafir children, whom the Boers have been lately purchasing from the Swazies at the rate of a horse for a child. I should like to see this man and his father as witnesses before an Imperial Commission. He let fall one or two incidents of the past which were brought to mind by the occurrences of the present. In 1864, he says, 'The Swazies accompanied the Boers against Males. The Boers did nothing but stand by and witness the fearful massacre. The men and women were also murdered. One poor woman sat clutching her baby of eight days old. The Swazies stabbed her through the body, and when she found that she could not live, she wrung the baby's neck with her own hands to save it from future misery. On the return of that Commando the children who became too weary to continue the journey were killed on the road. The survivors were sold as slaves to the farmers.'"

The same gentleman writes in the issue of the 12th December as follows:—"The whole world may know it, for it is true, and investigation will only bring out the horrible details, that through the whole course of this Republic's existence it has acted in contravention of the Sand River Treaty; and slavery has occurred not only here and there in isolated cases, but as an unbroken practice, and has been one of the peculiar institutions of the country, mixed up with all its social and political life. It has been at the root of most of its wars. It has been carried on regularly even in times of peace. It has been characterised by all those circumstances which have so often roused the British nation to an indignant protest, and to repeated efforts to banish the slave trade from the world. The Boers have not only fallen on unsuspecting kraals simply for the purpose of obtaining the women and children and cattle, but they have carried on a traffic through natives who have kidnapped the children of their weaker neighbours, and sold them to the white man. Again, the Boers have sold and exchanged their victims among themselves. Waggon-loads of slaves have been conveyed from one end of the country to the other for sale, and that with the cognisance of, and for the direct advantage of, the highest officials of the land. The writer has himself seen in a town, situated in the south of the Republic, the children who had been brought down from a remote northern district. One fine morning, in walking through the streets, he was struck with the number of little black strangers standing about certain houses, and wondered where they could have come from. He learnt a few hours later that they were part of loads which were disposed of on the outskirts of the town the day before. The circumstances connected with some of these kidnapping excursions are appalling, and the barbarities practised by cruel masters upon some of these defenceless creatures during the course of their servitude are scarcely less horrible than those reported from Turkey. It is no disgrace in this country for an official to ride a fine horse which was got for two Kafir children, to procure whom the father and mother were shot. No reproach is inherited by the mistress who, day after day, tied up her female servant in an agonising posture, and had her beaten until there was no sound part in her body, securing her in the stocks during the intervals of torture. That man did not lose caste who tied up another woman and had her thrashed until she brought forth at the whipping-post. These are merely examples of thousands of cases which could be proved were an Imperial Commission to sit, and could the wretched victims of a prolonged oppression recover sufficiently from the dread of their old tyrants to give a truthful report."

To come to some evidence more recently adduced. On the 9th May 1881, an affidavit was sworn to by the Rev. John Thorne, curate of St. John the Evangelist, Lydenburg, Transvaal, and presented to the Royal Commission appointed to settle Transvaal affairs, in which he states: — "That I was appointed to the charge of a congregation in Potchefstroom, about thirteen years ago, when the Republic was under the presidency of Mr. Pretorius.[*] I remember noticing one morning, as I walked through the streets, a number of young natives, whom I knew to be strangers. I inquired where they came from. I was told that they had just been brought from Zoutpansberg. This was the locality from which slaves were chiefly brought at that time, and were traded for under the name of 'Black Ivory.' One of these natives belonged to Mr. Munich, the State Attorney. It was a matter of common remark at that time, that the President of the Republic was himself one of the greatest dealers in slaves." In the fourth paragraph of the same affidavit Mr. Thorne says, "That the Rev. Doctor Nachtigal, of the Berlin Missionary Society, was the interpreter for Shatane's people in the private office of Mr. Roth, and, at the close of the interview, told me what had occurred. On my expressing surprise, he went on to relate that he had information on native matters which would surprise me more. He then produced the copy of a register, kept in the landdrost's office, of men, women, and children, to the number of four hundred and eighty (480), who had been disposed of by one Boer to another for a consideration. In one case an ox was given in exchange, in another goats, in a third a blanket, and so forth. Many of these natives he (Mr. Nachtigal) knew personally. The copy was certified as true and correct by an official of the Republic, and I would mention his name now, only that I am persuaded that it would cost the man his life if his act became known to the Boers."

[*] One of the famous Triumvirate.

On the 16th May 1881, a native, named Frederick Molepo, was examined by the Royal Commission. The following are extracts from his examination:—

"(Sir E. Wood.) Are you a Christian?—Yes.

"(Sir H. de Villiers.) How long were you a slave?—Half a year.

"How do you know that you were a slave? Might you not have been an apprentice?—No, I was not apprenticed.

"How do you know?—They got me from my parents, and ill-treated me.

"(Sir E. Wood.) How many times did you get the stick?—Every day.

"(Sir H. de Villiers.) What did the Boers do with you when they caught you?—They sold me.

"How much did they sell you for?—One cow and a big pot."

On the 28th May 1881, amongst the other documents handed in for the consideration of the Royal Commission, is the statement of a headman, whose name it has been considered advisable to omit in the blue book for fear the Boers should take vengeance on him. He says, "I say, that if the English Government dies I shall die too; I would rather die than be under the Boer Government. I am the man who helped to make bricks for the church you see now standing in the square here (Pretoria), as a slave without payment. As a representative of my people I am still obedient to the English Government, and willing to obey all commands from them, even to die for their cause in this country, rather than submit to the Boers.

"I was under Shambok, my chief, who fought the Boers formerly, but he left us, and we were *put up to auction* and sold among the Boers. I want to state this myself to the Royal Commission in Newcastle. I was bought by Fritz Botha and sold by Frederick Botha, who was then veld cornet (justice of the peace) of the Boers."[*]

[*] I have taken the liberty to quote all these extracts exactly as they stand in the original, instead of weaving

their substance into my narrative, in order that I may not
be accused, as so often happens to authors who write upon
this subject, of having presented a garbled version of the
truth. The original of every extract is to be found in blue
books presented to Parliament. I have thought it best to
confine myself to these, and avoid repeating stories of
cruelties and slavery, however well authenticated, that have
come to my knowledge privately, such stories being always
more or less open to suspicion.

It would be easy to find more reports of the slave-trading practices of the Boers, but as the above are fair samples it will not be necessary to do so. My readers will be able from them to form some opinion as to whether or not slavery or apprenticeship existed in the Transvaal. If they come to the conclusion that it did, it must be borne in mind that what existed in the past will certainly exist again in the future. Natives are not now any fonder of working for Boers than they were a few years back, and Boers must get labour somehow. If, on the other hand, it did not exist, then the Boers are a grossly slandered people, and all writers on the subject, from Livingstone down, have combined to take away their character.

Leaving native questions for the present, we must now return to the general affairs of the country. When President Burgers opened the special sitting of the Volksraad, on the 4th September, he appealed, it will be remembered, to that body for pecuniary aid to liquidate the expenses of the war. This appeal was responded to by the passing of a war tax, under which every owner of a farm was to pay 10 pounds, the owner of half a farm 5 pounds, and so on. The tax was not a very just one, since it fell with equal weight on the rich man, who held twenty farms, and the poor man, who held but one. Its justice or injustice was, however, to a great extent immaterial, since the free and independent burghers, including some of the members of the Volksraad who had imposed it, promptly refused to pay it, or indeed, whilst they were about it, any other tax. As the Treasury was already empty, and creditors were pressing, this refusal was most ill-timed, and things began to look very black indeed. Meanwhile, in addition to the ordinary expenditure, and the interest payable on debts, money had to be found to pay Von Schlickmann's volunteers. As there was no cash in the country, this was done by issuing Government promissory notes, known as "goodfors," or vulgarly as "good for nothings," and by promising them all booty, and to each man a farm of two thousand acres, lying east and north-east of the Loolu mountains; in other words, in Secocoeni's territory, which did not belong to the Government to give away. The officials were the next to suffer, and for six months before the Annexation these unfortunate individuals lived as best they could, for they certainly got no salary, except in the case of a postmaster, who was told to help himself to his pay in stamps. The Government issued large numbers of bills, but the banks refused to discount them, and in some cases the neighbouring Colonies had to advance money to the Transvaal post-cart contractors, who were carrying the mails, as a matter of charity. The Government even mortgaged the great salt-pan near Pretoria for the paltry sum of 400 pounds, whilst the leading officials of the Government were driven to pledging their own private credit in order to obtain the smallest article necessary to its continuance. In fact, to such a pass did things come that when the country was annexed a single threepenny bit (which had doubtless been overlooked) was found in the Treasury chest, together with acknowledgments of debts to the extent of nearly 300,000 pounds.

Nor was the refusal to pay taxes, which they were powerless to enforce, the only difficulty with which the Government had to contend. Want of money is as bad and painful a thing to a State as to an individual, but there are perhaps worse things than want of money, one of which is to be deserted by your own friends and household. This was the position of the Government of the Republic; no sooner was it involved in overwhelming difficulties than its own subjects commenced to bait it, more especially the English portion of its subjects. They complained to the English authorities about the commandeering of members of their family or goods; they petitioned the British Government to interfere, and generally made themselves as unpleasant as possible to the local Authorities. Such a course of action was perhaps natural, but it can hardly be said to be either quite logical or just. The Transvaal Government had never asked them to come and live in the country, and if they did so, it must be remembered that many of the agitators had accumulated property, to leave which would mean ruin; and they saw that, unless something was done, its value would be destroyed.

Under the pressure of all these troubles the Boers themselves split up into factions, as they are always ready to do. The Dopper party declared that they had had enough progress, and proposed the extremely conservative Paul Kruger as President, Burgers' time having nearly expired. Paul Kruger accepted the candidature, although he had previously promised his support to Burgers, and distrust of each other was added to the other difficulties of the Executive, the Transvaal becoming a house very much divided against itself. Natives, Doppers, Progressionists, Officials, English, were all pulling different ways, and each striving for his own advantage. Anything more hopeless than the position of the country on the 1st January 1877 it is impossible to conceive. Enemies surrounded it; on every border there was the prospect of a serious war. In the exchequer there was nothing but piles of overdue bills. The President was helpless, and mistrustful of his officers, and the officers were caballing against the President. All the ordinary functions of Government had ceased, and trade was paralysed. Now and then wild proposals were made to relieve the State of its burdens, some of which partook of the nature of repudiation, but these were the exception; the majority of the inhabitants, who would neither fight nor pay taxes, sat still and awaited the catastrophe, utterly careless of all consequences.

CHAPTER III.
THE ANNEXATION

Anxiety of Lord Carnarvon – Despatch of Sir T. Shepstone as Special Commissioner to the Transvaal – Sir T. Shepstone, his great experience and ability – His progress to Pretoria and reception there – Feelings excited by the arrival of the mission – The annexation not a foregone conclusion – Charge brought against Sir T. Shepstone of having called up the Zulu army to sweep the Transvaal – Its complete falsehood – Cetywayo's message to Sir T. Shepstone – Evidence on the matter summed up – General desire of the natives for English rule – Habitual disregard of their interests – Assembly of the Volksraad – Rejection of Lord Carnarvon's Confederation Bill and of President Burgers' new constitution – President Burgers' speeches to the Raad – His posthumous statement – Communication to the Raad of Sir T. Shepstone's intention to annex the country – Despatch of Commission to inquire into the alleged peace with Secocoeni – Its fraudulent character discovered – Progress of affairs in the Transvaal – Paul Kruger and his party – Restlessness of natives – Arrangements for the annexation – The annexation proclamation.

The state of affairs described in the previous chapter was one that filled the Secretary of State for the Colonies with alarm. During his tenure of office, Lord Carnarvon evidently had the permanent welfare of South Africa much at heart, and he saw with apprehension that the troubles that were brewing in the Transvaal were of a nature likely to involve the Cape and Natal in a native war. Though there is a broad line of demarcation between Dutch and English, it is not so broad but that a victorious nation like the Zulus might cross it, and beginning by fighting the Boer, might end by fighting the white man irrespective of race. When the reader reflects how terrible would be the consequences of a combination of native tribes against the Whites, and how easily such a combination might at that time have been brought about in the first flush of native successes, he will understand the anxiety with which all thinking men watched the course of events in the Transvaal in 1876.

At last they took such a serious turn that the Home Government saw that some action must be taken if the catastrophe was to be averted, and determined to despatch Sir Theophilus Shepstone as Special Commissioner to the Transvaal, with powers, should it be necessary, to annex the country to Her Majesty's dominions, "in order to secure the peace and safety of Our said colonies and of Our subjects elsewhere."

The terms of his Commission were unusually large, leaving a great deal to his discretionary power. In choosing that officer for the execution of a most difficult and delicate mission, the Government, doubtless, made a very wise selection. Sir Theophilus Shepstone is a man of remarkable tact and ability, combined with great openness and simplicity of mind, and one whose name will always have a leading place in South African history. During a long official lifetime he has had to do with most of the native races in South Africa, and certainly knows them and their ways better than any living man; whilst he is by them all regarded with a peculiar and affectionate reverence. He is *par excellence* their great white chief and "father," and a word from him, even now that he has retired from active life, still carries more weight than the formal remonstrances of any governor in South Africa.

With the Boers he is almost equally well acquainted, having known many of them personally for years. He possesses, moreover, the rare power of winning the regard and affection, as well as the respect, of those about him in such a marked degree that those who have served him once would go far to serve him again. Sir T. Shepstone, however, has enemies like other people, and is commonly reported among them to be a disciple of Machiavelli, and to have his mind steeped in all the darker wiles of Kafir policy. The Annexation of the Transvaal is by them attributed to a successful and vigorous use of those arts that distinguished the diplomacy of two centuries ago. Falsehood and bribery are supposed to have been the great levers used to effect the change, together with threats of extinction at the hands of a savage and unfriendly nation.

That the Annexation was a triumph of mind over matter is quite true, but whether or not that triumph was unworthily obtained, I will leave those who read this short chronicle of the events connected with it to judge. I saw it somewhat darkly remarked in a newspaper the other day that the history of the Annexation had evidently yet to be written; and I fear that the remark represents the feeling of most people about the event; implying as it did, that it was carried out, by means certainly mysterious, and presumably doubtful. I am afraid that those who think thus will be disappointed in what I have to say about the matter, since I know that the means employed to bring the Boers—

"Fracti bello, fatisque repulsi" —

under her Majesty's authority were throughout as fair and honest as the Annexation itself was, in my opinion, right and necessary.

To return to Sir T. Shepstone. He undoubtedly had faults as a ruler, one of the most prominent of which was that his natural mildness of character would never allow him to act with severity even when severity was necessary. The very criminals condemned to death ran a good chance of reprieve when he had to sign their death-warrants. He had also that worst of faults (so called), in one fitted by nature to become great—want of ambition, a failing that in such a man marks him the possessor of an even and a philosophic mind. It was no seeking of his own that raised him out of obscurity, and when his work was done to comparative obscurity he elected to return, though whether a man of his ability and experience in South African affairs should, at the present crisis, be allowed to remain there, is another question.

On the 20th December 1876, Sir T. Shepstone wrote to President Burgers, informing him of his approaching visit to the Transvaal, to secure, if possible, the adjustment of the existing troubles, and the adoption of such measures as might be best calculated to prevent their recurrence in the future.

On his road to Pretoria, Sir Theophilus received a hearty welcome from the Boer as well as the English inhabitants of the country. One of these addresses to him says: "Be assured, high honourable Sir, that we burghers, now assembled together, entertain the most friendly feeling towards your Government, and that we shall agree with anything you may do in conjunction with our Government for the progress of our State, the strengthening against our native enemies, and for the general welfare of all the inhabitants of the whole of South Africa. Welcome in Heidelberg, and welcome in the Transvaal."

At Pretoria the reception of the Special Commissioner was positively enthusiastic; the whole town came out to meet him, and the horses having been taken out of the carriage, he was dragged in triumph through the streets. In his reply to the address presented to him, Sir Theophilus shadowed forth the objects of his mission in these words: "Recent events in this country have shown to all thinking men the absolute necessity for closer union and more oneness of purpose among the Christian Governments of the southern portion of this Continent: the best interests of the native races, no less than the peace and prosperity of the white, imperatively demand it, and I rely upon you and upon your Government to co-operate with me in endeavouring to achieve the great and glorious end of inscribing on a general South African banner the appropriate motto—'Eendragt maakt magt' (Unity makes strength)."

A few days after his arrival a commission was appointed, consisting of Messrs. Henderson and Osborn, on behalf of the Special Commissioner, and Messrs. Kruger and Jorissen, on behalf of the Transvaal Government, to discuss the state of the country. This commission came to nothing, and was on both sides nothing more than a bit of by-play.

The arrival of the mission was necessarily regarded with mixed feelings by the inhabitants of the Transvaal. By one party it was eagerly greeted, viz., the English section of the population, who devoutly hoped that it had come to annex the country. With the exception of the Hollander element, the officials also were glad of its arrival, and secretly hoped that the country would be taken over, when there would be more chance of their getting their arrear pay. The better educated Boers also were for the most part satisfied that there was no hope for the country unless England helped it in some way, though they did not like having to accept the help. But the more bigoted and narrow-minded among them were undoubtedly opposed to English interference, and under their leader, Paul Kruger, who was at the time running for the President's chair, did their best to be rid of it. They found ready allies in the Hollander clientele, with which Mr. Burgers had surrounded himself, headed by the famous Dr. Jorissen, who was, like most of the rulers of this singular State, an ex-clergyman, but now an Attorney-general, not learned in the law. These men were for the most part entirely unfit for the positions they held, and feared that in the event of the country changing hands they might be ejected from them; and also, they did all Englishmen the favour to regard them, with that particularly virulent and general hatred which is a part of the secret creed of many foreigners, more especially of such as are under our protection. As may easily be imagined, what between all these different parties and the presence of the Special Commissioner, there were certainly plenty of intrigues going on in Pretoria during the first few months of 1877, and the political excitement was very great. Nobody knew how far Sir T. Shepstone was prepared to go, and everybody was afraid of putting out his hand further than he could pull it back, and trying to make himself comfortable on two stools at once. Members of the Volksraad and other prominent individuals in the country who had during the day been denouncing the Commissioner in no measured terms, and even proposing that he and his staff should be shot as a warning to the English Government, might be seen arriving at his house under cover of the shades of evening, to have a little talk with him, and express the earnest hope that it was his intention to annex the country as soon as possible. It is necessary to assist at a peaceable annexation to learn the depth of meanness human nature is capable of.

In Pretoria, at any rate, the ladies were of great service to the cause of the mission, since they were nearly all in favour of a change of government, and, that being the case, they naturally soon brought their husbands, brothers, and lovers to look at things from the same point of view. It was a wise man who said that in any matter where it is necessary to obtain the goodwill of a population you should win over the women; that done, you need not trouble yourself about the men.

Though the country was thus overflowing with political intrigues, nothing of the kind went on in the Commissioner's camp. It was not he who made the plots to catch the Transvaalers; on the contrary, they made the plots to catch him. For several months all that he did was to sit still and let the rival passions work their way, fighting what the Zulus afterwards called the "fight of sit down." When anybody came to see him he was very glad to meet them, pointed out the desperate condition of the country, and asked them if they could suggest a remedy. And that was about all he did do, beyond informing himself very carefully as to all that was going on in the country, and the movements of the natives within and outside its borders. There was no money spent on bribery, as has been stated, though it is impossible to imagine a state of affairs in which it would have been more easy to bribe, or in which it could have been done with greater effect; unless indeed the promise that some pension should be paid to President Burgers can be called a bribe, which it was certainly never intended to be, but simply a guarantee that after having spent all his private means on behalf of the State he should not be left destitute. The statement that the Annexation was effected under a threat that if the Government did not give its consent Sir T. Shepstone would let loose the Zulus on the country is also a wicked and malicious invention, but with this I shall deal more at length further on.

It must not, however, be understood that the Annexation was a foregone conclusion, or that Sir T. Shepstone came up to the Transvaal with the fixed intention of annexing the country without reference to its position, merely with a view of extending British influence, or, as has been absurdly stated, in order to benefit Natal. He had no fixed purpose, whether it were necessary or no, of exercising the full powers given to him by his commission; on the contrary, he was all along most anxious to find some internal resources within the State by means of which Annexation could be averted, and of this fact his various letters and despatches give full proof. Thus, in his letter to President Burgers, of the 9th April 1877, in which he announces his intention of annexing the country, he says: "I have more than once assured your Honour that if I could think of any plan by which the independence of the State could be maintained by its own internal resources I would most certainly not conceal that plan from you." It is also incidentally remarkably confirmed by a passage in Mr. Burgers' posthumous defence, in which he says: "Hence I met Shepstone alone in my house, and opened up the subject of his mission. With a candour that astonished me, he avowed that his purpose was to annex the country, as he had sufficient grounds for it, unless I could so alter as to satisfy his Government. My plan of a new constitution, modelled after that of America, of a standing police force of two hundred mounted men, was then proposed. He promised to give me time to call the Volksraad together, and to *abandon his design* if the Volksraad would adopt these measures, and the country be willing to submit to them, and to carry them out." Further on he says: "In justice to Shepstone I must say that I would not consider an officer of my Government to have acted faithfully if he had not done what Shepstone did."

It has also been frequently alleged in England, and always seems to be taken as the groundwork of argument in the matter of the Annexation, that the Special Commissioner represented that the majority of the inhabitants wished for the Annexation, and that it was sanctioned on that ground. This statement shows the great ignorance that exists in this country of South African affairs, an ignorance which in this case has been carefully fostered by Mr. Gladstone's Government for party purposes, they having found it necessary to assume, in order to make their position in the matter tenable, that Sir T. Shepstone and other Officials had been guilty of misrepresentation. Unfortunately, the Government and its supporters have been more intent upon making out their case than upon ascertaining the truth of their statements. If they had taken the trouble to refer to Sir T. Shepstone's despatches, they would have found that the ground on which the Transvaal was annexed was, not because the majority of the inhabitants wished for it, but because the State was drifting into anarchy, was bankrupt, and was about to be destroyed by native tribes. They would further have found that Sir T. Shepstone never represented that the majority of the Boers were in favour of Annexation. What he did say was that most thinking men in the country saw no other way out of the difficulty; but what proportion of the Boers can be called "thinking men?" He also said, in the fifteenth paragraph of his despatch to Lord Carnarvon of 6th March 1877, that petitions signed by 2500 people, representing every class of the community, out of a total adult population of 8000, had been presented to the Government of the Republic, setting forth its difficulties and dangers, and praying it "to treat with me for their amelioration or removal." He also stated, and with perfect truth, that many more would have signed had it not been for the terrorism that was exercised, and that all the towns and villages in the country desired the change, which was a patent fact.

This is the foundation on which the charge of misrepresentation is built—a charge which has been manipulated so skilfully, and with such a charming disregard for the truth, that the British public has been duped into believing it. When it is examined into, it vanishes into thin air.

But a darker charge has been brought against the Special Commissioner—a charge affecting his honour as a gentleman and his character as a Christian; and, strange to say, has gained a considerable credence, especially amongst a certain party in England. I allude to the statement that he called up the Zulu army with the intention of sweeping the Transvaal if the Annexation was objected to. I may state, from my own personal knowledge, that the report is a complete falsehood, and that no such threat was ever made, either by Sir T. Shepstone or by anybody connected with him, and I will briefly prove what I say.

When the mission first arrived at Pretoria, a message came from Cetywayo to the effect that he had heard that the Boers had fired at "Sompseu" (Sir T. Shepstone), and announcing his intention of attacking the Transvaal if "his father" was touched. About the middle of March alarming rumours began to spread as to the intended action of Cetywayo with reference to the Transvaal; but as Sir T. Shepstone did not think that the king would be likely to make any hostile movement whilst he was in the country, he took no steps in the matter. Neither did the Transvaal Government ask his advice and assistance. Indeed, a remarkable trait in the Boers is their supreme self-conceit, which makes them believe that they are capable of subduing all the natives in Africa, and of thrashing the whole British army if necessary. Unfortunately, the recent course of events has tended to confirm them in their opinion as regards their white enemies. To return: towards the second week in April, or the week before the proclamation of annexation was issued, things began to look very serious; indeed, rumours that could hardly be discredited reached the Special Commissioner that the whole of the Zulu army was collected in a chain of Impis or battalions, with the intention of bursting into the Transvaal and sweeping the country. Knowing how terrible would be the catastrophe if this were to happen, Sir T. Shepstone was much alarmed about the matter, and at a meeting with the Executive Council of the Transvaal Government he pointed out to them the great danger in which the country was placed. This was done in the presence of several officers of his Staff, and it was on this friendly exposition of the state of affairs that the charge that he had threatened the country with invasion by the Zulus was based. On the 11th of April, or the day before the Annexation, a message was despatched to Cetywayo, telling him of the reports that had reached Pretoria, and stating that if they were true he must forthwith give up all such intentions, as the Transvaal would at once be placed under the sovereignty of Her Majesty, and that if he had assembled any armies for purposes of aggression they must be disbanded at once. Sir T. Shepstone's message reached Zululand not a day too soon. Had the Annexation of the Transvaal been delayed by a few weeks even— and this is a point which I earnestly beg Englishmen to remember in connection with that act—Cetywayo's armies would have entered the Transvaal, carrying death before them, and leaving a wilderness behind them.

Cetywayo's answer to the Special Commissioner's message will sufficiently show, to use Sir Theophilus' own words in his despatch on the subject, "the pinnacle of peril which the Republic and South Africa generally had reached at the moment when the Annexation took place." He says, "I thank my Father Sompseu (Sir T. Shepstone) for his message. I am glad that he has sent it, because the Dutch have tired me out, and I intended to fight them once and once only, and to drive them over the Vaal. Kabana (name of messenger), you see my Impis (armies) are gathered. It was to fight the Dutch I called them together; now I will send them back to their homes. Is it well that two men ('amadoda-amabili') should be made 'iziula' (fools)? In the reign of my father Umpanda the Boers were constantly moving their boundary further into my country. Since his death the same thing has been done. I had therefore determined to end it once for all!" The message then goes on to other matters, and ends with a request to be allowed to fight the Amaswazi, because "they fight together and kill one another. This," says Cetywayo naively, "is wrong, and I want to chastise them for it."

This quotation will suffice to convince all reasonable men, putting aside all other matters, from what imminent danger the Transvaal was delivered by the much-abused Annexation.

Some months after that event, however, it occurred to the ingenious mind of some malicious individual in Natal that, properly used, much political capital might be made out of this Zulu incident, and the story that Cetywayo's army had been called up by Sir Theophilus himself to overawe, and, if necessary, subdue the Transvaal, was accordingly invented and industriously circulated. Although Sir T. Shepstone at once caused it to be authoritatively contradicted, such an astonishing slander naturally took firm root, and on the 12th April 1879 we have Mr. M. W. Pretorius, one of the Boer leaders, publicly stating at a meeting of the farmers that "previous to the Annexation Sir T. Shepstone had threatened the Transvaal with an attack from the Zulus as an argument for advancing the Annexation." Under such an imputation the Government could no longer keep silence, and accordingly Sir Owen Lanyon, who was then Administrator of the Transvaal, caused the matter to be officially investigated, with these results, which are summed up by him in a letter to Mr. Pretorius, dated 1st May 1879:—

1. The records of the Republican Executive Council contained no allusion to any such statement.

2. Two members of that Council filed statements in which they unreservedly denied that Sir T. Shepstone used the words or threats imputed to him.

3. Two officers of Sir T. Shepstone's staff, who were always present with him at interviews with the Executive Council, filed statements to the same effect.

"I have no doubt," adds Sir Owen Lanyon, "that the report has been originated and circulated by some evil-disposed persons."

In addition to this evidence we have a letter written to the Colonial Office by Sir T. Shepstone, dated London, August 12, 1879, in which he points out that Mr. Pretorius was not even present at any of the interviews with the Executive Council on which occasion he accuses him of having made use of the threats. He further shows that the use of such a threat on his part would have been the depth of folly, and "knowingly to court the instant and ignominious failure of my mission," because the Boers were so persuaded of their own prowess that they could not be convinced that they stood in any danger from native sources, and also because "such play with such keen-edged tools as the excited passions of savages are, and especially such savages as I knew the Zulus to be, is not what an experience of forty-two years in managing them inclined me to." And yet, in the face of all this accumulated evidence, this report continues to be believed, that is, by those who wished to believe it.

Such are the accusations that have been brought against the manner of the Annexation and the Officer who carried it out, and never were accusations more groundless. Indeed both for party purposes, and from personal animus, every means, fair or foul, has been used to discredit it and all connected with it. To take a single instance, one author (Miss Colenso, "History of the Zulu War") actually goes the length of putting a portion of a speech made by President Burgers into the mouth of Sir T. Shepstone, and then abusing him for his incredible profanity. Surely this exceeds the limits of fair criticism.

Before I go on to the actual history of the Annexation there is one point I wish to submit to my reader. In England the change of Government has always been talked of as though it only affected the forty thousand white inhabitants of the country, whilst everybody seems to forget that this same land had about a million human beings living on it, its original owners, and only, unfortunately for themselves, possessing a black skin, and therefore entitled to little consideration, — even at the hands of the most philanthropic Government in the world. It never seems to have occurred to those who have raised so much outcry on behalf of the forty thousand Boers, to inquire what was thought of the matter by the million natives. If they were to be allowed a voice in their own disposal, the country was certainly annexed by the wish of a very large majority of its inhabitants. It is true that Secocoeni, instigated thereto by the Boers, afterwards continued the war against us, but, with the exception of this one chief, the advent of our rule was hailed with joy by every native in the Transvaal, and even he was glad of it at the time. During our period of rule in the Transvaal the natives have had, as they foresaw, more peace than at any time since the white man set foot in the land. They have paid their taxes gladly, and there has been no fighting among themselves; but since we have given up the country we hear a very different tale. It is this million of men, women, and children who, notwithstanding their black skins, live and feel, and have intelligence as much as ourselves, who are the principal, because the most numerous sufferers from Mr. Gladstone's conjuring tricks, that can turn a Sovereign into a Suzerain as airily as the professor of magic brings a litter of guinea-pigs out of a top hat. It is our falsehood and treachery to them whom we took over "for ever," as we told them, and whom we have now handed back to their natural enemies to be paid off for their loyalty to the Englishman, that is the blackest stain in all this black business, and that has destroyed our prestige, and caused us to be looked on amongst them, for they do not hide their opinion, as "cowards and liars."

But very little attention, however, seems to have been paid to native views or claims at any time in the Transvaal; indeed they have all along been treated as serfs of the soil, to be sold with it, if necessary, to a new master. It is true that the Government, acting under pressure from the Aborigines Protection Society, made, on the occasion of the Surrender, a feeble effort to secure the independence of some of the native tribes; but when the Boer leaders told them shortly that they would have nothing of the sort, and that, if they were not careful, they would reoccupy Laing's Nek, the proposal was at once dropped, with many assurances that no offence was intended. The worst of the matter is that this treatment of our native subjects and allies will assuredly recoil on the heads of future innocent Governments.

Shortly after the appointment of the Joint-Commission alluded to at the beginning of this chapter, President Burgers, who was now in possession of the Special Commissioner's intentions, should he be unable to carry out reforms sufficiently drastic to satisfy the English Government, thought it best to call together the Volksraad. In the meantime, it had been announced that the "rebel" Secocoeni had sued for peace and signed a treaty declaring himself a subject of the Republic. I shall have to enter into the question of this treaty a little further on, so I will at present only say that it was the first business laid before the Raad, and, after some discussion, ratified. Next in order to the Secocoeni peace came the question of Confederation, as laid down in Lord Carnarvon's Permissive Bill. This proposal was laid before them in an earnest and eloquent speech by their President, who entreated them to consider the dangerous position of the Republic, and to face their difficulties like men. The question was referred to a committee, and an adverse report being brought up, was rejected without further consideration. It is just possible that intimidation had something to do with the summary treatment of so important a matter, seeing that whilst it was being argued a large mob of Boers, looking very formidable with their sea-cow hide whips, watched every move of their representatives through the windows of the Volksraad Hall. It was Mr. Chamberlain's caucus system in practical and visible operation.

A few days after the rejection of the Confederation Bill, President Burgers, who had frequently alluded to the desperate condition of the Republic, and stated that either some radical reform must be effected or the country must come under the British flag, laid before the Raad a brand new constitution of a very remarkable nature, asserting that they must either accept it or lose their independence.

The first part of this strange document dealt with the people and their rights, which remained much as they were before, with the exception that the secrecy of all letters entrusted to the post was to be inviolable. The recognition of this right is an amusing incident in the history of a free Republic. Under following articles the Volksraad was entrusted with the charge of the native inhabitants of the State, the provision for the administration of justice, the conduct of education, the regulation of money-bills, &c. It is in the fourth chapter, however, that we come to the real gist of the Bill, which was the endowment of the State President with the authority of a dictator. Mr. Burgers thought to save the State by making himself an absolute monarch. He was to be elected for a period of seven years instead of five years, and to be eligible for re-election. In him was vested the power of making all appointments without reference to the legislature. All laws were to be drawn up by him, and he was to have the right of veto on Volksraad resolutions, which body he could summon and dissolve at will. Finally, his Executive Council was to consist of heads of departments appointed by himself, and of one member of the Volksraad. The Volksraad treated this Bill in much the same way as they had dealt with the Permissive Confederation Bill, gave it a casual consideration, and threw it out.

The President, meanwhile, was doing his best to convince the Raad of the danger of the country; that the treasury was empty, whilst duns were pressing, that enemies were threatening on every side, and, finally, that Her Majesty's Special Commissioner was encamped within a thousand yards of them, watching their deliberations with some interest. He showed them that it was impossible at once to scorn reform and reject friendly offers, that it was doubtful if anything could save them, but that if they took no steps they were certainly lost as a nation. The "Fathers of the land," however, declined to dance to the President's piping. Then he took a bolder line. He told them that a guilty nation never can evade the judgment that follows its steps. He asked them "conscientiously to advise the people not obstinately to refuse a union with a powerful Government. He could not advise them to refuse such a union. . . . He did not believe that a new constitution would save them; for as little as the old constitution had brought them to ruin, so little would a new constitution bring salvation. . . . If the citizens of England had behaved towards the Crown as the burghers of this State had behaved to their Government, England would never have stood so long as she had." He pointed out to them their hopeless financial position. "To-day," he said, "a bill for 1100 pounds was laid before me for signature; but I would sooner have cut off my right hand than sign that paper—(cheers)—for I have not the slightest ground to expect that, when that bill becomes due, there will be a penny to pay it with." And finally, he exhorted them thus: "Let them make the best of the situation, and get the best terms they possibly could; let them agree to join their hands to those of their brethren in the south, and then from the Cape to the Zambesi there would be one great people. Yes, there was something grand in that, grander even than their idea of a Republic, something which ministered to their national feeling—(cheers)—and would this be so miserable? Yes, this would be miserable for those who would not be under the law, for the rebel and the revolutionist, but welfare and prosperity for the men of law and order."

These powerful words form a strong indictment against the Republic, and from them there can be little doubt that President Burgers was thoroughly convinced of the necessity and wisdom of the Annexation. It is interesting to compare them, and many other utterances of his made at this period, with the opinions he expresses in the posthumous document recently published, in which he speaks somewhat jubilantly of the lessons taught us on Laing's Nek and Majuba by such "an inherently weak people as the Boers," and points to them as striking instances of retribution. In this document he attributes the Annexation to the desire to advance English supremacy in South Africa, and to lay hold of the way to Central South Africa. It is, however, noticeable that he does not in any way indicate how it could have been averted, and the State continue to exist; and he seems all along to feel that his case is a weak one, for in explaining, or attempting to explain, why he had never defended himself from the charges brought against him in connection with the Annexation, he says: "Had I not endured in silence, had I not borne patiently all the accusations, but out of selfishness or fear told the plain truth of the case, the Transvaal would never have had the consideration it has now received from Great Britain. However unjust the Annexation was, my self-justification would have *exposed the Boers to such an extent*, and the state of the country in such a way, that it would have deprived them both of the sympathy of the world and the consideration of the English politicians." In other words, "If I had told the truth about things as I should have been obliged to do to justify myself, there would have been no more outcry about the Annexation, because the whole world, even the English Radicals, would have recognised how necessary it was, and what a fearful state the country was in."

But to let that pass, it is evident that President Burgers did not take the same view of the Annexation in 1877 as he did in 1881, and indeed his speeches to the Volksraad would read rather oddly printed in parallel columns with his posthumous statement. The reader would be forced to one of two conclusions, either on one of the two occasions he is saying what he does not mean, or he must have changed his mind. As I believe him to have been an honest man, I incline to the latter supposition; nor do I consider it so very hard to account for, taking into consideration his natural Dutch proclivities. In 1877 Burgers is the despairing head of a State driving rapidly to ruin, if not to actual extinction, when the strong hand of the English Government is held out to him. What wonder that he accepts it gladly on behalf of his country, which is by its help brought into a state of greater prosperity than it has ever before known? In 1881 the wheel has gone round, and great events have come about whilst he lies dying. The enemies of the Boers have been destroyed, the powers of the Zulus and Secocoeni are no more; the country has prospered under a healthy rule, and its finances have been restored. More, — glad tidings have come from Mid-Lothian, to the "rebel and the revolutionist," whose hopes were flagging, and eloquent words have been spoken by the new English Dictator that have aroused a great rebellion. And, to crown all, English troops have suffered one massacre and three defeats, and England sues for peace from the South African peasant, heedless of honour or her broken word, so that the prayer be granted.

With such events before him, that dying man may well have found cause to change his opinion. Doubtless the Annexation was wrong, since England disowns her acts; and may not that dream about the great South African Republic come true after all? Has not the pre-eminence of the Englishman received a blow from which it can never recover, and is not his control over Boers and natives irredeemably weakened? And must he,—Burgers,—go down to posterity as a Dutchman who tried to forward the interests of the English party? No, doubtless the Annexation was wrong; but it has done good, for it has brought about the downfall of the English: and we will end the argument in the very words of his last public utterance, with which he ends his statement: "South Africa gained more from this, and has made a larger step forward in the march of freedom than most people can conceive."

Who shall say that he is wrong? the words of dying men are sometimes prophetic! South Africa has made a great advance towards the "freedom" of a Dutch Republic.

This has been a digression, but I hope not an uninteresting one. To return—on the 1st March, Sir T. Shepstone met the Executive Council, and told them that in his opinion there was now but one remedy to be adopted, and that was that the Transvaal should be united with English Colonies of South Africa under one head, namely the Queen, saying at the same time that the only thing now left to the Republic was to make the best arrangements it could for the future benefit of its inhabitants, and to submit to that which he saw to be, and every thinking man saw to be, inevitable. So soon as this information was officially communicated to the Raad, for a good proportion of its members were already acquainted with it unofficially, it flew from a state of listless indifference into vigorous and hasty action. The President was censured, and a Committee was appointed to consider and report upon the situation, which reported in favour of the adoption of Burgers' new constitution. Accordingly, the greatest part of this measure, which had been contemptuously rejected a few days before, was adopted almost without question, and Mr. Paul Kruger was appointed Vice-President. On the following day, a very drastic treason law was passed, borrowed from the Statute book of the Orange Free State, which made all public expression of opinion, if adverse to the Government, or in any way supporting the Annexation party, high treason. This done, the Assembly prorogued itself until— October 1881.

During and after the sitting of the Raad, rumours arose that the Chief Secocoeni's signature to the treaty of peace, ratified by that body, had been obtained by misrepresentation. As ratified, this treaty consisted of three articles, according to which Secocoeni consented, first to become a subject of the Republic, and obey the laws of the country; secondly, to agree to a certain restricted boundary line and, thirdly, to pay 2000 head of cattle; which, considering he had captured quite 5000 head, was not exorbitant.

Towards the end of February a written message was received from Secocoeni by Sir T. Shepstone, dated after the signing of the supposed treaty. The original, which was written in Sisutu, was a great curiosity. The following is a correct translation:—

"For Myn Heer Sheepstone,—I beg you, Chief, come help me, the Boers are killing me, and I don't know the reasons why they should be angry with me; Chief, I beg you come with Myn Heer Merensky.—I am Sikukuni."

This message was accompanied by a letter from Mr. Merensky, a well-known and successful missionary, who had been for many years resident in Secocoeni's country, in which he stated that he heard on very good authority that Secocoeni had distinctly refused to agree to that article of the treaty by which he became a subject of the State. He adds that he cannot remain "silent while such tricks are played."

Upon this information, Sir T. Shepstone wrote to President Burgers, stating that "if the officer in whom you have placed confidence has withheld any portion of the truth from you, especially so serious a portion of it, he is guilty of a wrong towards you personally, as well as towards the Government, because he has caused you to assume an untenable position," and suggesting that a joint commission should be despatched to Secocoeni, to thoroughly sift the question in the interest of all concerned. This suggestion was after some delay agreed to, and a commission was appointed, consisting of Mr. Van Gorkom, a Hollander, and Mr. Holtshausen, a member of the Executive Council, on behalf of the Transvaal Government, and Mr. Osborn, R.M., and Captain Clarke, R.A., on behalf of the Commissioner, whom I accompanied as Secretary.

At Middelburg the native Gideon who acted as interpreter between Commandant Ferreira, C.M.G. (the officer who negotiated the treaty on behalf of the Boer Government), and Secocoeni was examined, and also two natives, Petros and Jeremiah, who were with him, but did not actually interpret. All these men persisted that Secocoeni had positively refused to become a subject of the Republic, and only consented to sign the treaty on the representations of Commandant Ferreira that it would only be binding, as regards to the two articles about the cattle and the boundary line.

The Commission then proceeded to Secocoeni's town, accompanied by a fresh set of interpreters, and had a long interview with Secocoeni. The chief's Prime Minister or "mouth," Makurupiji, speaking in his presence, and on his behalf and making use of the pronoun "I" before all the assembled headmen of the tribe, gave an account of the interview between Commandant Ferreira in the presence of that gentleman, who accompanied the commission and Secocoeni, in almost the same words as had been used by the interpreters at Middelburg. He distinctly denied having consented to become a subject of the Republic or to stand under the law, and added that he feared he "had touched the feather to" (signed) things that he did not know of in the treaty. Commandant Ferreira then put some questions, but entirely failed to shake the evidence; on the contrary, he admitted by his questions that Secocoeni had not consented to become a subject of the Republic. Secocoeni had evidently signed the piece of paper under the impression that he was acknowledging his liability to pay 2000 head of cattle, and fixing a certain portion of his boundary line, and on the distinct understanding that he was not to become a subject of the State.

Now it was the Secocoeni war that had brought the English Mission into the country, and if it could be shown that the Secocoeni war had come to a successful termination, it would go far towards helping the Mission out again. To this end, it was necessary that the Chief should declare himself a subject of the State, and thereby, by implication acknowledge himself to have been a rebel, and admit his defeat. All that was required was a signature, and that once obtained the treaty was published and submitted to the Raad for confirmation, without a whisper being heard of the conditions under which this ignorant Basutu was induced to sign. Had no Commission visited

Secocoeni, this treaty would afterwards have been produced against him in its entirety. Altogether, the history of the Secocoeni Peace Treaty does not reassure one as to the genuineness of the treaties which the Boers are continually producing, purporting to have been signed by native chiefs, and as a general rule presenting the State with great tracts of country in exchange for a horse or a few oxen. However fond the natives may be of their Boer neighbours, such liberality can scarcely be genuine. On the other hand, it is so easy to induce a savage to sign a paper, or even, if he is reticent, to make a cross for him, and once made, as we all know, *litera scripa manet*, and becomes title to the lands.

During the Secocoeni investigation, affairs in the Transvaal were steadily drifting towards anarchy. The air was filled with rumours; now it was reported that an outbreak was imminent amongst the English population at the Gold Fields, who had never forgotten Von Schlickmann's kind suggestion that they should be "subdued;" now it was said that Cetywayo had crossed the border, and might shortly be expected at Pretoria; now that a large body of Boers were on their road to shoot the Special Commissioner, his twenty-five policemen and Englishmen generally, and so on.

Meanwhile, Paul Kruger and his party were not letting the grass grow under their feet, but worked public feeling with great vigour, with the double object of getting Paul made President and ridding themselves of the English. Articles in his support were printed in the well-known Dutch paper "Die Patriot," published in the Cape Colony, which are so typical of the Boers and of the only literature that has the slightest influence over them, that I will quote a few extracts from one of them.

After drawing a very vivid picture of the wretched condition of the country as compared to what it was when the Kafirs had "a proper respect" for the Boers, before Burgers came into power, the article proceeds to give the cause of this state of affairs. "God's word," it says, "gives us the solution. Look at Israel, while the people have a godly king, everything is prosperous, but under a godless prince the land retrogrades, and the whole of the people must suffer. Read Leviticus, chapter 26, with attention, &c. In the day of the Voortrekkers (pioneers), a handful of men chased a thousand Kafirs and made them run; so also in the Free State War (Deut. xxxii. 30; Jos. xxiii.

10; Lev. xxvi. 8). But mark, now when Burgers became President, he knows no Sabbath, he rides through the land in and out of town on Sunday, he knows not the church and God's service (Lev. xxvi. 2-3) to the scandal of pious people. And he formerly was a priest too. And what is the consequence? No harvest (Lev. xxvi. 16), an army of 6,000 men runs because one man falls (Lev. xxvi. 17, &c.) What is now the remedy?" The remedy proves to be Paul Kruger, "because there is no other candidate. Because our Lord clearly points him out to be the man, for why is there no other candidate? Who arranged it this way?" Then follows a rather odd argument in favour of Paul's election, "Because he himself (P. Kruger) acknowledges in his own reply that he is *incompetent*, but that all his ability is from our Lord. Because he is a warrior. Because he is a Boer." Then Paul Kruger, the warrior and the Boer, is compared to Joan of Arc, "a simple Boer girl who came from behind the sheep." The Burghers of Transvaal are exhorted to acknowledge the hand of the Lord, and elect Paul Kruger, or look for still heavier punishment. (Lev. xxvi. 18 *et seq.*) Next the "Patriot" proceeds to give a bit of advice to "our candidate, Paul Kruger." He is to deliver the land from the Kafirs. "The Lord has given you the heart of a warrior, arise and drive them," a bit of advice quite suited to his well-known character. But this chosen vessel was not to get all the loaves and fishes; on the contrary, as soon as he had fulfilled his mission of "driving" the Kafirs, he was to hand over his office to a "good" president. The article ends thus: "If the Lord wills to use you now to deliver this land from its enemies, and a day of peace and prosperity arises again, and you see that you are not exactly the statesman to further govern the Republic, then it will be your greatest honour to say, 'Citizens, I have delivered you from the enemy, I am no statesman, but now you have peace and time to choose and elect a *good* President.'"

An article such as the above is instructive reading as showing the low calibre of the minds that are influenced by it. Yet such writings and sermons have more power among the Boers than any other arguments, appealing as they do to the fanaticism and vanity of their nature, which causes them to believe that the Divinity is continually interfering on their behalf at the cost of other people. It will be noticed that the references given are all to the Old Testament, and nearly all refer to acts of blood.

These doctrines were not, however, at all acceptable to Burgers' party, or the more enlightened members of the community, and so bitter did the struggle of rival opinions become that there is very little doubt that had the country not been annexed, civil war would have been added to its other calamities. Meanwhile the natives were from day to day becoming more restless, and messengers were constantly arriving at the Special Commissioner's camp, begging that their tribe might be put under the Queen, and stating that they would fight rather than submit any longer to the Boers.

At length on the 9th April, Sir T. Shepstone informed the Government of the Republic that he was about to declare the Transvaal British territory. He told them that he had considered and reconsidered his determination, but that he could see no possible means within the State by which it could free itself from the burdens that were sinking it to destruction, adding that if he could have found such means he would certainly not have hidden them from the Government. This intimation was received in silence, though all the later proceedings with reference to the Annexation were in reality carried out in concert with the Authorities of the Republic. Thus on the 13th March the Government submitted a paper of ten questions to Sir T. Shepstone as regards the future condition of the Transvaal under English rule, whether the debts of the State would be guaranteed, &c. To these questions replies were given which were on the whole satisfactory to the Government. As these replies formed the basis of the proclamation guarantees, it is not necessary to enter into them.

It was further arranged by the Republican Government that a formal protest should be entered against the Annexation, which was accordingly prepared and privately shown to the Special Commissioner. The annexation proclamation was also shown to President Burgers, and a paragraph eliminated at his suggestion. In fact, the Special Commissioner and the President, together with most of his Executive, were quite at one as regards the necessity of the proclamation being issued, their joint endeavours being directed to the prevention of any disturbance, and to secure a good reception for the change.

At length, after three months of inquiry and negotiation, the proclamation of annexation was on the 12th of April 1877 read by Mr. Osborn, accompanied by some other gentlemen of Sir T. Shepstone's staff. It was an anxious moment for all concerned. To use the words of the Special Commissioner in his despatch home on the subject, "Every effort had been made during the previous fortnight by, it is said, educated Hollanders, and who had but lately arrived in the country to rouse the fanaticism of the Boers and induce them to offer 'bloody' resistance to what it was known I intended to do. The Boers were appealed to in the most inflammatory language by printed manifestoes and memorials; . . . it was urged that I had but a small escort which could easily be overpowered." In a country so full of desperadoes and fanatical haters of anything English, it was more than possible than though such an act would have been condemned by the general sense of the country, a number of men could easily be found who would think they were doing a righteous act in greeting the "annexationists" with an ovation of bullets. I do not mean that the anxiety was personal, because I do not think the members of that small party set any higher value on their lives than other people, but it was absolutely necessary for the success of the act itself, and for the safety of the country, that not a single shot should be fired. Had that happened it is probable that the whole country would have been involved in confusion and bloodshed, the Zulus would have broken in, and the Kafirs would have risen; in fact, to use Cetywayo's words, "the land would have burned with fire."

It will therefore be easily understood what an anxious hour that was both for the Special Commissioner sitting up at Government House, and for his Staff down on the Market Square, and how thankful they were when the proclamation was received with hearty cheers by the crowd. Mr. Burgers' protest, which was read immediately afterwards, was received in respectful silence.

And thus the Transvaal Territory passed for a while into the great family of the English Colonies. I believe that the greatest political opponent of the act will bear tribute to the very remarkable ability with which it was carried out. When the variety and number of the various interests that had to be conciliated, the obstinate nature of the individuals who had to be convinced, as well as the innate hatred of the English name and ways which had to be overcome to carry out this act successfully, are taken into consideration: together with a thousand other matters, the neglect of any one of which would have sufficed to make failure certain, it will be seen what tact and skill, and knowledge of human nature were required to execute so difficult a task. It must be remembered that no force was used, and that there never was any threat of force. The few troops that were to enter the Transvaal were four weeks' march from Pretoria at the time. There was nothing whatsoever to prevent the Boers putting a summary stop to the proceedings of the Commissioner if they had thought fit.

That Sir Theophilus played a bold and hazardous game nobody will deny, but, like most players who combine boldness with coolness of head and justice of cause, he won; and, without shedding a single drop of blood, or even confiscating an acre of land, and at no cost, annexed a great country, and averted a very serious war. That same country four years later cost us a million of money, the loss of nearly a thousand men killed and wounded, and the ruin of many more confiding thousands, to surrender. It is true, however, that nobody can accuse the retrocession of having been conducted with judgment or ability—very much the contrary.

There can be no more ample justification of the necessity of the issue of the annexation proclamation than the proclamation itself—

First, it touches on the Sand River Convention of 1852, by which independence was granted to the State, and shows that the "evident objects and inciting motives" in granting such guarantee were to promote peace, free-trade and friendly intercourse, in the hope and belief that the Republic "would become a flourishing and self-sustaining State, a source of strength and security to neighbouring European communities, and a point from which Christianity and civilisation might rapidly spread toward Central Africa." It goes on to show how these hopes have been disappointed, and how that "increasing weakness in the State itself on the one side, and more than corresponding growth of real strength and confidence among the native tribes on the other have produced their natural and inevitable consequence . . . that after more or less of irritating conflict with aboriginal tribes to the north, there commenced about the year 1867 gradual abandonment to the natives in that direction of territory, settled by burghers of the Transvaal in well-built towns and villages and on granted farms."

It goes on to show that "this decay of power and ebb of authority in the north, is being followed by similar processes in the south under yet more dangerous circumstances. People of this State residing in that direction have been compelled within the last three months, at the bidding of native chiefs and at a moment's notice, to leave their farms and homes, their standing crops . . . all to be taken possession of by natives, but that the Government is more powerless than ever to vindicate its assumed rights or to resist the declension that is threatening its existence." It then recites how all the other colonies and communities of South Africa have lost confidence in the State, how it is in a condition of hopeless bankruptcy, and its commerce annihilated whilst the inhabitants are divided into factions, and the Government has fallen into "helpless paralysis." How also the prospect of the election of a new President, instead of being looked forward to with hope, would, in the opinion of all parties, be the signal for civil war, anarchy, and bloodshed. How that this state of things affords the very strongest temptation to the great neighbouring native powers to attack the country, a temptation that they were only too ready and anxious to yield to, and that the State was in far too feeble a condition to repel such attacks, from which it had hitherto only been saved by the repeated representations of the Government of Natal. The next paragraphs I will quote as they stand, for they sum up the reasons for the Annexation.

"That the Secocoeni war, which would have produced but little effect on a healthy constitution, has not only proved suddenly fatal to the resources and reputation of the Republic, but has shown itself to be a culminating point in the history of South Africa, in that a Makatee or Basutu tribe, unwarlike and of no account in Zulu estimation, successfully withstood the strength of the State, and disclosed for the first time to the native powers outside the Republic, from the Zambesi to the Cape, the great change that had taken place in the relative strength of the white and black races, that this disclosure at once shook the prestige of the white man in South Africa, and placed every European community in peril, that this common danger has caused universal anxiety, has given to all concerned the right to investigate its cause, and to protect themselves from its consequences, and has imposed the duty upon those who have the power to shield enfeebled civilisation from the encroachments of barbarism and inhumanity." It proceeds to point out that the Transvaal will be the first to suffer from the results of its own policy, and that it is for every reason perfectly impossible for Her Majesty's Government to stand by and see a friendly white State ravaged, knowing that its own possessions will be the next to suffer. That H. M. Government, being persuaded that the only means to prevent such a catastrophe would be by the annexation of the country, and, knowing that this was the wish of a large proportion of the inhabitants of the Transvaal, the step must be taken. Next follows the formal annexation.

Together with the proclamation, an address was issued by Sir T. Shepstone to the burghers of the State, laying the facts before them in a friendly manner, more suited to their mode of thought than it was possible to do in a formal proclamation. This document, the issue of which was one of those touches that ensured the success of the Annexation, was a powerful summing up in colloquial language of the arguments used in the proclamation strengthened by quotations from the speeches of the President. It ends with these words: "It remains only for me to beg of you to consider and weigh what I have said calmly and without undue prejudice. Let not mere feeling or sentiment prevail over your judgment. Accept what Her Majesty's Government intends shall be, and what you will soon find from experience, is a blessing not only to you and your children, but to the whole of South Africa through you, and I believe that I speak these words to you as a friend from my heart."

Two other proclamations were also issued, one notifying the assumption of the office of Administrator of the Government by Sir T. Shepstone, and the other repealing the war-tax, which was doubtless an unequal and oppressive impost.

I have in the preceding pages stated all the principal grounds of the Annexation and briefly sketched the history of that event. In the next chapter I propose to follow the fortunes of the Transvaal under British Rule.

CHAPTER IV.
THE TRANSVAAL UNDER BRITISH RULE

Reception of the annexation – Major Clarke and the Volunteers – Effect of the annexation on credit and commerce – Hoisting of the Union Jack – Ratification of the annexation by Parliament – Messrs. Kruger and Jorissen's mission to England – Agitation against the annexation in the Cape Colony – Sir T. Shepstone's tour – Causes of the growth of discontent among the Boers – Return of Messrs. Jorissen and Kruger – The Government dispenses with their services – Despatch of a second deputation to England – Outbreak of war with Secocoeni – Major Clarke, R.A. – The Gunn of Gunn plot – Mission of Captain Paterson and Mr. Sergeaunt to Matabeleland – Its melancholy termination – The Isandhlwana disaster – Departure of Sir T. Shepstone for England – Another Boer meeting – The Pretoria Horse – Advance of the Boers on Pretoria – Arrival of Sir B. Frere at Pretoria and dispersion of the Boers – Arrival of Sir Garnet Wolseley – His proclamation – The Secocoeni expedition – Proceedings of the Boers – Mr. Pretorius – Mr. Gladstone's Mid-Lothian speeches, their effect – Sir G. Wolseley's speech at Pretoria, its good results – Influx of Englishmen and cessation of agitation – Financial position of the country after three years of British rule – Letter of the Boer leaders to Mr. Courtney.

The news of the Annexation was received all over the country with a sigh of relief, and in many parts of it with great rejoicings. At the Gold Fields, for instance, special thanksgiving services were held, and "God save the Queen" was sung in church. Nowhere was there the slightest disturbance, but, on the contrary, addresses of congratulation and thanks literally poured in by every mail, many of them signed by Boers who have since been conspicuous for their bitter opposition to English rule. At first, there was some doubt as to what would be the course taken under the circumstances by the volunteers enlisted by the late Republic. Major Clarke, R.A., was sent to convey the news, and to take command of them, unaccompanied save by his Kafir servant. On arrival at the principal fort, he at once ordered the Republican flag to be hauled down and the Union Jack run up, and his orders were promptly obeyed. A few days afterwards some members of the force thought better of it, and having made up their minds to kill him, came to the tent where he was sitting to carry out their purpose. On learning their kind intentions, Major Clarke fixed his eye-glass in his eye, and, after steadily glaring at them through it for some time, said, "You are all drunk, go back to your tents." The volunteers, quite overcome by his coolness and the fixity of his gaze, at once slipped off, and there was no further trouble. About three weeks after the Annexation, the 1-13th Regiment arrived at Pretoria, having been very well received all along the road by the Boers, who came from miles round to hear the band play. Its entry into Pretoria was quite a sight; the whole population turned out to meet it; indeed the feeling of rejoicing and relief was so profound that when the band began to play "God save the Queen" some of the women burst into tears.

Meanwhile the effect of the Annexation on the country was perfectly magical. Credit and commerce were at once restored; the railway bonds that were down to nothing in Holland rose with one bound to par, and the value of landed property nearly doubled. Indeed it would have been possible for any one, knowing what was going to happen, to have realised large sums of money by buying land in the beginning of 1877, and selling it shortly after the Annexation.

On the 24th May, being Her Majesty's birthday, all the native chiefs who were anywhere within reach, were summoned to attend the first formal hoisting of the English flag. The day was a general festival, and the ceremony was attended by a large number of Boers and natives in addition to all the English. At mid-day, amidst the cheers of the crowd, the salute of artillery, and the strains of "God save the Queen," the Union Jack was run up a lofty flagstaff, and the Transvaal was formally announced to be British soil. The flag was hoisted by Colonel Brooke, R.E., and the present writer. Speaking for myself, I may say that it was one of the proudest moments of my life. Could I have foreseen that I should live to see that same flag, then hoisted with so much joyous ceremony, within a few years shamefully and dishonourably hauled down and buried,[*] I think it would have been the most miserable.

[*] The English flag was during the signing of the
Convention at Pretoria formally buried by a large crowd of
Englishmen and loyal natives.

The Annexation was as well received in England as it was in the Transvaal. Lord Carnarvon wrote to Sir T. Shepstone to convey "the Queen's entire approval of your conduct since you received Her Majesty's commission, with a renewal of my own thanks on behalf of the Government for the admirable prudence and discretion with which you have discharged a great and unwonted responsibility." It was also accepted by Parliament with very few dissentient voices, since it was not till afterwards, when the subject became useful as an electioneering howl, that the Liberal party, headed by our "powerful popular minister," discovered the deep iniquity that had been perpetrated in South Africa. So satisfied were the Transvaal Boers with the change that Messrs. Kruger, Jorissen, and Bok, who formed the deputation to proceed to England and present President Burgers' formal protest against the Annexation, found great difficulty in raising one-half of the necessary expenses—something under one thousand pounds—towards the cost of the undertaking. The thirst for independence cannot have been very great when all the wealthy burghers in the Transvaal put together would not subscribe a thousand pounds towards retaining it. Indeed, at this time the members of the deputation themselves seem to have looked upon their undertaking as being both doubtful and undesirable, since they informed Sir T. Shepstone that they were going to Europe to discharge an obligation which had been imposed upon them, and if the mission failed, they would have done their duty. Mr. Kruger said that if they did fail, he would be found to be as faithful a subject under the new form of government as he had been under the old; and Dr. Jorissen admitted with equal frankness that "the change was inevitable, and expressed his belief that the cancellation of it would be calamitous."

Whilst the Annexation was thus well received in the country immediately interested, a lively agitation was commenced in the Western Province of the Cape Colony, a thousand miles away, with a view of inducing the Home Government to repudiate Sir T. Shepstone's act. The reason of this movement was that the Cape Dutch party, caring little or nothing for the real interests of the Transvaal, did care a great deal about their scheme to turn all the white communities of South Africa into a great Dutch Republic, to which they thought the Annexation would be a deathblow. As I have said elsewhere, it must be borne in mind that the strings of the anti-annexation agitation have all along been pulled in the Western Province, whilst the Transvaal Boers have played the parts of puppets. The instruments used by the leaders of the movement in the Cape were, for the most part, the discontented and unprincipled Hollander element, a newspaper of an extremely abusive nature called the "Volkstem," and another in Natal known as the "Natal Witness," lately edited by the notorious Aylward, which has an almost equally unenviable reputation.

On the arrival of Messrs. Jorissen and Kruger in England, they were received with great civility by Lord Carnarvon, who was, however, careful to explain to them that the Annexation was irrevocable. In this decision they cheerfully acquiesced, assuring his lordship of their determination to do all they could to induce the Boers to accept the new state of things, and expressing their desire to be allowed to serve under the new Government.

Whilst these gentlemen were thus satisfactorily arranging matters with Lord Carnarvon, Sir T. Shepstone was making a tour round the country which resembled a triumphal progress more than anything else. He was everywhere greeted with enthusiasm by all classes of the community, Boers, English, and natives, and numerous addresses were presented to him couched in the warmest language, not only by Englishmen but also by Boers.

It is very difficult to reconcile the enthusiasm of a great number of the inhabitants of the Transvaal for English rule, and the quite acquiescence of the remainder, at this time, with the decidedly antagonistic attitude assumed later on. It appears to me, however, that there are several reasons that go far towards accounting for it. The Transvaal, when we annexed it, was in the position of a man with a knife at his throat, who is suddenly rescued by some one stronger than he, on certain conditions which at the time he gladly accepts, but afterwards, when the danger is passed, wishes to repudiate. In the same way the inhabitants of the South African Republic, were in the time of need very thankful for our aid, but after a while, when the recollection of their difficulties had grown faint, when their debts had been paid and their enemies defeated, they began to think that they would like to get rid of us again, and start fresh on their own account, with a clean sheet. What fostered agitation more than anything else, however, was the perfect impunity in which it was allowed to be carried on. Had only a little firmness and decision been shown in the first instance there would have been no further trouble. We might have been obliged to confiscate half-a-dozen farms, and perhaps imprison as many free burghers for a few months, and there it would have ended. Neither Boers or natives understand our namby-pamby way of playing at government; they put it down to fear. What they want, and what they expect, is to be governed with a just but a firm hand. Thus when the Boers found that they could agitate with impunity, they naturally enough continued to agitate. Anybody who knows them will understand that it was very pleasant to them to find themselves in possession of that delightful thing, a grievance, and, instead of stopping quietly at home on their farms, to feel obliged to proceed, full of importance and long words, to a distant meeting, there to spout and listen to the spouting of others. It is so much easier to talk politics than to sow mealies. Some attribute the discontent among the Boers to the postponement of the carrying out of the annexation proclamation promises with reference to the free institutions to be granted to the country, but in my opinion it had little or nothing to do with it. The Boers never understood the question of responsible government, and never wanted that institution; what they did want was to be free of all English control, and this they said twenty times in the most outspoken language. I think there is little doubt the causes I have indicated are the real sources of the agitation, though there must be added to them their detestation of our mode of dealing with natives, and of being forced to pay taxes regularly, and also the ceaseless agitation of the Cape wire-pullers, through their agents the Hollanders, and their organs in the press.

On the return of Messrs. Kruger and Jorissen to the Transvaal, the latter gentleman resumed his duties as Attorney-General, on which occasion, if I remember aright, I myself had the honour of administering to him the oath of allegiance to Her Majesty, that he afterwards kept so well. The former reported the proceedings of the deputation to a Boer meeting, when he took a very different tone to that in which he addressed Lord Carnarvon, announcing that if there existed a majority of the people in favour of independence, he still was Vice-President of the country.

Both these gentlemen remained for some time in the pay of the British Government, Mr. Jorissen as Attorney-General, and Mr. Kruger as member of the Executive Council. The Government, however, at length found it desirable to dispense with their services, though on different grounds. Mr. Jorissen had, like several other members of the Republican Government, been a clergyman, and was quite unfit to hold the post of Attorney-General in an important colony like the Transvaal, where legal questions were constantly arising requiring all the attention of a trained mind; and after he had on several occasions been publicly admonished from the bench, the Government retired him on liberal terms. Needless to say, his opposition to English rule then became very bitter. Mr. Kruger's appointment expired by law in November 1877, and the Government did not think it advisable to re-employ him. The terms of his letter of dismissal can be found of Blue Book (c. 144), and involving as they do a serious charge of misrepresentation in money matters, are not very creditable to him. After this event he also pursued the cause of independence with increased vigour.

During the last months of 1877 and the first part of 1878 agitation against British rule went on unchecked, and at last grew to alarming proportions, so much so that Sir T. Shepstone, on his return from the Zulu border in March 1878, where he had been for some months discussing the vexed and dangerous question of the boundary line with the Zulus, found it necessary to issue a stringent proclamation warning the agitators that their proceedings and meetings were illegal, and would be punished according to law. This document which was at the time vulgarly known as the "Hold-your-jaw" proclamation, not being followed by action, produced but little effect.

On the 4th April 1878 another Boer meeting was convened, at which it was decided to send a second deputation to England, to consist this time of Messrs. Kruger and Joubert, with Mr. Bok as secretary. This deputation proved as abortive as the first, Sir M. Hicks Beach assuring it, in a letter dated 6th August 1878, that it is "impossible, for many reasons, ... that the Queen's sovereignty should now be withdrawn."

Whilst the Government was thus hampered by internal disaffection, it had also many other difficulties on its hands. First, there was the Zulu boundary question, which was constantly developing new dangers to the country. Indeed, it was impossible to say what might happen in that direction from one week to another. Nor were its relations with Secocoeni satisfactory. It will be remembered that just before the Annexation this chief had expressed his earnest wish to become a British subject, and even paid over part of the fine demanded from him by the Boer Government to the Civil Commissioner, Major Clarke. In March 1878, however, his conduct towards the Government underwent a sudden change, and he practically declared war. It afterwards appeared, from Secocoeni's own statement, that he was instigated to this step by a Boer, Abel Erasmus by name—the same man who was concerned in the atrocities in the first Secocoeni war—who constantly encouraged him to continue the struggle. I do not propose to minutely follow the course of this long war, which, commencing in the beginning of 1878, did not come to an end till after the Zulu war: when Sir Garnet Wolseley attacked Secocoeni's stronghold with a large force of troops, volunteers, and Swazi allies, and took it with great slaughter. The losses on our side were not very heavy, so far as white men were concerned, but the Swazies are reported to have lost 400 killed and 500 wounded.

The struggle was, during the long period preceding the final attack, carried on with great courage and ability by Major Clarke, R.A., C.M.G., whose force, at the best of times, only consisted of 200 volunteers and 100 Zulus. With this small body of men he contrived, however, to keep Secocoeni in check, and to take some important strongholds. It was marked also by some striking acts of individual bravery, of which one, performed by Major Clarke himself, whose reputation for cool courage and presence of mind in danger is unsurpassed in South Africa, is worthy of notice; and which, had public attention been more concentrated on the Secocoeni war, would doubtless have won him the Victoria Cross. On one occasion, on visiting one of the outlying forts, he found that a party of hostile natives, who were coming down to the fort on the previous day with a flag of truce, had been accidentally fired upon, and had at once retreated. As his system in native warfare was always to try and inspire his enemy with perfect faith in the honour of Englishmen, and their contempt of all tricks and treachery even towards a foe, he was very angry at this occurrence, and at once, unarmed and unattended save by his native servant, rode up into the mountains to the kraal from which the white flag party had come on the previous day, and apologised to the Chief for what had happened. When I consider how very anxious Secocoeni's natives were to kill or capture Clarke, whom they held in great dread, and how terrible the end of so great a captain would in all probability have been had he taken alive by these masters of refined torture, I confess that I think this act of gentlemanly courage is one of the most astonishing things I ever heard of. When he rode up those hills he must have known that he was probably going to meet his death at the hands of justly incensed savages. When Secocoeni heard of what Major Clarke had done he was so pleased that he shortly afterwards released a volunteer whom he had taken prisoner, and who would otherwise, in all probability, have been tortured to death. I must add that Major Clarke himself never reported to or alluded to this incident, but an account of it can be found in a despatch written by Sir O. Lanyon to the Secretary of State, dated 2d February 1880.

Concurrently with, though entirely distinct from, the political agitation that was being carried on among the Boers having for object the restoration of independence, a private agitation was set on foot by a few disaffected persons against Sir T. Shepstone, with the view of obtaining his removal from office in favour of a certain Colonel Weatherley. The details of this impudent plot are so interesting, and the plot itself so typical of the state of affairs with which Sir T. Shepstone had to deal, that I will give a short account of it.

After the Annexation had taken place, there were naturally enough a good many individuals who found themselves disappointed in the results so far as they personally were concerned; I mean that they did not get so much out of it as they expected. Among these was a gentleman called Colonel Weatherley, who had come to the Transvaal as manager of a gold-mining company, but getting tired of that had taken a prominent part in the Annexation, and who, being subsequently disappointed about an appointment, became a bitter enemy of the Administrator. I may say at once that Colonel Weatherley seems to me to have been throughout the dupe of the other conspirators.

The next personage was a good-looking desperado, who called himself Captain Gunn of Gunn, and who was locally somewhat irreverently known as the very Gunn of very Gunn. This gentleman, whose former career had been of a most remarkable order, was, on the annexation of the country, found in the public prison charged with having committed various offences, but on Colonel Weatherley's interesting himself strongly on his behalf, he was eventually released without trial. On his release, he requested the Administrator to publish a Government notice declaring him innocent of the charges brought against him. This Sir T. Shepstone declined to do, and so, to use his own words, in a despatch to the High Commissioner on the subject, Captain Gunn of Gunn at once became "what in this country is called a patriot."

The third person concerned was a lawyer, who had got into trouble on the Diamond Fields, and who felt himself injured because the rules of the High Court did not allow him to practise as an advocate. The quartet was made up by Mr. Celliers, the editor of the patriotic organ, the "Volkstem," who, since he had lost the Government printing contract, found that no language could be too strong to apply to the *personnel* of the Government, more especially its head. Of course, there was a lady in it; what plot would be complete without? She was Mrs. Weatherley, now, I believe, Mrs. Gunn of Gunn. These gentlemen began operations by drawing up a long petition to Sir Bartle Frere as High Commissioner, setting forth a string of supposed grievances, and winding up with a request that the Administrator might be "promoted to some other sphere of political usefulness." This memorial was forwarded by the "committee," as they called themselves, to various parts of the country for signature, but without the slightest success, the fact of the matter being that it was not the Annexor but the Annexation that the Boers objected to.

At this stage in the proceedings Colonel Weatherley went to try and forward the good cause with Sir Bartle Frere at the Cape. His letters to Mrs. Weatherley from thence, afterwards put into Court in the celebrated divorce case, contained many interesting accounts of his attempts in that direction. I do not think, however, that he was cognisant of what was being concocted by his allies in Pretoria, but being a very vain, weak man, was easily deceived by them. With all his faults he was a gentleman. As soon as he was gone a second petition was drawn up by the "committee," showing "the advisability of immediately suspending our present Administrator, and temporarily appointing and recommending for Her Majesty's royal and favourable consideration an English gentleman of high integrity and honour, in whom the country at large has respect and confidence."

The English gentleman of high integrity and honour of course proves to be Colonel Weatherley, whose appointment is, further on, "respectfully but earnestly requested," since he had "thoroughly gained the affections, confidence, and respect of Boers, English, and other Europeans in this country." But whilst it is comparatively easy to write petitions, there is sometimes a difficulty in getting people to sign them, as proved to be the case with reference to the documents under consideration. When the "committee" and the employes in the office of the "Volkstem" had affixed their valuable signatures it was found to be impossible to induce anybody else to follow their example. Now, a petition with some half dozen signatures attached would not, it was obvious, carry much weight with the Imperial Government, and no more could be obtained.

But really great minds rise superior to such difficulties, and so did the "committee," or some of them, or one of them. If they could not get genuine signatures to their petitions, they could at any rate manufacture them. This great idea once hit out, so vigorously was it prosecuted that they, or some of them, or one of them, produced in a very little while no less than 3883 signatures, of which sixteen were proved to be genuine, five were doubtful, and all the rest fictitious. But the gentleman, whoever he was, who was the working partner in the scheme—and I may state, by way of parenthesis, that when Gunn of Gunn was subsequently arrested, petitions in process of signature were found under the mattress of his bed—calculated without his host. He either did not know, or had forgotten, that on receipt of such documents by a superior officer, they are at once sent to the officer accused to report upon. This course was followed in the present case, and the petitions were discovered to be gross impostures. The ingenuity exercised by their author or authors was really very remarkable, for it must be remembered that not one of the signatures was forged; they were all invented, and had, of course, to be written in a great variety of hands. The plan generally pursued was to put down the names of people living in the country, with slight variations. Thus "De Villiers" became "De Williers," and "Van Zyl" "Van Zul." I remember that my own name appeared on one of the petitions with some slight alteration. Some of the names were evidently meant to be facetious. Thus there was a "Jan Verneuker," which means "John the Cheat."

Of the persons directly or indirectly concerned in this rascally plot, the unfortunate Colonel Weatherly subsequently apologised to Sir T. Shepstone for his share in the agitation, and shortly afterwards died fighting bravely on Kambula. Captain Gunn of Gunn and Mrs. Weatherley, after having given rise to the most remarkable divorce case I ever heard,—it took fourteen days to try—were, on the death of Colonel Weatherley, united in the bonds of holy matrimony, and are, I believe, still in Pretoria. The lawyer vanished I know not where, whilst Mr. Celliers still continues to edit that admirably conducted journal the "Volkstem;" nor, if I may judge from the report of a speech made by him recently at a Boer festival, which, by the way, was graced by the presence of our representative, Mr. Hudson, the British Resident: has his right hand forgotten its cunning, or rather his tongue lost the use of those peculiar and recherche epithets that used to adorn the columns of the "Volkstem." I see that he, on this occasion, denounced the English element as being "poisonous and dangerous" to a State, and stated, amidst loud cheers, that "he despised" it. Mr. Cellier's lines have fallen in pleasant places; in any other country he would long ago have fallen a victim to the stern laws of libel. I recommend him to the notice of enterprising Irish newspapers. Such is the freshness and vigour of his style that I am confident he would make the fortune of any Hibernian journal.

Some little time after the Gunn of Gunn frauds a very sad incident happened in connection with the Government of the Transvaal. Shortly after the Annexation, the Home Government sent out Mr. Sergeaunt, C.M.G., one of the Crown Agents for the Colonies, to report on the financial condition of the country. He was accompanied, in an unofficial capacity, amongst other gentlemen, by Captain Patterson and his son, Mr. J Sergeaunt; and when he returned to England, these two gentlemen remained behind to go on a shooting expedition. About this time Sir Bartle Frere was anxious to send a friendly mission to Lo Bengula, king of the Matabele, a branch of the Zulu tribe, living up towards the Zambesi. This chief had been making himself unpleasant by causing traders to be robbed, and it was thought desirable to establish friendly relations with him, so it was suggested to Captain Patterson and Mr. Sergeaunt that they should combine business with pleasure, and go on a mission to Lo Bengula, an offer which they accepted, and shortly afterwards started for Matabeleland with an interpreter and a few servants. They reached their destination in safety; and having concluded their business with the king, started on a visit to the Zambesi Falls on foot, leaving the interpreter with the wagon. The falls were about twelve days' walk from the king's kraal, and they were accompanied thither by young Mr. Thomas, the son of the local missionary, two Kafir servants, and twenty native bearers supplied by Lo Bengula. The next thing that was heard of them was that they had all died through drinking poisoned water, full details of the manner of their deaths being sent down by Lo Bengula.

In the first shock and confusion of such news it was not very closely examined, at any rate by the friends of the dead men, but, on reflection, there were several things about it that appeared strange. For instance, it was well known that Captain Patterson had a habit, for which indeed, we had often laughed at him, of, however thirsty he might be, always having his water boiled when he was travelling, in order to destroy impurities: and it seemed odd, that he should on this one occasion, have neglected the precaution. Also, it was curious that the majority of Lo Bengula's bearers appeared to have escaped, whereas all the others were, without exception, killed; nor even in that district is it usual to find water so bad that it will kill with the rapidity it had been supposed to do in this case, unless indeed it had been designedly poisoned. These doubts of the poisoning-by-water-story resolved themselves into certainty when the waggon returned in charge of the interpreter, when, by putting two and two together, we were able to piece out the real history of the diabolical murder of our poor friends with considerable accuracy, a story which shows what bloodthirsty wickedness a savage is capable of when he fancies his interests are threatened.

It appeared that, when Captain Patterson first interviewed Lo Bengula, he was not at all well received by him. I must, by way of explanation, state that there exists a Pretender to his throne, Kruman by name, who, as far as I can make out, is the real heir to the kingdom. This man had, for some cause or other, fled the country, and for a time acted as gardener to Sir T. Shepstone in Natal. At the date of Messrs. Patterson and Sergeaunt's mission to Matabeleland he was living, I believe, in the Transvaal. Captain Patterson, on finding himself so ill received by the king, and not being sufficiently acquainted with the character of savage chiefs, most unfortunately, either by accident or design, dropped some hint in the course of conversation about this Kruman. From that moment, Lo Bengula's conduct towards the mission entirely changed, and, dropping his former tone, he became profusely civil; and from that moment, too, he doubtless determined to kill them, probably fearing that they might forward some scheme to oust him and place Kruman, on whose claim a large portion of his people looked favourably, on the throne.

When their business was done, and Captain Patterson told the king that they were anxious, before returning, to visit the Zambesi Falls, he readily fell in with their wish, but, in the first instance, refused permission to young Thomas, the son of the missionary, to accompany them, only allowing him to do so on the urgent representation of Captain Patterson. The reason for this was, no doubt, that he had kindly feelings towards the lad, and did not wish to include him in the slaughter.

Captain Patterson was a man of extremely methodical habits, and, amongst other things, was in the habit of making notes of all that he did. His note-book had been taken off his body, and sent down to Pretoria with the other things. In it we found entries of his preparations for the trip, including the number and names of the bearers provided by Lo Bengula. We also found the chronicle of the first three days' journey, and that of the morning of the fourth day, but there the record stopped. The last entry was probably made a few minutes before he was killed; and it is to be observed that there was no entry of the party having been for several days without water, as stated by the messengers, and then finding the poisoned water.

This evidence by itself would not have amounted to much, but now comes the curious part of the story, showing the truth of the old adage, "Murder will out." It appears that when the waggon was coming down to Pretoria in charge of the interpreter, it was outspanned one day outside the borders of Lo Bengula's country, when some Kafirs— Bechuanas, I think—came up, asked for some tobacco, and fell into conversation with the driver, remarking that he had come up with a full waggon, and now he went down with an empty one. The driver replied by lamenting the death by poisoned water of his masters, whereupon one of the Kafirs told him the following story:—He said that a brother of his was out hunting, a little while back, in the desert for ostriches, with a party of other Kafirs, when hearing shots fired some way off, they made for the spot, thinking that white men were out shooting, and that they would be able to beg meat. On reaching the spot, which was by a pool of water, they saw the bodies of three white men lying on the ground, and also those of a Hottentot and a Kafir, surrounded by an armed party of Kafirs. They at once asked the Kafirs what they had been doing killing the white men, and were told to be still, for it was by "order of the king." They then learned the whole story. It appeared that the white men had made a mid-day halt by the water, when one of the bearers, who had gone to the edge of the pool, suddenly shouted to them to come and look at a great snake in the water. Captain Patterson ran up, and, as he leaned over the edge, was instantly killed by a blow with an axe; the others were then shot and assegaied. The Kafir further described the clothes that his brother had seen on the bodies, and also some articles that had been given to his party by the murderers, that left little doubt as to the veracity of his story. And so ended the mission to Matabeleland.

No public notice was taken of the matter, for the obvious reason that it was impossible to get at Lo Bengula to punish him; nor would it have been easy to come by legal evidence to disprove the ingenious story of the poisoned water, since anybody trying to reach the spot of the massacre would probably fall a victim to some similar accident before he got back again. It is devoutly to be hoped that the punishment he deserves will sooner or later overtake the author of this devilish and wholesale murder.

The beginning of 1879 was signalised by the commencement of operations in Zululand and by the news of the terrible disaster at Isandhlwana, which fell on Pretoria like a thunderclap. It was not, however, any surprise to those who were acquainted with Zulu tactics and with the plan of attack adopted by the English commanders. In fact, I know that one solemn warning of what would certainly happen to him, if he persisted in his plan of advance, was addressed to Lord Chelmsford, through the officer in command at Pretoria, by a gentlemen whose position and long experience of the Zulus and their mode of attack should have carried some weight. If it ever reached him, he took, to the best of my recollection, no notice of it whatever.

But though some such disaster was daily expected by a few, the majority of both soldiers and civilians never dreamed of anything of the sort, the general idea being that the conquest of Cetywayo was a very easy undertaking: and the shock produced by the news of Isandhlwana was proportionally great, especially as it reached Pretoria in a much exaggerated form. I shall never forget the appearance of the town that morning; business was entirely suspended, and the streets were filled with knots of men talking, with scared faces, as well they might: for there was scarcely anybody but had lost a friend, and many thought that their sons or brothers were among the dead on that bloody field. Among others, Sir T. Shepstone lost one son, and thought for some time that he had lost three.

Shortly after this event Sir T. Shepstone went to England to confer with the Secretary of State on various matters connected with the Transvaal, carrying with him the affection and respect of all who knew him, not excepting the majority of the malcontent Boers. He was succeeded by Colonel, now Sir Owen Lanyon, who was appointed to administer the Government during the absence of Sir T. Shepstone.

By the Boers, however, the news of our disaster was received with great and unconcealed rejoicing, or at least by the irreconcilable portion of that people. England's necessity was their opportunity, and one of which they certainly meant to avail themselves. Accordingly, notices were sent out summoning the burghers of the Transvaal to attend a mass meeting on the 18th March, at a place about thirty miles from Pretoria. Emissaries were also sent to native chiefs, to excite them to follow Cetywayo's example, and massacre all the English within reach, of whom a man called Solomon Prinsloo was one of the most active. The natives, however, notwithstanding the threats used towards them, one and all declined the invitation.

It must not be supposed that all the Boers who attended these meetings did so of their own free will; on the contrary, a very large number came under compulsion, since they found that the English authorities were powerless to give them protection. The recalcitrants were threatened with all sorts of pains and penalties if they did not attend, a favourite menace being that they should be made "biltong" of when the country was given back (i.e., be cut into strips and hung in the sun to dry). Few, luckily for themselves, were brave enough to tempt fortune by refusing to come, but those who did, have had to leave the country since the war. Whatever were the means employed, the result was an armed meeting of about 3000 Boers, who evidently meant mischief.

Just about this time a corps had been raised in Pretoria, composed, for the most part, of gentlemen, and known as the Pretoria Horse; for the purpose of proceeding to the Zulu border, where cavalry, especially cavalry acquainted with the country, was earnestly needed. In the emergency of the times officials were allowed to join this corps, a permission of which I availed myself, and was elected one of the lieutenants.[*] The corps was not, after all, allowed to go to Zululand on account of the threatening aspect adopted by the Boers, against whom it was retained for service. In my capacity as an officer of the corps I was sent out with a small body of picked men, all good riders and light weights, to keep up a constant communication between the Boer camp and the Administrator, and found the work both interesting and exciting. My head-quarters were at an inn about twenty-five miles from Pretoria, to which our agents in the meeting used to come every evening and report how matters were proceeding, whereupon, if the road was clear, I despatched a letter to head-quarters; or, if I feared that the messengers would be caught *en route* by Boer patrols and searched, I substituted different coloured ribbons according to what I wished to convey. There was a relief hidden in the trees or rocks every six miles, all day and most of the night, whose business it was to take the despatch or ribbon and gallop on with it to the next station, in which way we used to get the despatches into town in about an hour and a quarter.

[*] *It is customary in South African volunteer forces to allow the members to elect their own officers, provided the men elected are such as the Government approves. This is done, so that the corps may not afterwards be able to declare that they have no confidence in their officers in action, or to grumble at their treatment by them.*

On one or two occasions the Boers came to the inn and threatened to shoot us, but as our orders were to do nothing unless our lives were actually in danger, we took no notice. The officer who came out to relieve me had not, however, been there more than a day or two before he and all his troopers, were hunted back into Pretoria by a large mob of armed Boers whom they only escaped by very hard riding.

Meanwhile the Boers were by degrees drawing nearer and nearer to the town, till at last they pitched their laagers within six miles, and practically besieged it. All business was stopped, the houses were loopholed and fortified, and advantageous positions were occupied by the military and the various volunteer corps. The building, normally in the occupation of the Government mules, fell to the lot of the Pretoria Horse, and, though it was undoubtedly a post of honour, I honestly declare that I have no wish to sleep for another month in a mule stable that has not been cleaned out for several years. However, by sinking a well, and erecting bastions and a staging for sharp-shooters, we converted it into an excellent fortress, though it would not have been of much use against artillery. Our patrols used to be out all night, since we chiefly feared a night attack, and generally every preparation was made to resist the onset that was hourly expected, and I believe that it was that state of preparedness that alone prevented it.

Whilst this meeting was going on, and when matters had come to a point that seemed to render war inevitable, Sir B. Frere arrived at Pretoria and had several interviews with the Boer leaders, at which they persisted in demanding their independence, and nothing short of it. After a great deal of talk the meeting finally broke up without any actual appeal to arms, though it had, during its continuance, assumed many of the rights of government, such as stopping post-carts and individuals, and sending armed patrols about the country. The principal reason of its break-up was that the Zulu war was now drawing to a close, and the leaders saw that there would soon be plenty of troops available to suppress any attempt at revolt, but they also saw to what lengths they could go with impunity. They had for a period of nearly two months been allowed to throw the whole country into confusion, to openly violate the laws, and to intimidate and threaten Her Majesty's loyal subjects with war and death. The lesson was not lost on them; but they postponed action till a more favourable opportunity offered.

Sir Bartle Frere before his departure took an opportunity at a public dinner given him at Potchefstroom of assuring the loyal inhabitants of the country that the Transvaal would never be given back.

Meanwhile a new Pharaoh had arisen in Egypt, in the shape of Sir G. Wolseley, and on the 29th June 1879 we find him communicating the fact to Sir O. Lanyon in very plain language, telling him that he disapproved of his course of action with regard to Secocoeni, and that "in future you will please take orders only from me."

As soon as Sir Garnet had completed his arrangements for the pacification of Zululand, he proceeded to Pretoria, and having caused himself to be sworn in as Governor, set vigorously to work. I must say that in his dealings with the Transvaal he showed great judgment and a keen appreciation of what the country needed, namely, strong government; the fact of the matter being, I suppose, that being very popular with the Home authorities he felt that he could more or less command their support in what he did, a satisfaction not given to most governors, who never know but that they may be thrown overboard in emergency, in lighten the ship.

One of his first acts was to issue a proclamation, stating that "Whereas it appears that, notwithstanding repeated assurances of the contrary given by Her Majesty's representatives in this territory, uncertainty or misapprehension exists amongst some of Her Majesty's subjects as to the intention of Her Majesty's Government regarding the maintenance of British rule and sovereignty over the territory of the Transvaal: and whereas it is expedient that all grounds for such uncertainty or misapprehension should be removed once and for all beyond doubt or question: now therefore I do hereby proclaim and make known, in the name and on behalf of Her Majesty the Queen, that it is the will and determination of Her Majesty's Government that this Transvaal territory shall be, *and shall continue to be for ever*, an integral portion of Her Majesty's dominions in South Africa."

Alas! Sir G. Wolseley's estimate of the value of a solemn pledge thus made in the name of Her Majesty, whose word has hitherto been held to be sacred, differed greatly to that of Mr. Gladstone and his Government.

Sir Garnet Wolseley's operations against Secocoeni proved eminently successful, and were the best arranged bit of native warfare that I have yet heard of in South Africa. One blow was struck, and only one, but that was crushing. Of course the secret of his success lay in the fact that he had an abundance of force; but it was not ensured by that alone, good management being very requisite in an affair of the sort, especially where native allies have to be dealt with. The cost of the expedition, not counting other Secocoeni war expenditure, amounted to over 300,000 pounds, all of which is now lost to this country.

Another step in the right direction undertaken by Sir Garnet was the establishment of an Executive Council and also of a Legislative Council, for the establishment of which Letters Patent were sent from Downing Street in November 1880.

Meanwhile the Boers, paying no attention to the latter proclamation, for they guessed that it, like other proclamations in the Transvaal, would be a mere *brutum fulmen*, had assembled for another mass meeting, at which they went forward a step, and declared a Government which was to treat with the English authorities. They had now learnt that they could do what they liked with perfect impunity, provided they did not take the extreme course of massacring the English. They had yet to learn that they might even do that. At the termination of this meeting, a vote of thanks was passed to "Mr. Leonard Courtney of London, and other members of the British Parliament." It was wise of the Boer leaders to cultivate Mr. Courtney of London. As a result of this meeting, Pretorius, one of the principal leaders, and Bok, the secretary, were arrested on a charge of treason, and underwent a preliminary examination; but as the Secretary of State, Sir M. Hicks Beach, looked rather timidly on the proceeding, and the local authorities were doubtful of securing a verdict, the prosecution was abandoned, and necessarily did more harm than good, being looked upon as another proof of the impotence of the Government.

Shortly afterwards, Sir G. Wolseley changed his tactics, and, instead of attempting to imprison Pretorius, offered him a seat on the Executive Council, with a salary attached. This was a much more sensible way of dealing with him, and he at once rose to the bait, stating his willingness to join the Government after a while, but that he could not publicly do so at the moment lest he should lose his influence with those who were to be brought round through him. It does not, however, appear that Mr. Pretorius ever did actually join the Executive, probably because he found public opinion too strong to allow him to do so.

In December 1879, a new light broke upon the Boers, for, in the previous month Mr. Gladstone had been delivering his noted attack on the policy of the Conservative Government. Those Mid-Lothian speeches did harm, it is said, in many parts of the world; but I venture to think that they have proved more mischievous in South Africa than anywhere else; at any rate, they have borne fruit sooner. It is not to be supposed that Mr. Gladstone really cared anything about the Transvaal or its independence when he was denouncing the hideous outrage that had been perpetrated by the Conservative Government in annexing it. On the contrary, as he acquiesced in the Annexation at the time (when Lord Kimberley stated that it was evidently unavoidable), and declined to rescind it when he came into power, it is to be supposed that he really approved of it, or at the least looked on it as a necessary evil. However this may be, any stick will do to beat a dog with, and the Transvaal was a convenient point on which to attack the Government. He probably neither knew nor cared what effect his reckless words might have on ignorant Boers thousands of miles away; and yet, humanly speaking, many a man would have been alive and strong to-day, whose bones now whiten the African Veldt, had those words never been spoken. Then, for the first time, the Boers learnt that, if they played their cards properly and put on sufficient pressure, they would, in the event of the Liberal party coming to office, have little difficulty in coercing it as they wished.

There was a fair chance at the time of the utterance of the Mid-Lothian speeches that the agitation would, by degrees, die away; Sir G. Wolseley had succeeded in winning over Pretorius, and the Boers in general were sick of mass meetings. Indeed, a memorial was addressed to Sir G. Wolseley by a number of Boers in the Potchefstroom district, protesting against the maintenance of the movement against Her Majesty's rule, which, considering the great amount of intimidation exercised by the malcontents, may be looked upon as a favourable sign.

But when it slowly came to be understood among the Boers that a great English Minister had openly espoused their cause, and that he would perhaps soon be all-powerful, the moral gain to them was incalculable. They could now go to the doubting ones and say,—we must be right about the matter, because, putting our own feelings out of the question, the great Gladstone says we are. We find the committee of the Boer malcontents, at their meeting in March 1880, reading a letter to Mr. Gladstone, "in which he was thanked for the great sympathy shown to their fate," and a hope expressed that, if he succeeded in getting power, he would not forget them. In fact, a charming unanimity prevailed between our great Minister and the Boer rebels, for their interests were the same, the overthrow of the Conservative Government. If, however, every leader of the Opposition were to intrigue, or countenance intrigues with those who are seeking to undermine the authority of Her Majesty, whether they be Boers or Irishmen, in order to help himself to power, the country might suffer in the long run.

But whatever feelings may have prompted Her Majesty's opposition, the Home Government, and their agent, Sir Garnet Wolseley, blew no uncertain blast, if we may judge from their words and actions. Thus we find Sir Garnet speaking as follows at a banquet given in his honour at Pretoria:—

"I am told that these men (the Boers) are told to keep on agitating in this way, for a change of Government in England may give them again the old order of things. Nothing can show greater ignorance of English politics than such an idea; I tell you that there is no Government, Whig or Tory, Liberal, Conservative, or Radical, *who would dare under any circumstances to give back this country*. They would not dare, because the English people would not allow them. To give back the country, what would it mean? To give it back to external danger, to the danger of attack by hostile tribes on its frontier, and who, if the English Government were removed for one day, would make themselves felt the next. Not an official of Government paid for months; it would mean national bankruptcy. No taxes being paid, the same thing recurring again which had existed before would mean danger without, anarchy and civil war within, every possible misery; the strangulation of trade, and the destruction of property."

It is very amusing to read this passage by the light of after events. On other occasions Sir Garnet Wolseley will probably not be quite so confident as to the future when it is to be controlled by a Radical Government.

This explicit and straightforward statement of Sir Garnet's produced a great effect on the loyal inhabitants of the Transvaal, which was heightened by the publication of the following telegram from the

Secretary of State:—"You may fully confirm explicit statements made from the time to time as to inability of Her Majesty's Government to entertain *any proposal* for withdrawal of the Queen's sovereignty."

On the faith of these declarations many Englishmen migrated to the Transvaal and settled there, whilst those who were in the country now invested all their means, being confident that they would not lose their property through its being returned to the Boers. The excitement produced by Mr. Gladstone's speeches began to quiet down and be forgotten for the time, arrear taxes were paid up by the malcontents, and generally the aspect of affairs was such, in Sir Garnet Wolseley's opinion, as justified him in writing, in April 1880, to the Secretary of State expressing his belief that the agitation was dying out.[*] Indeed, so sanguine was he on that point that he is reported to have advised the withdrawal of the cavalry regiment stationed in the territory, a piece of economy that was one of the immediate causes of the revolt.

The reader will remember the financial condition of the country at the time of the Annexation, which was one of utter bankruptcy. After three years of British rule, however, we find, notwithstanding the constant agitation that had been kept up, that the total revenue receipts for the first quarter of 1879 and 1880 amounted to 22,773 pounds, and 44,982 pounds respectively. That is to say, that, during the last year of British rule, the revenue of the country more than doubled itself, and amounted to about 160,000 pounds a-year, taking the quarterly returns at the low average of 40,000 pounds. It must, however, be remembered that this sum would have been very largely increased in subsequent years, most probably doubled. At any rate the revenue would have been amply sufficient to make the province one of the most prosperous in South Africa, and to have enabled it to shortly repay all debts due to the British Government, and further to provide for its own defence. Trade also, which in April 1877, was completely paralysed, had increased enormously. So early as the middle of 1879, the Committee of the Transvaal Chamber of Commerce pointed out, in a resolution adopted by them, that the trade of the country had in two years, risen from almost nothing to the considerable sum of two millions sterling per annum, and that it was entirely in the hands of those favourable to British rule. They also pointed out that more than half the land tax was paid by Englishmen, or other Europeans adverse to Boer Government. Land, too, had risen greatly in value, of which

I can give the following instance. About a year after the Annexation I, together with a friend, bought a little property on the outskirts of Pretoria, which, with a cottage we put up on it, cost some 300 pounds. Just before the rebellion we fortunately determined to sell it, and had no difficulty in getting 650 pounds for it. I do not believe that it would now fetch a fifty pound note.

[*] *In Blue Book No. (C. 2866) of September 1881, which is descriptive of various events connected with the Boer rising, is published, as an appendix, a despatch from Sir Garnet Wolseley, dated October 1879. This despatch declares the writer's opinion that the Boer discontent is on the increase. Its publication thus – apropos des bottes – nearly two years after it was written, is rather an amusing incident. It certainly gives one the idea that Sir Garnet Wolseley, fearing that his reputation for infallibility might be attacked by scoffers for not having foreseen the Boer rebellion, and perhaps uneasily conscious of other despatches very different in tenor and subsequent in date: and, mindful of the withdrawal of the cavalry regiment by his advice, had caused it to be tacked on to the Blue Book as a documentary "I told you so," and a proof that, whoever else was blinded, he foresaw. It contains, however, the following remarkable passage: – "Even were it not impossible, for many other reasons, to contemplate a withdrawal of our authority from the Transvaal, the position of insecurity in which we should leave this loyal and important section of the community (the English inhabitants), by exposing them to the certain retaliation of the Boers, would constitute, in my opinion, an insuperable obstacle to retrocession. Subjected to the same danger, moreover, would be those of the Boers, whose superior intelligence and courageous*

character has rendered them loyal to our Government."

As the Government took the trouble to publish the despatch,

it is a pity that they did not think fit to pay more

attention to its contents.

I cannot conclude this chapter better than by drawing attention to a charming specimen of the correspondence between the Boer leaders and their friend Mr. Courtney. The letter in question, which is dated 26th June, purports to be written by Messrs. Kruger and Joubert, but it is obvious that it owes its origin to some member or members of the Dutch party at the Cape, from whence, indeed, it is written. This is rendered evident both by its general style, and also by the use of such terms as "Satrap," and by references to Napoleon III. and Cayenne, about whom Messrs. Kruger and Joubert know no more than they do of Peru and the Incas.

After alluding to former letters, the writers blow a blast of triumph over the downfall of the Conservative Government, and then make a savage attack on the reputation of Sir Bartle Frere. The "stubborn Satrap" is throughout described as a liar, and every bad motive imputed to him. Really, the fact that Mr. Courtney should encourage such epistles as this is enough to give colour to the boast made by some of the leading Boers, after the war, that they had been encouraged to rebel by a member of the British Government.

At the end of this letter, and on the same page of the Blue Book, is printed the telegram recalling Sir Bartle Frere, dated 1st August 1880. It really reads as though the second document was consequent to the first. One thing is very clear, the feelings of Her Majesty's new Government towards Sir Bartle Frere differed only in the method of their expression, from those set forth by the Boer leaders in their letter to Mr. Courtney, whilst their object, namely, to be rid of him, was undoubtedly identical with that of the Dutch party in South Africa.

CHAPTER V.
THE BOER REBELLION

Accession of Mr. Gladstone to power – His letters to the Boer leaders and the loyals – His refusal to rescind the annexation – The Boers encouraged by prominent members of the Radical party – The Bezuidenhout incident – Despatch of troops to Potchefstroom – Mass meeting of the 8th December 1880 – Appointment of the Triumvirate and declaration of the republic – Despatch of Boer proclamation to Sir O. Lanyon – His reply – Outbreak of hostilities at Potchefstroom – Defence of the court-house by Major Clarke – The massacre of the detachment of the 94th under Colonel Anstruther – Dr. Ward – The Boer rejoicings – The Transvaal placed under martial law – Abandonment of their homes by the people of Pretoria – Sir Owen Lanyon's admirable defence organisation – Second proclamation issued by the Boers – Its complete falsehood – Life at Pretoria during the siege – Murders of natives by the Boers – Loyal conduct of the native chiefs – Difficulty of preventing them from attacking the Boers – Occupation of Lang's Nek by the Boers – Sir George Colley's departure to Newcastle – The condition of that town – The attack on Lang's Nek – Its desperate nature – Effect of victory on the Boers – The battle at the Ingogo – Our defeat – Sufferings of the wounded – Major Essex – Advance of the Boers into Natal – Constant alarms – Expected attack on Newcastle – Its unorganised and indefensible condition – Arrival of the reinforcements and retreat of the Boers to the Nek – Despatch of General Wood to bring up more reinforcements – Majuba Hill – Our disaster, and death of Sir George Colley – Cause of our defeat – A Boer version of the disaster – Sir George Colley's tactics.

When the Liberal ministry became an accomplished fact instead of a happy possibility, Mr. Gladstone did not find it convenient to adopt the line of policy with reference to the Transvaal, that might have been expected from his utterances whilst leader of the Opposition. On the contrary, he declared in Parliament that the Annexation could not be cancelled, and on the 8th June 1880 we find him, in answer to a Boer petition, written with the object of inducing him to act up to the spirit of his words and rescind the Annexation, writing thus:—"Looking to all circumstances, both of the Transvaal and the rest of South Africa, and to the necessity of preventing a renewal of disorders which might lead to disastrous consequences, not only to the Transvaal, but to the whole of South Africa, our judgment is, that the *Queen cannot be advised to relinquish her sovereignty over the Transvaal;* but, consistently with the maintenance of that sovereignty, we desire that the white inhabitants of the Transvaal should, without prejudice to the rest of the population, enjoy the fullest liberty to manage their local affairs. We believe that this liberty may be most easily and promptly conceded to the Transvaal as a member of a South African confederation."

Unless words have lost their signification, this passage certainly means that the Transvaal must remain a British colony, but that England will be prepared to grant it responsible government, more especially if it will consent to a confederation scheme. Mr. Gladstone, however, in a communication dated 1st June 1881, and addressed to the unfortunate Transvaal loyals, for whom he expresses "respect and sympathy," interprets his meaning thus: "It is stated, as I observe, that a promise was given to me that the Transvaal should never be given back. There is no mention of the terms or date of this promise. If the reference be to my letter, of 8th June 1880, to Messrs. Kruger and Joubert, I do not think the language of that letter justifies the description given. Nor am I sure in what manner or to what degree the fullest liberty to manage their local affairs, which I then said Her Majesty's Government desired to confer on the white population of the Transvaal, differs from the settlement now about being made in its bearing on the interests of those whom your Committee represents."

Such twisting of the meaning of words would, in a private person, be called dishonest. It will also occur to most people that Mr. Gladstone might have spared the deeply wronged and loyal subjects of Her Majesty whom he was addressing, the taunt he levels at them in the second paragraph I have quoted. If asked, he would no doubt say that he had not the slightest intention of laughing at them; but when he deliberately tells them that it makes no difference to their interests whether they remain Her Majesty's subjects under a responsible Government, or become the servants of men who were but lately in arms against them and Her Majesty's authority, he is either mocking them, or offering an insult to their understandings.

By way of comment on his remarks, I may add that he had, in a letter replying to a petition from these same loyal inhabitants, addressed to him in May 1880, informed them that he had already told the Boer representatives that the Annexation could not be rescinded. Although Mr. Gladstone is undoubtedly the greatest living master of the art of getting two distinct and opposite sets of meanings out of one set of words, it would try even his ingenuity to make out, to the satisfaction of an impartial mind, that he never gave any pledge about the retention of the Transvaal.

Indeed, it is from other considerations clear that he had no intention of giving up the country to the Boers, whose cause he appears to have taken up solely for electioneering purposes. Had he meant to do so, he would have carried out his intention on succeeding to office, and, indeed, as things have turned out, it is deeply to be regretted that he did not; for, bad as such a step would have been, it would at any rate have had a better appearance than our ultimate surrender after three defeats. It would also have then been possible to secure the repayment of some of the money owing to this country, and to provide for the proper treatment of the natives, and the compensation of the loyal inhabitants who could no longer live there: since it must naturally have been easier to make terms with the Boers before they had defeated our troops.

On the other hand, we should have missed the grandest and most soul-stirring display of radical theories, practically applied, that has as yet lightened the darkness of this country. But although Mr. Gladstone gave his official decision against returning the country, there seems to be little doubt that communications on the subject were kept up with the Boer leaders through some prominent members of the Radical party, whom, it was said, went so far as to urge the Boers to take up arms against us. When Mr. White came to this country on behalf of the loyalists, after the surrender, he stated that this was so at a public meeting, and said further that he had in his possession proofs of his statements. He even went so far as to name the gentleman he accused, and to challenge him to deny it. I have not been able to gather that Mr. White's statements were contradicted.

However this may be, after a pause, agitation in the Transvaal suddenly recommenced with redoubled vigour. It began through a man named Bezuidenhout, who refused to pay his taxes. Thereupon a waggon was seized in execution under the authority of the court and put up to auction, but its sale was prevented by a crowd of rebel Boers, who kicked the auctioneer off the waggon and dragged the vehicle away. This was on the 11th November 1880. When this intelligence reached Pretoria, Sir Owen Lanyon sent down a few companies of the 21st Regiment, under the command of Major Thornhill, to support the Landdrost in arresting the rioters, and appointed Captain Raaf, C.M.G., to act as special messenger to the Landdrost's Court at Potchefstroom, with authority to enrol special constables to assist him to carry out the arrests. On arrival at Potchefstroom Captain Raaf found that, without an armed force, it was quite impossible to effect any arrest. On the 26th November Sir Owen Lanyon, realising the gravity of the situation, telegraphed to Sir George Colley, asking that the 58th Regiment should be sent back to the Transvaal. Sir George replied that he could ill spare it on account of "daily expected outbreak of Pondos and possible appeal for help from Cape Colony," and that the Government must be supported by the loyal inhabitants.

It will be seen that the Boers had, with some astuteness, chosen a very favourable time to commence operations. The hands of the Cape Government were full with the Basutu war, so no help could be expected from it. Sir G. Wolseley had sent away the only cavalry regiment that remained in the country, and lastly, Sir Owen Lanyon had quite recently allowed a body of 300 trained volunteers, mostly, if not altogether, drawn from among the loyalists, to be raised for service in the Basutu war, a serious drain upon the resources of a country so sparsely populated as the Transvaal.

Meanwhile a mass meeting had been convened by the Boers for the 8th January to consider Mr. Gladstone's letter, but the Bezuidenhout incident had the effect of putting forward the date of assembly by a month, and it was announced that it would be held on the 8th December. Subsequently the date was shifted to the 15th, and then back again to the 8th. Every effort was made, by threats of future vengeance, to secure the presence of as many burghers as possible; attempts were also made to persuade the native chiefs to send representatives, and to promise to join in an attack on the English. These entirely failed. The meeting was held at a place called Paarde Kraal, and resulted in the sudden declaration of the Republic and the appointment of the famous triumvirate Kruger, Joubert, and

Pretorius. It then moved into Heidelberg, a little town about sixty miles from Pretoria, and on the 16th December the Republic was formally proclaimed in a long proclamation, containing a summary of the events of the few preceding years, and declaring the arrangements the malcontents were willing to make with the English authorities. The terms offered in this document are almost identical with those finally accepted by Her Majesty's Government, with the exception that in the proclamation of the 16th December the Boer leaders declare their willingness to enter into confederation, and to guide their native policy by general rules adopted in concurrence "with the Colonies and States of South Africa." This was a more liberal offer than that which we ultimately agreed to, but then the circumstances had changed.

This proclamation was forwarded to Sir Owen Lanyon with a covering letter, in which the following words occur:—"We declare in the most solemn manner that we have no desire to spill blood, and that from our side we do not wish war. It lies in your hands to force us to appeal to arms in self-defence. . . . . We expect your answer within twice twenty-four hours."

I beg to direct particular attention to these paragraphs, as they have a considerable interest in view of what followed.

The letter and proclamation reached Government House, Pretoria, at 10.30 on the evening of Friday the 17th December. Sir Owen Lanyon's proclamation, written in reply, was handed to the messenger at noon on Sunday, 19th December, or within about thirty-six hours of his arrival, and could hardly have reached the rebel camp, sixty miles off, before dawn the next day, the 20th December, on which day, at about one o'clock, a detachment of the 94th was ambushed and destroyed on the road between Middelburg and Pretoria, about eighty miles off, by a force despatched from Heidelburg for that purpose some days before. On the 16th December, or the *same day* on which the Triumvirate had despatched the proclamation to Pretoria containing their terms, and expressing in the most solemn manner that they had no desire to shed blood, a large Boer force was attacking Potchefstroom.

So much then for the sincerity of the professions of their desire to avoid bloodshed.

The proclamation sent by Sir O. Lanyon in reply recited in its preamble the various acts of which the rebels had been guilty, including that of having "wickedly sought to incite the said loyal native inhabitants throughout the province to take up arms against Her Majesty's Government," announced that matters had now been put into the hands of the officer commanding Her Majesty's troops, and promised pardon to all who would disperse to their homes.

It was at Potchefstroom, which town had all along been the nursery of the rebellion, that actual hostilities first broke out. Potchefstroom as a town is much more Boer in its sympathies than Pretoria, which is, or rather was, almost purely English. Sir Owen Lanyon had, as stated before, sent a small body of soldiers thither to support the civil authorities, and had also appointed Major Clarke, C.M.G., an officer of noted coolness and ability, to act as Special Commissioner for the district.

Major Clarke's first step was to try, in conjunction with Captain Raaf, to raise a corps of volunteers, in which he totally failed. Those of the townsfolk who were not Boers at heart had too many business relations with the surrounding farmers, and perhaps too little faith in the stability of English rule after Mr. Gladstone's utterances, to allow them to indulge in patriotism. At the time of the outbreak, between seventy and eighty thousand sterling was owing to firms in Potchefstroom by neighbouring Boers, a sum amply sufficient to account for their lukewarmness in the English cause. Subsequent events have shown that the Potchefstroom shopkeepers were wise in their generation.

On the 15th December a large number of Boers came into the town and took possession of the printing-office in order to print the proclamation already alluded to. Major Clarke made two attempts to enter the office and see the leaders, but without success.

On the 16th a Boer patrol fired on some of the mounted infantry, and the fire was returned. These were the first shots fired during the war, and they were fired by Boers. Orders were thereupon signalled to Clarke by Lieutenant-Colonel Winsloe, 21st Regiment, now commanding at the fort which he afterwards defended so gallantly, that he was to commence firing. Clarke was in the Landdrost's office on the Market Square with a force of about twenty soldiers under Captain Falls and twenty civilians under Captain Raaf, C.M.G., a position but ill-suited for defensive purposes, from whence fire was accordingly opened, the Boers taking up positions in the surrounding houses commanding the office. Shortly after the commencement of the fighting, Captain Falls was shot dead whilst talking to Major Clarke, the latter having a narrow escape, a bullet grazing his head just above the ear. The fighting continued during the 17th and till the morning of the 18th, when the Boers succeeded in firing the roof, which was of thatch, by throwing fire-balls on to it. Major Clarke then addressed the men, telling them that, though personally he did not care about his own life, he did not see that they could serve any useful purpose by being burned alive, so he should surrender, which he did, with a loss of about six killed and wounded. The camp meanwhile had repulsed with loss the attack made on it, and was never again directly attacked.

Whilst these events were in progress at Potchefstroom, a much more awful tragedy was in preparation on the road between Middelburg and Pretoria.

On the 23rd November Colonel Bellairs, at the request of Sir Owen Lanyon, directed a concentration on Pretoria of most of the few soldiers that there were in the territory, in view of the disturbed condition of the country. In accordance with these orders, Colonel Anstruther marched from Lydenburg, a town about 180 miles from Pretoria, on the 5th December, with the headquarters and two companies of the 94th Regiment, being a total of 264 men, three women, and two children, and the disproportionately large train of thirty-four ox-waggons, or an ox-waggon capable of carrying five thousand pounds' weight to every eight persons. And here I may remark that it is this enormous amount of baggage, without which it appears to be impossible to move the smallest body of men, that renders infantry regiments almost useless for service in South Africa except for garrisoning purposes. Both Zulus and Boers can get over the ground at thrice the pace possible to the unfortunate soldier, and both races despise them accordingly. The Zulus call our infantry "pack oxen." In this particular instance, Colonel Anstruther's defeat, or rather, annihilation, is to a very great extent referable to his enormous baggage train; since, in the first place, had he not lost valuable days in collecting more waggons, he would have been safe in Pretoria before danger arose. It must also be acknowledged that his arrangements on the line of march were somewhat reckless, though it can hardly be said that he was ignorant of his danger. Thus we find that Colonel Bellairs wrote to Colonel Anstruther, warning him of the probability of an attack, and impressing on him the necessity of keeping a good look-out, the letter being received and acknowledged by the latter on the 17th December.

To this warning was added a still more impressive one, that came to my knowledge privately. A gentleman well known to me received, on the morning after the troops had passed through the town of Middelburg on their way to Pretoria, a visit from an old Boer with whom he was on friendly terms, who had purposely come to tell him that a large patrol was out to ambush the troops on the Pretoria road. My informant having convinced himself of the truth of the statement, at once rode after the soldiers, and catching them up some distance from Middelburg, told Colonel Anstruther what he had heard, imploring him, he said, with all the energy he could command, to take better precautions against surprise. The Colonel, however, laughed at his fears, and told him that if the Boers came "he would frighten them away with the big drum."

At one o'clock on Sunday, the 20th December, the column was marching along about a mile and a half from a place known as Bronker's Spruit, and thirty-eight miles from Pretoria, when suddenly a large number of mounted Boers were seen in loose formation on the left side of the road. The band was playing at the time, and the column was extended over more than half a mile, the rear-guard being about a hundred yards behind the last waggon. The band stopped playing on seeing the Boers, and the troops halted, when a man was seen advancing with a white flag, whom Colonel Anstruther went out to meet, accompanied by Conductor Egerton, a civilian. They met about one hundred and fifty yards from the column, and the man gave Colonel Anstruther a letter, which announced the establishment of the South African Republic, stated that until they heard Lanyon's reply to their proclamation they did not know if they were at war or not; that, consequently, they could not allow any movements of troops which would be taken as a declaration of war. This letter was signed by Joubert, one of the Triumvirate. Colonel Anstruther replied that he was ordered to Pretoria, and to Pretoria he must go.

Whilst this conference was going on, the Boers, of whom there were quite five hundred, had gradually closed round the column, and took up positions behind rocks and trees which afforded them excellent cover, whilst the troops were on a bare plain, and before Colonel Anstruther reached his men a murderous fire was poured in upon them from all sides. The fire was hotly returned by the soldiers. Most of the officers were struck down by the first volley, having, no doubt, been picked out by the marksmen. The firing lasted about fifteen minutes, and at the end of that time seven out of the nine officers were down killed and wounded; an eighth (Captain Elliot), one of two who escaped untouched, being reserved for an even more awful fate. The majority of the men were also down, and had the hail of lead continued much longer it is clear that nobody would have been left. Colonel Anstruther, who was lying badly wounded in five places, seeing what a hopeless state affairs were in, ordered the bugler to sound the cease firing, and surrendered. One of the three officers who were not much hurt was, most providentially, Dr. Ward, who had but a slight wound in the thigh; all the others, except Captain Elliot and one lieutenant, were either killed or died from the effects of their wounds. There were altogether 56 killed and 101 wounded, including a woman, Mrs. Fox. Twenty more afterwards died of their wounds. The Boer loss appears to have been very small.

After the fight Conductor Egerton, with a sergeant, was allowed to walk into Pretoria to obtain medical assistance, the Boers refusing to give him a horse, or even to allow him to use his own. The Boer leader also left Dr. Ward eighteen men and a few stores for the wounded, with which he made shift as best he could. Nobody can read this gentleman's report without being much impressed with the way in which, though wounded himself, he got through his terrible task of, without assistance, attending to the wants of 101 sufferers. Beginning the task at two P.M., it took him till six the next morning before he had seen the last man. It is to be hoped that his services have met with some recognition. Dr. Ward remained near the scene of the massacre with his wounded men till the declaration of peace, when he brought them down to Maritzburg, having experienced great difficulty in obtaining food for them during so many weeks.

This is a short account of what I must, with reluctance, call a most cruel and carefully planned massacre. I may mention that a Zulu driver, who was with the rear-guard, and escaped into Natal, stated that the Boers shot all the wounded men who formed that body. His statement was to a certain extent borne out by the evidence of one of the survivors, who stated that all the bodies found in that part of the field (nearly three-quarters of a mile away from the head of the column), had a bullet hole through the head or breast in addition to their other wounds.

The Administrator in the Transvaal in council thus comments on the occurrence in an official minute: — "The surrounding and gradual hemming in under a flag of truce of a force, and the selection of spots from which to direct their fire, as in the case of the unprovoked attack by the rebels upon Colonel Anstruther's force, is a proceeding of which very few like incidents can be mentioned in the annals of civilised warfare."

The Boer leaders, however, were highly elated at their success, and celebrated it in a proclamation of which the following is an extract: — "Inexpressible is the gratitude of the burghers for this blessing conferred on them. Thankful to the brave General F. Joubert and his men who have upheld the honour of the Republic on the battlefield. Bowed down in the dust before Almighty God, who had thus stood by them, and, with a loss of over a hundred of the enemy, only allowed two of ours to be killed."

In view of the circumstances of the treacherous hemming in and destruction of this small body of unprepared men, most people would think this language rather high-flown, not to say blasphemous.

On the news of this disaster reaching Pretoria, Sir Owen Lanyon issued a proclamation placing the country under martial law. As the town was large, straggling, and incapable of defence, all the inhabitants, amounting to over four thousand souls, were ordered up to camp, where the best arrangements possible were made for their convenience. In these quarters they remained for three months, driven from their comfortable homes, and cheerfully enduring all the hardships, want, and discomforts consequence on their position, whilst they waited in patience for the appearance of that relieving column that never came. People in England hardly understand what these men and women went through because they chose to remain loyal. Let them suppose that all the inhabitants of an ordinary English town, with the exception of the class known as poor people, which can hardly be said to exist in a colony, were at an hour's notice ordered—all, the aged, and the sick, delicate women, and tiny children—to leave their homes to the mercy of the enemy, and crowd up in a little space under shelter of a fort, with nothing but canvas tents or sheds to cover them from the fierce summer suns and rains, and the coarsest rations to feed them; whilst the husbands and brothers were daily engaged with a cunning and dangerous enemy, and sometimes brought home wounded or dead. They will, then, have some idea of what was gone through by the loyal people of Pretoria, in their weak confidence in the good faith of the English Government.

The arrangements made for the defence of the town were so ably and energetically carried out by Sir Owen Lanyon, assisted by the military officers, that no attack upon it was ever attempted. It seems to me that the organisation that could provide for the penning up of four thousand people for months, and carry it out without the occurrence of a single unpleasantness or expression of discontent, must have had something remarkable about it. Of course, it would have been impossible without the most loyal co-operation on the part of those concerned. Indeed, everybody in the town lent a helping hand; judges served out rations, members of the Executive inspected nuisances, and so forth. There was only one instance of "striking;" and then, of all people in the world, it was the five civil doctors who, thinking it a favourable opportunity to fleece the Government, combined to demand five guineas a-day each for their services. I am glad to say that they did not succeed in their attempt at extortion.

On the 23d December, the Boer leaders issued a second proclamation in reply to that of Sir O. Lanyon of the 18th, which is characterised by an utter absence of regard for the truth, being, in fact, nothing but a tissue of impudent falsehoods. It accuses Sir O. Lanyon of having bombarded women and children, of arming natives against the Boers, and of firing on the Boers without declaring war. Not one of these accusations has any foundation in fact, as the Boers well knew; but they also knew that Sir Owen, being shut up in Pretoria, was not in a position to rebut their charges, which they hoped might, to some extent, be believed, and create sympathy for them in other parts of the world. This was the reason for the issue of the proclamation, which well portrays the character of its framers.

Life at Pretoria was varied by occasional sorties against the Boer laagers, situated at different points in the neighbourhood, generally about six or eight miles from the town. These expeditions were carried out with considerable success, though with some loss, the heaviest incurred being when the Boers, having treacherously hoisted the white flag, opened a heavy fire on the Pretoria forces, as soon as they, beguiled into confidence, emerged from their cover. In the course of the war, one in every four of the Pretoria mounted volunteers was killed or wounded.

But perhaps the most serious of all the difficulties the Government had to meet, was that of keeping the natives in check. As has before been stated they were devotedly attached to our rule, and, during the three years of its continuance, had undergone what was to them a strange experience, they had neither been murdered, beaten, or enslaved. Naturally they were in no hurry to return to the old order of things, in which murder, flogging, and slavery were events of everyday occurrence. Nor did the behaviour of the Boers on the outbreak of the war tend to reconcile them to any such idea. Thus we find that the farmers had pressed a number of natives from Waterberg into one of their laagers (Zwart Koppies); two of them tried to run away, a Boer saw them and shot them both. Again, on the 7th January a native reported to the authorities at Pretoria that he and some others were returning from the Diamond Fields driving some sheep. A Boer came and asked them to sell the sheep. They refused, whereupon he went away, but returning with some other Dutchmen fired on the Kafirs, killing one.

On the 2d January information reached Pretoria that on the 26th December some Boers fired on some natives who were resting outside Potchefstroom and killed three; the rest fled, whereupon the Boers took the cattle they had with them.

On the 11th January some men, who had been sent from Pretoria with despatches for Standerton, were taken prisoners. Whilst prisoners they saw ten men returning from the Fields stopped by the Boers and ordered to come to the laager. They refused and ran away, were fired on, five being killed and one getting his arm broken.

These are a few instances of the treatment meted out to the unfortunate natives, taken at haphazard from the official reports.

There are plenty more of the same nature if anybody cares to read them.

As soon as the news of the rising reached them, every chief of any importance sent in to offer aid to Government, and many of them, especially Montsoia, our old ally in the Keate Award district, took the loyals of the neighbourhood under their protection. Several took charge of Government property and cattle during the disturbances, and one had four or five thousand pounds in gold, the product of a recently collected tax given him to take care of by the Commissioner of his district, who was afraid that the money would be seized by the Boers. In every instance the property entrusted to their charge was returned intact. The loyalty of all the native chiefs under very trying circumstances (for the Boers were constantly attempting to cajole or frighten them into joining them) is a remarkable proof of the great affection of the Kafirs, more especially those of the Basutu tribes, who love peace better than war, for the Queen's rule. The Government of Pretoria need only have spoken one word, to set an enormous number of armed men in motion against the Boers, with the most serious results to the latter. Any other Government in the world would, in its extremity, have spoken that word, but, fortunately for the Boers, it is against English principles to set black against white under any circumstances.

Besides the main garrison at Pretoria there were forts defended by soldiery and loyals at the following places:—Potchefstroom, Rustenburg, Lydenburg, Marabastad, and Wakkerstroom, none of which were taken by the Boers.[*]

[*] *Colonel Winsloe, however, being short of provisions, was beguiled by the fraudulent representations and acts of the Boer commander into surrendering the fort at Potchefstroom during the armistice.*

One of the first acts of the Triumvirate was to despatch a large force from Heidelberg with orders to advance into Natal Territory, and seize the pass over the Drakensberg known as Lang's Nek, so as to dispute the advance of any relieving column. This movement was promptly executed, and strong Boer troops patrolled Natal country almost up to Newcastle.

The news of the outbreak, followed as it was by that of the Bronker's Spruit massacre, and Captain Elliot's murder, created a great excitement in Natal. All available soldiers were at once despatched up country, together with a naval brigade, who, on arrival at Newcastle, brought up the strength of the Imperial troops of all arms to about a thousand men. On the 10th January Sir George Colley left Maritzburg to join the force at Newcastle, but at this time nobody dreamt that he meant to attack the Nek with such an insignificant column. It was known that the loyals and troops who were shut up in the various towns in the Transvaal had sufficient provisions to last for some months, and that there was therefore nothing to necessitate a forlorn hope. Indeed the possibility of Sir George Colley attempting to enter the Transvaal was not even speculated upon until just before his advance, it being generally considered as out of the question.

The best illustration I can give of the feeling that existed about the matter is to quote my own case. I had been so unfortunate as to land in Natal with my wife and servants just as the Transvaal troubles began, my intention being to proceed to a place I had near Newcastle. For some weeks I remained in Maritzburg, but finding that the troops were to concentrate on Newcastle, and being besides heartily wearied of the great expense and discomfort of hotel life in that town, I determined to go on up country, looking on it as being as safe as any place in the Colony. Of course the possibility of Sir George attacking the Nek before the arrival of the reinforcements did not enter into my calculations, as I thought it a venture that no sensible man would undertake. On the day of my start, however, there was a rumour about the town that the General was going to attack the Boer position. Though I did not believe it, I thought it as well to go and ask the Colonial Secretary, Colonel Mitchell, privately, if there was any truth in it, adding that if there was, as I had a pretty intimate knowledge of the Boers and their shooting powers, and what the inevitable result of such a move would be, I should certainly prefer, as I had ladies with me, to remain where I was. Colonel Mitchell told me frankly that he knew no more about Sir George's plans than I did; but he added I might be sure that so able and prudent a soldier would not do anything rash. His remark concurred with my own opinion; so I started, and on arrival at Newcastle a week later was met by the intelligence that Sir George had advanced that morning to attack the Nek. To return was almost impossible, since both horses and travellers were pretty nearly knocked up. Also, anybody who has travelled with his family in summer-time over the awful track of alternate slough and boulders between Maritzburg and Newcastle, known in the Colony as a road, will understand, that at the time, the adventurous voyagers would far rather risk being shot than face a return journey.

The only thing to do under the circumstances was to await the course of events, which were now about to develop themselves with startling rapidity. The little town of Newcastle was at this time an odd sight, and remained so all through the war. The hotels were crowded to overflowing with refugees, and on every spare patch of land were erected tents, mud huts, canvas houses, and every kind of covering that could be utilised under the pressure of necessity, to house the many homeless families who had succeeded in effecting their escape from the Transvaal, many of whom were reduced to great straits.

On the morning of the 28th January, anybody listening attentively in the neighbourhood of Newcastle could hear the distant boom of heavy guns. We were not kept long in suspense, for in the afternoon news arrived that Sir George had attacked the Nek, and failed with heavy loss. The excitement in the town was intense, for, in addition to other considerations, the 58th Regiment, which had suffered most, had been quartered there for some time, and both the officers and men were personally known to the inhabitants.

The story of the fight is well known, and needs little repetition, and a sad story it is. The Boers, who at that time were some 2000 strong, were posted and entrenched on steep hills, against which Sir George Colley hurled a few hundred soldiers. It was a forlorn hope, but so gallant was the charge, especially that of the mounted squadron led by Major Bronlow, that at one time it nearly succeeded. But nothing could stand under the withering fire from the Boer schanses, and as regards the foot soldiers, they never had a chance. Colonel Deane tried to take them up the hill with a rush, with the result that by the time they reached the top, some of the men were actually sick from exhaustion, and none could hold a rifle steady. There on the bare hill-top, they crouched and lay, while the pitiless fire from redoubt and rock lashed them like hail, till at last human nature could bear it no longer, and what was left of them retired slowly down the slope. But for many, that gallant charge was their last earthly action.

As they charged they fell, and where they fell they were afterwards buried. The casualties, killed and wounded, amounted to 195, which, considering the small number of troops engaged in the actual attack, is enormously heavy, and shows more plainly than words can tell, the desperate nature of the undertaking. Amongst the killed were Colonel Deane, Major Poole, Major Hingeston, and Lieutenant Elwes. Major Essex was the only staff officer engaged who escaped, the same officer who was one of the fortunate four who lived through Isandhlwana. On this occasion his usual good fortune attended him, for though his horse was killed and his helmet knocked off, he was not touched. The Boer loss was very trivial.

Sir George Colley, in his admirably lucid despatch about this occurrence addressed to the Secretary of State for War, does not enter much into the question as to the motives that prompted him to attack, simply stating that his object was to relieve the besieged towns. He does not appear to have taken into consideration, what was obvious to anybody who knew the country and the Boers, that even if he had succeeded in forcing the Nek, in itself almost an impossibility, he could never have operated with any success in the Transvaal with so small a column, without cavalry, and with an enormous train of waggons. He would have been harassed day and night by the Boer skirmishers, his supplies cut off, and his advance made practically impossible. Also the Nek would have been re-occupied behind him, since he could not have detached sufficient men to hold it, and in all probability Newcastle, his base of supplies, would have fallen into the hands of the enemy.

The moral effect of our defeat on the Boers was very great. Up to this time there had been many secret doubts amongst a large section of them as to what the upshot of an encounter with the troops might be; and with this party, in the same way that defeat, or even the anxiety of waiting to be attacked, would have turned the scale one way, victory turned it the other. It gave them unbounded confidence in their own superiority, and infused a spirit of cohesion and mutual reliance into their ranks which had before been wanting. Waverers wavered no longer, but gave a loyal adherence to the good cause, and, what was still more acceptable, large numbers of volunteers,— whatever President Brand may say to the contrary,—poured in from the Orange Free State.

What Sir George Colley's motive was in making so rash a move is, of course, quite inexplicable to the outside observer. It was said at the time in Natal that he was a man with a theory: namely, that small bodies of men properly handled were as useful and as likely to obtain the object in view as a large force. Whether or no this was so, I am not prepared to say; but it is undoubtedly the case that very clever men have sometimes very odd theories, and it may be that he was a striking instance in point.

For some days after the battle at Lang's Nek affairs were quiet, and it was hoped that they would remain so till the arrival of the reinforcements, which were on their way out. The hope proved a vain one. On the 7th February it was reported that the escort proceeding from Newcastle to the General's camp with the post, a distance of about eighteen miles, had been fired on and forced to return.

On the 8th, about mid-day, we were all startled by the sound of fighting, proceeding apparently from a hill known as Scheins Hoogte, about ten miles from Newcastle. It was not know that the General contemplated any move, and everybody was entirely at a loss to know what was going on, the general idea being, however, that the camp near Lang's Nek had been abandoned, and that Sir George was retiring on Newcastle.

The firing grew hotter and hotter, till at last it was perfectly continuous, the cannon evidently being discharged as quickly as they could be loaded, whilst their dull booming was accompanied by the unceasing crash and roll of the musketry. Towards three o'clock the firing slackened, and we thought it was all over, one way or the other, but about five o'clock it broke out again with increased vigour. At dusk it finally ceased. About this time some Kafirs came to my house and told us that an English force was hemmed in on a hill this side of the Ingogo River, that they were fighting bravely, but that "their arms were tired," adding that they thought they would be all killed at night.

Needless to say we spent that night with heavy hearts, expecting every minute to hear the firing begin again, and ignorant of what fate had befallen our poor soldiers on the hill. Morning put an end to our suspense, and we then learnt that we had suffered what, under the circumstances, amounted to a crushing defeat. It appears that Sir George had moved out with a force of five companies of the 60th

Regiment, two guns, and a few mounted men, to, in his own words, "patrol the road, and meet and escort some waggons expected from Newcastle." As soon as he passed the Ingogo he was surrounded by a body of Boers sent after him from Lang's Nek, on a small triangular plateau, and sharply assailed on all sides. With a break of about two hours, from three to five, the assault was kept up till nightfall, with very bad results so far as we were concerned, seeing that out of a body of about 500 men, over 150 were killed and wounded. The reinforcements sent for from the camp apparently did not come into action. For some unexplained reason the Boers did not follow up their attack that night, perhaps because they did not think it possible that our troops could effect their escape back to the camp, and considered that the next morning would be soon enough to return and finish the business. The General, however, determined to get back, and scratch teams of such mules, riding-horses, and oxen as had lived through the day being harnessed to the guns, the dispirited and exhausted survivors of the force managed to ford the Ingogo, now swollen by rain which had fallen in the afternoon, poor Lieutenant Wilkinson, the Adjutant of the 60th, losing his life in the operation, and to struggle through the dense darkness back to camp.

On the hill-top they had lately held, the dead lay thick. There, too, exposed to the driving rain and bitter wind lay the wounded, many of whom would be dead before the rising of the morrow's sun. It must, indeed, have been a sight never to be forgotten by those who saw it. The night—I remember well—was cold and rainy, the great expanses of hill and plain being sometimes lit by the broken gleams of an uncertain moon, and sometimes plunged into intensest darkness by the passing of a heavy cloud. Now and again flashes of lightning threw every crag and outline into vivid relief, and the deep muttering of distant thunder made the wild gloom more solemn. Then a gust of icy wind would come tearing down the valleys to be followed by a pelting thunder shower—and thus the night wore away.

When one reflects what discomfort, and even danger, an ordinary healthy person would suffer if left after a hard day's work to lie all night in the rain and wind on the top of a stony mountain, without food, or even water to assuage his thirst, it becomes to some degree possible to realise what the sufferings of our wounded after the battle of Ingogo must have been. Those who survived were next day taken to the hospital at Newcastle.

What Sir George Colley's real object was in exposing himself to the attack has never transpired. It can hardly have been to clear the road, as he says in his despatch, because the road was not held by the enemy, but only visited occasionally by their patrols. The result of the battle was to make the Boers, whose losses were trifling, more confident than ever, and to greatly depress our soldiers. Sir George had now lost between three and four hundred men, out of his column of little over a thousand, which was thereby entirely crippled. Of his staff Officers Major Essex now alone survived, his usual good fortune having carried him safe through the battle of Ingogo. What makes his repeated escapes the more remarkable is that he was generally to be found in the heaviest firing. A man so fortunate as Major Essex ought to be rewarded for his good fortune if for no other reason, though, if reports are true, there would be no need to fall back on that to find grounds on which to advance a soldier who has always borne himself so well.

Another result of the Ingogo battle was that the Boers, knowing that we had no force to cut them off, and always secure of a retreat into the Free State, passed round Newcastle in Free State Territory, and descended from fifteen hundred to two thousand strong into Natal for the purpose of destroying the reinforcements which were now on their way up under General Wood. This was on the 11th of February, and from that date till the 18th, the upper districts of Natal were in the hands of the enemy, who cut the telegraph wires, looted waggons, stole herds of cattle and horses, and otherwise amused themselves at the expense of Her Majesty's subjects in Natal.

It was a very anxious time for those who knew what Boers are capable of, and had women and children to protect, and who were never sure if their houses would be left standing over their heads from one day to another.

Every night we were obliged to place out Kafirs as scouts to give us timely warning of the approach of marauding parties, and to sleep with loaded rifles close to our hands, and sometimes, when things looked very black, in our clothes, with horses ready saddled in the stable. Nor were our fears groundless, for one day a patrol of some five hundred Boers encamped on the next place, which by the way belonged to a Dutchman, and stole all the stock on it, the property of an Englishman. They also intercepted a train of waggons, destroyed the contents, and burnt them. Numerous were the false alarms it was our evil fortune to experience. For instance, one night I was sitting in the drawing-room reading, about eleven o'clock, with a door leading on to the verandah slightly ajar, for the night was warm, when suddenly I heard myself called by name in a muffled voice, and asked if the place was in the possession of the Boers. Looking towards the door I saw a full-cocked revolver coming round the corner, and on opening it in some alarm, I could indistinctly discern a line of armed figures in a crouching attitude stretching along the verandah into the garden beyond. It turned out to be a patrol of the mounted police, who had received information that a large number of Boers had seized the place and had come to ascertain the truth of the report. As we gathered from them that the Boers were certainly near, we did not pass a very comfortable night.

Meanwhile, we were daily expecting to hear that the troops had been attacked along the line of march, and knowing the nature of the country and the many opportunities it affords for ambuscading and destroying one of our straggling columns encumbered with innumerable waggons, we had the worst fears for the result. At length a report reached us to the effect that the reinforcements were expected on the morrow, and that they were not going to cross the Ingagaan at the ordinary drift, which was much commanded by hills, but at a lower drift on our own place, about three miles from Newcastle, which was only slightly commanded. We also heard that it was the intention of the Boers to attack them at this point and to fall back on my house and the hills beyond. Accordingly, we thought it about time to retreat, and securing a few valuables such as plate, we made our way into the town, leaving the house and its contents to take their chance. At Newcastle an attack was daily expected, if for no other reason, to obtain possession of the stores collected there.

The defences of the place were, however, in a wretched condition, no proper outlook was kept, and there was an utter want of effective organisation. The military element at the camp had enough to do to look after itself, and did not concern itself with the safety of the town; and the mounted police—a Colonial force paid by the Colony—had been withdrawn from the little forts round Newcastle, as the General wanted them for other purposes, and a message sent that the town must defend its own forts. There were, it is true, a large number of able-bodied men in the place who were willing to fight, but they had no organisation. The very laager was not finished until the danger was past.

Then there was a large party who were for surrendering the town to the Boers, because if they fought it might afterwards injure their trade. With this section of the population the feeling of patriotism was strong, no doubt, but that of pocket was stronger. I am convinced that the Boers would have found the capture of Newcastle an easy task, and I confess that what I then saw did not inspire me with great hopes of the safety of the Colony when it gets responsible government, and has to depend for protection on burgher forces. Colonial volunteer forces are, I think, as good troops as any in the world; but an unorganised colonial mob, pulled this way and that by different sentiments and interests, is as useless as any other mob, with the difference that it is more impatient of control.

For some unknown reason the Boer leaders providentially changed their minds about attacking the reinforcements, and their men were withdrawn to the Nek as swiftly and silently as they had been advanced, and on the 17th February the reinforcements marched into Newcastle to the very great relief of the inhabitants, who had been equally anxious for their own safety and that of the troops. Personally, I was never in my life more pleased to see Her Majesty's uniform; and we were equally rejoiced on returning home to find that nothing had been injured. After this we had quiet for a while.

On the 21st February, we heard that two fresh regiments had been sent up to the camp at Lang's Nek, and that General Wood had been ordered down country by Sir George Colley to bring up more reinforcements. This item of news caused much surprise, as nobody could understand, why, now that the road was clear, and that there was little chance of its being again blocked, a General should be sent down to do work, which could, to all appearance, have been equally well done by the Officers in command of the reinforcing regiments, with the assistance of their transport riders. It was, however, understood that an agreement had been entered into between the two Generals, that no offensive operations should be undertaken till Wood returned.

With the exception of occasional scares, there was no further excitement till Sunday the 27th February, when, whilst sitting on the verandah after lunch, I thought I heard the sound of distant artillery. Others present differed with me, thinking the sound was caused by thunder, but as I adhered to my opinion, we determined to ride into town and see. On arrival there, we found the place full of rumours, from which we gathered that some fresh disaster had occurred: and that messages were pouring down the wires from Mount Prospect camp. We then went on to camp, thinking that we should learn more there, but they knew nothing about it, several officers asking us what new "shave" we had got hold of. A considerable number of troops had been marched from Newcastle that morning to go to Mount Prospect, but when it was realised that something had occurred, they were stopped, and marched back again. Bit by bit we managed to gather the truth. At first we heard that our men had made a most gallant resistance on the hill, mowing down the advancing enemy by hundreds, till at last, their ammunition failing, they fought with their bayonets, using stones and meat tins as missiles. I wish that our subsequent information had been to the same effect.

It appears that on the evening of the 26th, Sir George Colley, after mess, suddenly gave orders for a force of a little over six hundred men, consisting of detachments from no less than three different regiments, the 58th, 60th, 92d, and the Naval Brigade, to be got ready for an expedition, without revealing his plans to anybody, until late in the afternoon: and then without more ado, marched them up to the top of Majuba—a great square-topped mountain to the right of, and commanding the Boer position at Lang's Nek. The troops reached the top about three in the morning, after a somewhat exhausting climb, and were stationed at different points of the plateau in a scientific way. Whilst the darkness lasted, they could, by the glittering of the watch-fires, trace from this point of vantage the position of the Boer laagers that lay 2000 yards beneath them, whilst the dawn of day revealed every detail of the defensive works, and showed the country lying at their feet like a map.

On arrival at the top, it was represented to the General that a rough entrenchment should be thrown up, but he would not allow it to be done on account of the men being wearied with their marching up. This was a fatal mistake. Behind an entrenchment, however slight, one would think that 600 English soldiers might have defied the whole Boer army, and much more the 200 or 300 men by whom they were hunted down Majuba. It appears that about 10.15 A.M. Colonel Steward and Major Fraser again went to General Colley "to arrange to start the sailors on an entrenchment" . . . "Finding the ground so exposed, the General did not give orders to entrench."

As soon as the Boers found out that the hill was in the occupation of the English, their first idea was to leave the Nek, and they began to inspan with that object, but discovering that there were no guns commanding them, they changed their mind, and set to work to storm the hill instead. As far as I have been able to gather, the number of Boers who took the mountain was about 300, or possibly 400; I do not think there were more than that. The Boers themselves declare solemnly that they were only 100 strong, but this I do not believe. They slowly advanced up the hill till about 11.30, when the real attack began, the Dutchmen coming on more rapidly and confidently, and shooting with ever-increasing accuracy, as they found our fire quite ineffective.

About a quarter to one, our men retreated to the last ridge, and General Colley was shot through the head. After this, the retreat became a rout, and the soldiers rushed pell-mell down the precipitous sides of the hill, the Boers knocking them over by the score as they went, till they were out of range. A few were also, I heard, killed by the shells from the guns that were advanced from the camp to cover the retreat, but as this does not appear in the reports, perhaps it is not true. Our loss was about 200 killed and wounded, including Sir George Colley, Drs. Landon and Cornish, and Commander Romilly, who was shot with an explosive bullet, and died after some days' suffering. When the wounded Commander was being carried to a more sheltered spot, it was with great difficulty that the Boers were prevented from massacring him as he lay, they being under the impression that he was Sir Garnet Wolseley. As was the case at Ingogo, the wounded were left on the battlefield all night in very inclement weather, to which some of them succumbed. It is worthy of note that after the fight was over, they were treated with considerable kindness by the Boers.

Not being a soldier, of course I cannot venture to give any military reasons as to how it was, that what was after all a considerable force, was so easily driven from a position of great natural strength; but I think I may, without presumption, state my opinion was to the real cause, which was the villanous shooting of the British soldier. Though the troops did not, as was said at the time, run short of ammunition, it is clear that they fired away a great many rounds at men who, in storming the hill, must necessarily have exposed themselves more or less, of whom they managed to hit—certainly not more than six or seven,—which was the outside of the Boer casualties. From this it is clear that they can neither judge distance nor hit a moving object, nor did they probably know that when shooting down hill it is necessary to aim low. Such shooting as the English soldier is capable of may be very well when he has an army to aim at, but it is useless in guerilla warfare against a foe skilled in the use of the rifle and the art of taking shelter.

A couple of months after the storming of Majuba, I, together with a friend, had a conversation with a Boer, a volunteer from the Free State in the late war, and one of the detachment that stormed Majuba, who gave us a circumstantial account of the attack with the greatest willingness. He said that when it was discovered that the English had possession of the mountain, they thought that the game was up, but after a while bolder counsels prevailed, and volunteers were called for to storm the hill. Only seventy men could be found to perform the duty, of whom he was one. They started up the mountain in fear and trembling, but soon found that every shot passed over their heads, and went on with greater boldness. Only three men, he declared, were hit on the Boer side; one was killed, one was hit in the arm, and he himself was the third, getting his face grazed by a bullet, of which he showed us the scar. He stated that the first to reach the top ridge was a boy of twelve, and that as soon as the troops saw them they fled, when, he said, he paid them out for having nearly killed him, knocking them over one after another "like bucks" as they ran down the hill, adding that it was "alter lecker" (very nice). He asked us how many men we had lost during the war, and when we told him about seven hundred killed and wounded, laughed in our faces, saying he knew that our dead amounted to several thousands. On our assuring him that this was not the case, he replied, "Well, don't let's talk of it any more, because we are good friends now, and if we go on you will lie, and I shall lie, and then we shall get angry. The war is over now, and I don't want to quarrel with the English; if one of them takes off his hat to me I always acknowledge it." He did not mean any harm in talking thus; it is what Englishmen have to put up with now in South Africa; the Boers have beaten us, and act accordingly.

This man also told us that the majority of the rifles they picked up were sighted for 400 yards, whereas the latter part of the fighting had been carried on within 200.

Sir George Colley's death was much lamented in the Colony, where he was deservedly popular; indeed, anybody who had the honour of knowing that kind-hearted gentleman, could not do otherwise than deeply regret his untimely end. What his motive was in occupying Majuba in the way he did, has never, so far as I am aware, transpired. The move, in itself, would have been an excellent one, had it been made in force, or accompanied by a direct attack on the Nek—but, as undertaken, seems to have been objectless. There were, of course, many rumours as to the motives that prompted his action, of which the most probable seems to be that, being aware of what the Home Government intended to do with reference to the Transvaal, he determined to strike a blow to try and establish British Supremacy first, knowing how mischievous any apparent surrender would be. Whatever his faults may have been as a General, he was a brave man, and had the honour of his country much at heart.

It was also said by soldiers who saw him the night the troops marched up Majuba, that the General was "not himself," and it was hinted that continual anxiety and the chagrin of failure had told upon his mind. As against this, however, must be set the fact that his telegrams to the Secretary of State for War, the last of which he must have despatched only about half-an-hour before he was shot, are cool and collected, and written in the same unconcerned tone, — as though he were a critical spectator of an interesting scene—that characterises all his communications, more especially his despatches. They at any rate give no evidence of shaken nerve or unduly excited brain, nor can I see that any action of his with reference to the occupation of

Majuba is out of keeping with the details of his generalship upon other occasions. He was always confident to rashness, and possessed by the idea that every man in the ranks was full of as high a spirit, and as brave as he was himself. Indeed most people will think, that so far from its being a rasher action, the occupation of Majuba, bad generalship as it seems, was a wiser move than either the attack on the Nek or the Ingogo fiasco.

But at the best, all his movements are difficult to be understand by a civilian, though they may, for ought we know, have been part of an elaborate plan, perfected in accordance with the rules of military science, of which, it is said, he was a great student.

CHAPTER VI.
THE RETROCESSION OF THE TRANSVAAL

The Queen's Speech – President Brand and Lord Kimberley – Sir Henry de Villiers – Sir George Colley's plan – Paul Kruger's offer – Sir George Colley's remonstrance – Complimentary telegrams – Effect of Majuba on the Boers and English Government – Collapse of the Government – Reasons of the Surrender – Professional sentimentalists – The Transvaal Independence Committee – Conclusion of the armistice – The preliminary peace – Reception of the news in Natal – Newcastle after the declaration of peace – Exodus of the loyal inhabitants of the Transvaal – The value of property in Pretoria – The Transvaal officials dismissed – The Royal Commission – Mode of trial of persons accused of atrocities – Decision of the Commission and its results – The severance of territory question – Arguments pro *and* con *– Opinion of Sir E. Wood – Humility of the Commissioners and its cause – Their decision on the Keate award question – The Montsoia difficulty – The compensation and financial clauses of the report of the Commission – The duties of the British Resident – Sir E. Wood's dissent from the report of the Commission – Signing of the Convention – Burial of the Union Jack – The native side of the question – Interview between the Commissioners and the native chiefs – Their opinion of the surrender – Objections of the Boer Volksraad to the Convention – Mr. Gladstone temporises – The ratification – Its insolent tone – Mr. Hudson, the British Resident – The Boer festival – The results of the Convention – The larger issue of the matter – Its effect on the Transvaal – Its moral aspects – Its effect on the native mind.*

When Parliament met in January 1881, the Government announced, through the mediumship of the Queen's Speech, that it was their intention to vindicate Her Majesty's authority in the Transvaal. I have already briefly described the somewhat unfortunate attempts to gain this end by force of arms: and I now propose to follow the course of the diplomatic negotiations entered into by the Ministry with the same object.

As soon as the hostilities in the Transvaal took a positive form, causing great dismay among the Home authorities, whose paths, as we all know, are the paths of peace—at any price; and whilst, in the first confusion of calamity, they knew not where to turn, President Brand stepped upon the scene in the character of "Our Mutual Friend," and, by the Government at any rate, was rapturously welcomed.

This gentleman has for many years been at the head of the Government of the Orange Free State, whose fortunes he had directed with considerable ability. He is a man of natural talent and kind-hearted disposition, and has the advancement of the Boer cause in South Africa much at heart. The rising in the Transvaal was an event that gave him a great and threefold opportunity: first, of interfering with the genuinely benevolent object of checking bloodshed; secondly, of advancing the Dutch cause throughout South Africa under the cloak of amiable neutrality, and striking a dangerous blow at British supremacy over the Dutch and British prestige with the natives; and, thirdly, of putting the English Government under a lasting obligation to him. Of this opportunity he has availed himself to the utmost in each particular.

So soon as things began to look serious, Mr. Brand put himself into active telegraphic communication with the various British authorities with the view of preventing bloodshed by inducing the English Government to accede to the Boer demands. He was also earnest in his declarations that the Free State was not supporting the Transvaal; which, considering that it was practically the insurgent base of supplies, where they had retired their women, children, and cattle, and that it furnished them with a large number of volunteers, was perhaps straining the truth.

About this time also we find Lord Kimberley telegraphing to Mr. Brand that "if *only* the Transvaal Boers will desist from armed opposition to the Queen's authority," he thinks some arrangement might be made. This is the first indication made public of what was passing in the minds of Her Majesty's Government, on whom its radical supporters were now beginning to put the screw, to induce or threaten them into submitting to the Boer demands.

Again, on the 11th January, the President telegraphed to Lord Kimberley through the Orange Free State Consul in London, suggesting that Sir H. de Villiers, the Chief Justice at the Cape, should be appointed a Commissioner to go to the Transvaal to settle matters. Oddly enough, about the same time the same proposition emanated from the Dutch party in the Cape Colony, headed by Mr. Hofmeyer, a coincidence that inclines one to the opinion that these friends of the Boers had some further reason for thus urging Sir Henry de Villiers' appointment as Commissioner beyond his apparent fitness for the post, of which his high reputation as a lawyer and in his private capacity was a sufficient guarantee.

The explanation is not hard to find, the fact being that, rightly or wrongly, Sir Henry de Villiers, who is himself of Dutch descent, is noted throughout South Africa for his sympathies with the Boer cause, and both President Brand and the Dutch party in the Cape shrewdly suspected, that, if the settling of differences were left to his discretion, the Boers and their interests would receive very gentle handling. The course of action adopted by him, when he became a member of the Royal Commission, went far to support this view, for it will be noticed in the Report of the Commissioners that in every single point he appears to have taken the Boer side of the contention. Indeed so blind was he to their faults, that he would not even admit that the horrible Potchefstroom murders and atrocities, which are condemned both by Sir H. Robinson and Sir Evelyn Wood in language as strong as the formal terms of a report will allow, were acts contrary to the rules of civilised warfare. If those acts had been perpetrated by Englishmen on Boers, or even on natives, I venture to think Sir Henry de Villiers would have looked at them in a very different light.

In the same telegram in which President Brand recommends the appointment of Sir Henry de Villiers, he states that the allegations made by the Triumvirate in the proclamation in which they accused Sir Owen Lanyon of committing various atrocities, deserve to be investigated, as they maintain that the collision was commenced by the authorities. Nobody knew better than Mr. Brand that any English official would be quite incapable of the conduct ascribed to Sir Owen Lanyon, whilst, even if the collision had been commenced by the authorities, which as it happened it was not, they would under the circumstances have been amply justified in so commencing it. This remark by President Brand in his telegram was merely an attempt to throw an air of probability over a series of slanderous falsehoods.

Messages of this nature continued to pour along the wires from day to day, but the tone of those from the Colonial Office grew gradually humbler; thus we find Lord Kimberley telegraphing on the 8th February, that if the Boers would desist from armed opposition all reasonable guarantees would be given as to their treatment after submission, and that a scheme would be framed for the "permanent friendly settlement of difficulties." It will be seen that the Government had already begun to water the meaning of their declaration that they would vindicate Her Majesty's authority. No doubt Mr. Chamberlain, Mr. Courtney, and their followers, had given another turn to the Radical screw.

It is, however, clear that at this time no idea of the real aims of the Government had entered into the mind of Sir George Colley, since on the 7th February he telegraphed home a plan which he proposed to adopt on entering the Transvaal, which included a suggestion that he should grant a complete amnesty only to those Boers who would sign a declaration of loyalty.

In answer to this he was ordered to do nothing of the sort, but to promise protection to everybody and refer everything home.

Then came the battle of Ingogo, which checked for the time the flow of telegrams, or rather varied their nature, for those despatched during the next few days deal with the question of reinforcements. On the 13th February, however, negotiations were reopened by Paul Kruger, one of the Triumvirate, who offered, if all the troops were ordered to withdraw from the Transvaal to give them a free passage through the Nek, to disperse the Boers and to consent to the appointment of a Commission.

The offer was jumped at by Lord Kimberley, who, without making reference to the question of withdrawing the soldiers, offered, if only the Boers would disperse, to appoint a Commission with extensive powers to develop the "permanent friendly settlement" scheme. The telegram ends thus: "Add, that if this proposal is accepted, you now are authorised to agree to suspension of hostilities on our part." This message was sent to General Wood, because the Boers had stopped the communications with Colley. On the 19th, Sir George Colley replies in these words, which show his astonishment at the policy adopted by the Home Government, and which, in the opinion of most people, redound to his credit—

"Latter part of your telegram to Wood not understood. There can be no hostilities if no resistance is made, but am I to leave Lang's Nek in Natal territory in Boer occupation, and our garrisons isolated and short of provisions, or occupy former and relieve latter?" Lord Kimberley hastens to reply that the garrisons must be left free to provision themselves, "but we do not mean that you should march to the relief of garrisons or occupy Lang's Nek, if an arrangement proceeds."

It will be seen that the definition of what vindication of Her Majesty's authority consisted grew broader and broader; it now included the right of the Boers to continue to occupy their positions in the Colony of Natal.

Meanwhile the daily fire of complimentary messages was being kept up between President Brand and Lord Kimberley, who alternatively gave "sincere thanks to Lord Kimberley" and "fully appreciated the friendly spirit" of President Brand, till on the 21st February the latter telegraphs through Colley: "Hope of amicable settlement by negotiation, but this will be greatly facilitated if somebody on spot and friendly disposed to both, could by personal communication with both endeavour to smooth difficulties. Offers his services to Her Majesty's Government, and Kruger and Pretorius and Joubert are willing." Needless to say his services were accepted.

Presently, however, on 27th February, Sir George Colley made his last move, and took possession of Majuba. His defeat and death had the effect of causing another temporary check in the peace negotiations, whilst Sir Frederick Roberts with ample reinforcements was despatched to Natal. It had the further effect of increasing the haughtiness of the Boer leaders, and infusing a corresponding spirit of pliability or generosity into the negotiations of Her Majesty's Government.

Thus on 2d March, the Boers, through President Brand and Sir Evelyn Wood, inform the Secretary of State for the Colonies, that they are willing to negotiate, but decline to submit or cease opposition. Sir Evelyn Wood, who evidently did not at all like the line of policy adopted by the Government, telegraphed that he thought the best thing to do would be for him to engage the Boers, and disperse them *vi et armis*, without any guarantees, "considering the disasters we have sustained," and that he should, "if absolutely necessary," be empowered to promise life and property to the leaders, but that they should be banished from the country. In answer to this telegram, Lord Kimberley informs him that Her Majesty's Government will amnesty *everybody* except those who have committed acts contrary to the rules of civilised warfare, and that they will agree to anything, and appoint a Commission to carry out the details, and "be ready for friendly communications with *any persons* appointed by the Boers."

Thus was Her Majesty's authority finally re-established in the Transvaal.

It was not a very grand climax, nor the kind of arrangement to which Englishmen are accustomed, but perhaps, considering the circumstances, and the well-known predilections of those who made the settlement, it was as much as could be expected.

The action of the Government must not be considered, as though they were unfettered in their judgment; it can never be supposed that they acted as they did, because they thought such action right or even wise, for that would be to set them down as men of a very low order of intelligence, which they certainly are not.

It is clear that no set of sensible men, who had after much consideration given their decision that under all the circumstances, the Transvaal must remain British territory, and who, on a revolt subsequently breaking out in that territory, had declared that Her Majesty's rule must be upheld, would have, putting aside all other circumstances, deliberately stultified themselves by almost unconditionally, and of their own free will, abandoning the country, and all Her Majesty's subjects living in it. That would be to pay a poor tribute to their understanding, since it is clear that if reasons existed for retaining the Transvaal before the war, as they were satisfied there did, those reasons would exist with still greater force after a war had been undertaken and three crushing defeats sustained, which if left unavenged must, as they knew, have a most disastrous effect on our prestige throughout the South African continent.

I prefer to believe that the Government was coerced into acting as it did by Radical pressure, both from outside, and from its immediate supporters in the House, and that it had to choose between making an unconventional surrender in the Transvaal and losing the support of a very powerful party. Under these circumstances it, being Liberal in politics, naturally followed its instincts, and chose surrender.

If such a policy was bad in itself, and necessarily mischievous in its consequences, so much the worse for those who suffered by it; it was clear that the Government could not be expected to lose votes in order to forward the true interests of countries so far off as the South African Colonies, which had had the misfortune to be made a party question of, and must take the consequences.

There is no doubt that the interest brought to bear on the Government was very considerable, for not only had they to deal with their own supporters, and with the shadowy caucus that was ready to let the lash of its displeasure descend even on the august person of Mr. Gladstone, should he show signs of letting slip so rich an opportunity for the vindication of the holiest principles of advanced Radicalism, but also with the hydra-headed crowd of visionaries and professional sentimentalists who swarm in this country, and who are always ready to take up any cause, from that of Jumbo, or of a murderer, to that of oppressed peoples, such as the Bulgarians, or the Transvaal Boers.

These gentlemen, burning with zeal, and filled with that confidence which proverbially results from the hasty assimilation of imperfect and erroneous information, found in the Transvaal question a great opportunity of making a noise: and—as in a disturbed farmyard the bray of the domestic donkey, ringing loud and clear among the utterances of more intelligent animals, overwhelms and extinguishes them—so, and with like effect, amongst the confused sound of various English opinions about the Boer rising, rose the trumpet-note of the Transvaal Independence Committee and its supporters.

As we have seen, they did not sound in vain.

On the 6th of March an armistice with the Boers had been entered into by Sir Evelyn Wood, which was several times prolonged, up to the 21st March, when Sir Evelyn Wood concluded a preliminary peace with the Boer leaders, which, under certain conditions, guaranteed the restoration of the country within six months, and left all other points to be decided by a Royal Commission.

The news of this peace was at first received in the Colony in the silence of astonishment. Personally, I remember, I would not believe that it was true. It seemed to us, who had been witnesses of what had passed, and knew what it all meant, something so utterly incredible that we thought there must be a mistake.

If there had been any one redeeming circumstance about it, if the English arms had gained a single decisive victory, it might have been so, but it was hard for Englishmen, just at first, to understand that not only had the Transvaal been to all appearance wrested from them by force of arms, but that they were henceforth to be subject, as they well knew would be the case, to the coarse insults of victorious Boers, and the sarcasms of keener-witted Kafirs.

People in England seem to fancy that when men go to the Colonies they lose all sense of pride in their country, and think of nothing but their own advantage. I do not think that this is the case, indeed, I believe that, individual for individual, there exists a greater sense of loyalty, and a deeper pride in their nationality, and in the proud name of England, among Colonists, than among Englishmen proper. Certainly the humiliation of the Transvaal surrender was more keenly felt in South Africa than it was at home; but, perhaps, the impossibility of imposing upon people in that country with the farrago of nonsense about blood-guiltiness and national morality, which was made such adroit use of at home, may have made the difference.

I know that personally I would not have believed it possible that I could feel any public event so keenly as I did this; indeed, I quickly made up my mind that if the peace was confirmed, the neighbourhood of the Transvaal would be no fit or comfortable residence for an Englishman, and that I would, at any cost, leave the country,—which I accordingly did.

Newcastle was a curious sight the night after the peace was declared, every hotel and bar was crowded with refugees, who were trying to relieve their feelings, by cursing the name of Gladstone, with a vigour, originality, and earnestness, that I have never heard equalled; and declaring in ironical terms how proud they were to be citizens of England—a country that always kept its word. Then they set to work with many demonstrations of contempt to burn the effigy of the Right Honourable Gentleman at the head of Her Majesty's Government, an example, by the way, that was followed throughout South Africa.

Even Sir Evelyn Wood, who is very popular in the Colony, was hissed as he walked through the town, and great surprise was expressed that a soldier who came out expressly to fight the Boers, should consent to become the medium of communication in such a dirty business. And, indeed, there was some excuse for all this bitterness, for the news meant ruin to very many.

But if people in Natal and at the Cape received the news with astonishment, how shall I describe its effect upon the unfortunate loyal inhabitants in the Transvaal, on whom it burst like a thunderbolt?

They did not say much however, and indeed, there was nothing to be said, they simply began to pack up such things as they could carry with them, and to leave the country, which they well knew would henceforth be utterly untenable for Englishmen or English sympathisers. In a few weeks they came pouring down through Newcastle by hundreds; it was the most melancholy exodus that can be imagined. There were people of all classes, officials, gentlefolk, work-people, and loyal Boers, but they had a connecting link; they had all been loyal, and they were all ruined.

Most of these people had gone to the Transvaal since it became a British Colony, and invested all they had in it, and now their capital was lost and their labour rendered abortive; indeed, many of them whom one had known as well to do in the Transvaal, came down to Natal hardly knowing how they would feed their families next week.

It must be understood that so soon as the Queen's sovereignty was withdrawn the value of landed and house property in the Transvaal went down to nothing, and has remained there ever since. Thus a fair-sized house in Pretoria brought in a rental varying from ten to twenty pounds a month during British occupation, but after the declaration of peace, owners of houses were glad to get people to live in them to keep them from falling into ruin. Those who owned land or had invested money in businesses suffered in the same way; their property remains, neither profitable or saleable, and they themselves are precluded by their nationality from living on it, the art of "Boycotting" not being peculiar to Ireland.

Nor were they the only sufferers, the officials, many of whom had taken to the Government service as a permanent profession, in which they expected to pass their lives, were suddenly dismissed, mostly with a small gratuity, which would about suffice to pay their debts, and told to find their living as best they could. It was indeed a case of *vae victis,* — woe to the conquered loyalists.[*]

[*] *The following extract is clipped from a recent issue of the "Transvaal Advertiser." It describes the present condition of Pretoria: —*
"The streets grown over with rank vegetation, the water-furrows uncleaned and unattended, emitting offensive and unhealthy stenches, the houses showing evident signs of dilapidation and decay, the side paths, in many places, dangerous to pedestrians; in fact, everything the eye can rest upon indicates the downfall which has overtaken this once prosperous city. The visitor can, if he be so minded, betake himself to the outskirts and suburbs, where he will perceive the same sad evidences of neglect, public grounds unattended, roads uncared for, mills and other public works crumbling into ruin. These palpable signs of decay most strongly impress him. A blight seems to have come over this lately fair and prosperous town. Rapidly it is becoming a 'deserted village,' a 'city of the dead.'"

The Commission appointed by Her Majesty's Government consisted of Sir Hercules Robinson, Sir Henry de Villiers, and Sir Evelyn Wood, President Brand being also present in his capacity of friend of both parties, and to their discretion were left the settlement of all outstanding questions. Amongst these, were the mode of trial of those persons who had been guilty of acts contrary to the rules of civilised warfare, the question of severance of territory from the Transvaal on the Eastern boundary, the settlement of the boundary in the Keate-Award districts, the compensation for losses sustained during the war, the functions of the British Resident, and other matters. Their place of meeting was at Newcastle in Natal, and from thence they proceeded to Pretoria.

The first question of importance that came before the Commission was the mode of trial to be adopted in the cases of those persons accused of acts contrary to the usages of civilised warfare, such as murder. The Attorney-General for the Transvaal strongly advised that a special

Tribunal should be constituted to try these cases, principally because "after a civil war in which all the inhabitants of a country, with very few exceptions, have taken part, a jury of fair and impartial men, truly unbiassed, will be very difficult to get together." It is satisfactory to know that the Commissioners gave this somewhat obvious fact "their grave consideration," which, according to their Report, resulted in their determining to let the cases go before the ordinary court, and be tried by a jury, because in referring them to a specially constituted court which would have done equal justice without fear or favour, "the British Government would have made for itself, among the Dutch population of South Africa, a name for vindictive oppression, which no generosity in other affairs could efface."

There is more in this determination of the Commissioners, or rather of the majority of them—for Sir E. Wood, to his credit be it said, refused to agree in their decision—than meets the eye, the fact of the matter being that it was privately well known to them, that, though the Boer leaders might be willing to allow a few of the murderers to undergo the form of a trial, neither they nor the Boers themselves, meant to permit the farce to go any further. Had the men been tried by a special tribunal they would in all probability have been condemned to death, and then would have come the awkward question of carrying out the sentence on individuals whose deeds were looked on, if not with general approval, at any rate without aversion by the great mass of their countrymen. In short, it would probably have become necessary either to reprieve them or to fight the Boers again, since it was very certain that they would not have allowed them to be hung. Therefore the majority of the Commissioners, finding themselves face to face with a dead wall, determined to slip round it instead of boldly climbing it, by referring the cases to the Transvaal High Court, cheerfully confident of what the result must be.

After all, the matter was, much cry about little wool, for of all the crimes committed by the Boers—a list of some of which will be found in the Appendix to this book—in only three cases were a proportion of the perpetrators produced and put through the form of trial. Those three were, the dastardly murder of Captain Elliot, who was shot by his Boer escort while crossing the Vaal river on parole; the murder of a man named Malcolm, who was kicked to death in his own house by Boers, who afterwards put a bullet through his head to make the job "look better;" and the murder of a doctor named Barber, who was shot by his escort on the border of the Free State. A few of the men concerned in the first two of these crimes were tried in Pretoria: and it was currently reported at that time, that in order to make their acquittal certain our Attorney-General received instructions not to exercise his right of challenging jurors on behalf of the Crown. Whether or not this is true I am not prepared to say, but I believe it is a fact that he did not exercise that right, though the counsel of the prisoners availed themselves of it freely, with the result that in Elliot's case, the jury was composed of eight Boers and one German, nine being the full South African jury. The necessary result followed; in both cases the prisoners were acquitted in the teeth of the evidence. Barber's murderers were tried in the Free State, and were, as might be expected, acquitted.

Thus it will be seen that of all the perpetrators of murder and other crimes during the course of the war not one was brought to justice.

The offence for which their victims died was, in nearly every case, that they had served, were serving, or were loyal to Her Majesty the Queen. In no single case has England exacted retribution for the murder of her servants and citizens; but nobody can read through the long list of these dastardly slaughters without feeling that they will not go unavenged. The innocent blood that has been shed on behalf of this country, and the tears of children and widows now appeal to a higher tribunal than that of Mr. Gladstone's Government, and assuredly they will not appeal in vain.

The next point of importance dealt with by the Commission was the question whether or no any territory should be severed from the Transvaal, and kept under English rule for the benefit of the native inhabitants. Lord Kimberley, acting under pressure put upon him by members of the Aborigines Protection Society, instructed the Commission to consider the advisability of severing the districts of Lydenburg and Zoutpansberg, and also a strip of territory bordering on Zululand and Swazieland from the Transvaal, so as to place the inhabitants of the first two districts out of danger of maltreatment by the Boers, and to interpose a buffer between Zulus, and Swazies, and Boer aggression, and *vice versa*.

The Boer leaders had, it must be remembered, acquiesced in the principle of such a separation in the preliminary peace signed by Sir Evelyn Wood and themselves. The majority of the Commission, however (Sir Evelyn Wood dissenting), finally decided against the retention of either of these districts, a decision which I think was a wise one, though I arrive at that conclusion on very different grounds to those adopted by the majority of the Commission.

Personally, I cannot see that it is the duty of England to play policeman to the whole world. To have retained these native districts would have been to make ourselves responsible for their good government, and to have guaranteed them against Boer encroachment, which I do not think that we were called upon to do. It is surely not incumbent upon us, having given up the Transvaal to the Boers, to undertake the management of the most troublesome part of it, the Zulu border. Besides, bad as the abandonment of the Transvaal is, I think that if it was to be done at all, it was best to do it thoroughly, since to have kept some natives under our protection, and to have handed over the rest to the tender mercies of the Boers, would only be to render our injustice more obvious, whilst weakening the power of the natives themselves to combine in self-defence; since those under our protection would naturally have little sympathy with their more unfortunate brethren—their interests and circumstances being different.

The Commission do not seem to have considered the question from these points of view, but putting them on one side, there are many other considerations connected with it, which are ably summed up in their Report. Amongst these is the danger of disturbances commenced between Zulus or Swazies and Boers, spreading into Natal, and the probability of the fomenting of disturbances amongst the Zulus by Boers. The great argument for the retention of some territory, if only as a symbol that the English had not been driven out of the country, is, however, set forth in the forty-sixth paragraph of the Report, which runs as follows:—"The moral considerations that determine the actions of civilised Governments are not easily understood by barbarians, in whose eyes successful force is alone the sign of superiority, and it appeared possible that the surrender by the British Crown of one of its possessions to those who had been in arms against it, might be looked upon by the natives in no other way than as a token of the defeat and decay of the British Power, and that thus a serious shock might be given to British authority in South Africa, and the capacity of Great Britain to govern and direct the vast native population within and without her South African dominions—a capacity resting largely on the renown of her name— might be dangerously impaired."

These words coming from so unexpected a source do not, though couched in such mild language, hide the startling importance of the question discussed. On the contrary, they accurately and with double weight convey the sense and gist of the most damning argument against the policy of the retrocession of the Transvaal in its entirety; and proceeding from their own carefully chosen commissioners, can hardly have been pleasant reading to Lord Kimberley and his colleagues.

The majority of the Commission then proceeds to set forth the arguments advanced by the Boers against the retention of any territory, which appear to have been chiefly of a sentimental character, since we are informed that "the people, it seemed certain, would not have valued the restoration of a mutilated country. Sentiment in a great measure had led them to insurrection, and the force of such it was impossible to disregard." Sir E. Wood in his dissent, states, that he cannot even agree with the premises of his colleagues' argument, since he is convinced that it was not sentiment that had led to the outbreak, but a "general and rooted aversion to taxation." If he had added, and a hatred not only of English rule, but of all rule, he would have stated the complete cause of the Transvaal rebellion. In the next paragraph of the Report, however, we find the real cause of the pliability of the Commission in the matter, which is the same that influenced them in their decision about the mode of trial of the murderers and other questions:—they feared that the people would appeal to arms if they decided against their wishes.

Discreditable and disgraceful as it may seem, nobody can read this Report without plainly seeing that the Commissioners were, in treating with the Boers on these points, in the position of ambassadors from a beaten people getting the best terms they could. Of course, they well knew that this was not the case, but whatever the Boer leaders may have said, the Boers themselves did not know this, or even pretend to look at the matter in any other light. When we asked for the country back, said they, we did not get it; after we had three times defeated the English we did get it; the logical conclusion from the facts being that we got it because we defeated the English. This was their tone, and it is not therefore surprising that whenever the Commission threatened to decide anything against them, they, with a smile, let it know that if it did, they would be under the painful necessity of re-occupying Lang's Nek. It was never necessary to repeat the threat, since the majority of the Commission would thereupon speedily find a way to meet the views of the Boer representatives.

Sir Evelyn Wood, in his dissent, thus correctly sums up the matter:—"To contend that the Royal Commission ought not to decide contrary to the wishes of the Boers, because such decision might not be accepted, is to deny to the Commission the very power of decision that it was agreed should be left in its hands." Exactly so. But it is evident that the Commission knew its place, and so far from attempting to exercise any "power of decision," it was quite content with such concessions as it could obtain by means of bargaining. Thus, as an additional reason against the retention of any territory, it is urged that if this territory was retained "the majority of your Commissioners . . . would have found themselves in no favourable position for obtaining the concurrence of the Boer leaders as to other matters." In fact, Her Majesty's Commission appointed, or supposed to be appointed, to do Her Majesty's will and pleasure, shook in its shoes before men who had lately been rebels in arms against Her authority, and humbly submitted itself to their dicta.

The majority of the Commission went on to express their opinion, that by giving away about the retention of territory they would be able to obtain better terms for the natives generally, and larger powers for the British Resident. But, as Sir Evelyn Wood points out in his Report, they did nothing of the sort, the terms of the agreement about the Resident and other native matters being all consequent on and included in the first agreement of peace. Besides, they seem to have overlooked the fact that such concessions as they did obtain are only on paper, and practically worthless, whilst all *bona fide* advantages remained with the Boers.

The decision of the Commissioners in the question of the Keate Award, which next came under their consideration, appears to have been a judicious one, being founded on the very careful Report of

Colonel Moysey, R.E., who had been for many months collecting information on the spot. The Keate Award Territory is a region lying to the south-west of the Transvaal, and was, like many other districts in that country, originally in the possession of natives, of the Baralong and Batlapin tribes. Individual Boers having, however, *more suo* taken possession of tracts of land in the district, difficulties speedily arose between their Government and the native chiefs, and in 1871 Mr. Keate, Lieutenant-Governor of Natal, was by mutual consent called in to arbitrate on the matter. His decision was entirely in favour of the natives, and was accordingly promptly and characteristically repudiated by the Boer Volksraad. From that time till the rebellion the question remained unsettled, and was indeed a very thorny one to deal with. The Commission, acting on the principle *in medio tutissimus ibis*, drew a line through the midst of the disputed territory, or, in other words, set aside Mr. Keate's award and interpreted the dispute in favour of the Boers.

This decision was accepted by all parties at the time, but it has not resulted in the maintenance of peace. The principal Chief, Montsoia, is an old ally and staunch friend of the English, a fact which the Boers were not able to forget or forgive, and they appear to have stirred up rival Chiefs to attack him, and to have allowed volunteers from the Transvaal to assist them. Montsoia has also enlisted some white volunteers, and several fights have taken place, in which the loss of life has been considerable. Whether or no the Transvaal Government is directly concerned it is impossible to say, but from the fact that cannon are said to have been used against Montsoia it would appear that it is, since private individuals do not, as a rule, own Armstrong guns.[*]

[*] *I beg to refer any reader interested in this matter to the letter of "Transvaal" to the "Standard," which I have republished in the Appendix to this book.*

Amongst the questions remaining for the consideration of the Commissioners was that of what compensation should be given for losses during the war. Of course, the great bulk of the losses sustained were of an indirect nature, resulting from the necessary and enormous depreciation in the value of land and other property, consequent on the retrocession. Into this matter the Home Government declined to enter, thereby saving its pocket at the price of its honour, since it was upon English guarantees that the country would remain a British possession, that the majority of the unfortunate loyals invested their money in it. It was, however, agreed by the Commission (Sir H. de Villiers dissenting) that the Boers should be liable for compensation in cases where loss had been sustained through commandeering seizure, confiscation, destruction, or damage of property. The sums awarded under these heads have already amounted to about 110,000 pounds, which sum has been defrayed by the Imperial Government, the Boer authorities stating that they were not in a position to pay it.

In connection with this matter, I will pass to the Financial clauses of the Report. When the country was annexed, the public debt amounted to 301,727 pounds. Under British rule this debt was liquidated to the extent of 150,000 pounds, but the total was brought up by a Parliamentary grant, a loan from the Standard Bank, and sundries to 390,404 pounds, which represented the public debt of the Transvaal on the 31st December 1880. This was further increased by moneys advanced by the Standard Bank and English Exchequer during the war, and till the 8th August 1881, during which time the country yielded no revenue, to 457,393 pounds. To this must be added an estimated sum of 200,000 pounds for compensation charges, pension allowances, &c., and a further sum of 383,000 pounds, the cost of the successful expedition against Secocoeni, that of the unsuccessful one being left out of account, bringing up the total public debt to over a million, of which about 800,000 pounds is owing to this country.

This sum, with the characteristic liberality that distinguished them in their dealings with the Boers, but which was not so marked where loyals were concerned, the Commissioners (Sir Evelyn Wood dissenting) reduced by a stroke of the pen to 265,000 pounds, thus entirely remitting an approximate sum of 500,000 pounds, or 600,000 pounds. To the sum of 265,000 pounds still owing, must be added say another 150,000 pounds for sums lately advanced to pay the compensation claims, bringing up the actual amount now owing to England to something under half a million, of which I say with confidence she will never see a single 10,000 pounds. As this contingency was not contemplated, or if contemplated, not alluded to by the Royal Commission, provision was made for a sinking fund, by means of which the debt, which is a second charge on the revenues of the States, is to be extinguished in twenty-five years.

It is a strange instance of the proverbial irony of fate, that whilst the representatives of the Imperial Government were thus showering gifts of hundreds of thousands of pounds upon men who had spurned the benefits of Her Majesty's rule, made war upon her forces, and murdered her subjects, no such consideration was extended to those who had remained loyal to her throne. Their claims for compensation were passed by unheeded; and looking from the windows of the room in which they sat in Newcastle, the members of the Commission might have seen them flocking down from a country that could no longer be their home; those that were rich among them made poor, and those that were poor reduced to destitution.

The only other point which it will be necessary for me to touch on in connection with this Report is the duties of the British Resident and his relations to the natives. He was to be invested as representative of the Suzerain with functions for securing the execution of the terms of peace as regards: (1.) The control of the foreign relations of the State; (2.) The control of the frontier affairs of the State; and (3.) The protection of the interests of the natives in the State.

As regards the first of these points, it was arranged that the interests of subjects of the Transvaal should be left in the hands of Her Majesty's representatives abroad. Since Boers are, of all people in the world, the most stay-at-home, our ambassadors and consuls are not likely to be troubled much on their account. With reference to the second point, the Commission made stipulations that would be admirable if there were any probability of their being acted up to. The Resident is to report any encroachment on native territory by Boers to the High Commissioner, and when the Resident and the Boer Government differ, the decision of the Suzerain is to be final. This is a charming way of settling difficulties, but the Commission forgets to specify how the Suzerain's decision is to be enforced. After what has happened, it can hardly have relied on awe of the name of England to bring about the desired obedience!

But besides thus using his beneficent authority to prevent subjects of the Transvaal from trespassing on their neighbour's land, the Resident is to exercise a general supervision over the interests of all the natives in the country. Considering that they number about a million, and are scattered over a territory larger than France, one would think that this duty alone would have taken up the time of any ordinary man; and, indeed, Sir Evelyn Wood was in favour of the appointment of sub-residents to assist him. The majority of the Commission refused, however, to listen to any such suggestion—believing, they said, "that the least possible interference with the independent Government of the State would be the wisest." Quite so, but I suppose it never occurred to them to ask the natives what their views of the matter were! The Resident was also to be a member of a Native Location Committee, which was at some future time, to provide land for natives to live on.

In perusing this Report it is easy to follow with more or less accuracy the individual bent of its framers. Sir Hercules Robinson figures throughout as a man who has got a disagreeable business to carry out, in obedience to instructions that admit of no trifling with, and who has set himself to do the best he can for his country, and those who suffer through his country's policy, whilst obeying those instructions. He has evidently choked down his feelings and opinions as an individual, and turned himself into an official machine, merely registering in detail the will of Lord Kimberley. With Sir Henry de Villiers the case is very different, one feels throughout that the task is to him a congenial one, and that the Boer cause has in him an excellent friend. Indeed, had he been an advocate of their cause instead of a member of the Commission, he could not have espoused their side on every occasion with greater zeal. According to him they were always in the right, and in them he could find no guile. Mr. Hofmeyer and President Brand exercised a wise discretion from their own point of view, when they urged his appointment as Special Commissioner. I now come to Sir Evelyn Wood, who was in the position of an independent Englishman, neither prejudiced in favour of the Boers, or the reverse, and on whom, as a military man, Lord Kimberley would find it difficult to put the official screw. The results of his happy position are obvious in the paper attached to the end of the Report, and signed by him, in which he totally and entirely differs from the majority of the Commission on every point of importance. Most people will think that this very outspoke and forcible dissent deducts somewhat from the value of the Report, and throws a shadow of doubt on the wisdom of its provisions.

The formal document of agreement between Her Majesty's Government and the Boer leaders, commonly known as the

Convention, was signed by both parties at Pretoria on the afternoon of the 3d August 1881, in the same room in which, nearly four years before, the Annexation Proclamation was signed by Sir T. Shepstone.

Whilst this business was being transacted in Government House, a curious ceremony was going on just outside, and within sight of the windows. This was the ceremonious burial of the Union Jack, which was followed to the grave by a crowd of about 2000 loyalists and native chiefs. On the outside of the coffin was written the word "Resurgam," and an eloquent oration was delivered over the grave. Such demonstrations are, no doubt, foolish enough, but they are not entirely without political significance.

But a more unpleasant duty awaited the Commissioners than that of attaching their signatures to a document,—consisting of the necessity of conveying Her Majesty's decision as to the retrocession, to about a hundred native Chiefs, until now Her Majesty's subjects, who had been gathered together to hear it. It must be borne in mind that the natives had not been consulted as to the disposal of the country, although they outnumber the white people in the proportion of twenty to one, and that, beyond some worthless paper stipulations, nothing had been done for their interests.

Personally, I must plead guilty to what I know is by many, especially by those who are attached to the Boer cause, considered as folly if not worse, namely, a sufficient interest in the natives, and sympathy with their sufferings to bring me to the conclusion, that in acting thus we have inflicted a cruel injustice upon them. It seems to me, that as they were the original owners of the soil, they were entitled to some consideration in the question of its disposal, and consequently and incidentally, of their own. I am aware that it is generally considered that the white man has a right to the black man's possessions and land, and that it is his high and holy mission to exterminate the wretched native and take his place. But with this conclusion I venture to differ. So far as my own experience of natives has gone, I have found that in all the essential qualities of mind and body, they very much resemble white men, with the exception that they are, as a race, quicker-witted, more honest, and braver, than the ordinary run of white men. Of them might be aptly quoted the speech Shakespeare puts into Shylock's mouth: "Hath not a Jew eyes? hath not a Jew hands, organs, dimensions, senses, affections, passions?"

In the same way I ask, Has a native no feelings or affections? does he not suffer when his parents are shot, or his children stolen, or when he is driven a wanderer from his home? Does he not know fear, feel pain, affection, hate and gratitude? Most certainly he does; and this being so, I cannot believe that the Almighty, who made both white and black, gave to the one race the right or mission of exterminating, or even of robbing or maltreating the other, and calling the process the advance of civilisation. It seems to me, that on only one condition, if at all, have we the right to take the black man's land; and that is, that we provide them with an equal and a just Government, and allow no maltreatment of them, either as individuals or tribes: but, on the contrary, do our best to elevate them, and wean them from savage customs. Otherwise, the practice is surely undefensible.

I am aware, however, that with the exception of a small class, these are sentiments which are not shared by the great majority of the public, either at home or abroad. Indeed, it can be plainly seen how little sympathy they command, from the fact that but scanty remonstrance was raised at the treatment meted out to our native subjects in the Transvaal, when they were, to the number of nearly a million, handed over from the peace, justice, and security, that on the whole characterise our rule, to a state of things, and possibilities of wrong and suffering which I will not try to describe.

To the chiefs thus assembled Sir Hercules Robinson, as President of the Royal Commission, read a statement, and then retired, refusing to allow them to speak in answer. The statement informed the natives that "Her Majesty's Government, with that sense of justice which befits a great and powerful nation," had returned the country to the Boers, "whose representatives, Messrs. Kruger, Pretorius, and Joubert, I now," said Sir Hercules, "have much pleasure in introducing to you." If reports are true, the native Chiefs had, many of them personally, and all of them by reputation, already the advantage of a very intimate acquaintance with all three of these gentlemen, so that an introduction was somewhat superfluous.

Sir Hercules went on to explain to them that locations would be allotted to them at some future time; that a British Resident would be appointed, whose especial charge they would be, but that they must bear in mind that he was not the ruler of the country, but the Government, "subject to Her Majesty's suzerain rights." Natives were, no doubt, expected to know by intuition what suzerain rights are. The statement then goes on to give them good advice as to the advantages of indulging in manual labour when asked to do so by the Boers, and generally to show them how bright and happy is the future that lies before them. Lest they should be too elated by such good tidings, they are, however, reminded that it will be necessary to retain the law relating to passes, which is, in the hands of a people like the Boers, about as unjust a regulation as a dominant race can invent for the oppression of a subject people, and had, in the old days of the Republic, been productive of much hardship. The statement winds up by assuring them that their "interests will never be forgotten or neglected by Her Majesty's Government." Having read the document the Commission hastily withdrew, and after their withdrawal the Chiefs were "allowed" to state their opinions to the Secretary for Native Affairs.

In availing themselves of this permission, it is noticeable that no allusion was made to all the advantages they were to reap under the Convention, nor did they seem to attach much importance to the appointment of the British Resident. On the contrary, all their attention was given to the great fact that the country had been ceded to the Boers, and that they were no longer the Queen's subjects. We are told, in Mr. Shepstone's Report, that they "got very excited," and "asked whether it was thought that they had no feelings or hearts, that they were thus treated as a stick or piece of tobacco, which could be passed from hand to hand without question." Umgombarie, a Zoutpansberg Chief, said, "I am Umgombarie. I have fought with the Boers, and have many wounds, and they know that what I say is true. . . . I will never consent to place myself under their rule. I belong to the English Government. I am not a man who eats with both sides of his jaw at once; I only use one side. I am English, I have said." Silamba said, "I belong to the English. I will never return under the Boers. You see me, a man of my rank and position, is it right that such as I should be seized and laid on the ground and flogged, as has been done to me and other chiefs?"

Sinkanhla said: "We hear and yet do not hear, we cannot understand. We are troubling you, Chief, by talking in this way; we hear the Chiefs say that the Queen took the country because the people of the country wished it, and again that the majority of the owners of the country did not wish their rule, and that therefore the country was given back. We should like to have the man pointed out from among us black people who objects to the rule of the Queen. We are the real owners of the country; we were here when the Boers came, and without asking leave, settled down and treated us in every way badly. The English Government then came and took the country; we have now had four years of rest and peaceful and just rule. We have been called here to-day, and are told that the country, our country, has been given to the Boers by the Queen. This is a thing which surprises us. Did the country, then, belong to the Boers? Did it not belong to our fathers and forefathers before us, long before the Boers came here? We have heard that the Boers' country is at the Cape. If the Queen wishes to give them their land, why does she not give them back the Cape?"

I have quoted this speech at length, because, although made by a despised native, it sets forth their case more powerfully and in happier language than I can do.

Umyethile said: "We have no heart for talking. I have returned to the country from Sechelis, where I had to fly from Boer oppression. Our hearts are black and heavy with grief to-day at the news told us, we are in agony, our intestines are twisting and writhing inside of us, just as you see a snake do when it is struck on the head. . . . We do not know what has become of us, but we feel dead; it may be that the Lord may change the nature of the Boers, and that we will not be treated like dogs and beasts of burden as formerly, but we have no hope of such a change, and we leave you with heavy hearts and great apprehension as to the future." In his Report, Mr. Shepstone (the Secretary for Native Affairs) says: "One chief, Jan Sibilo, who has been, he informed me, personally threatened with death by the Boers after the English leave, could not restrain his feelings, but cried like a child."

I have nothing to add to these extracts, which are taken from many such statements. They are the very words of the persons most concerned, and will speak for themselves.

The Convention was signed on the 3d August 1881, and was to be formally ratified by a Volksraad or Parliament of the Burghers within three months of that date, in default of which it was to fall to the ground and become null and void.

Anybody who has followed the course of affairs with reference to the retrocession of the Transvaal, or who has even taken the trouble to read through this brief history, will probably come to the conclusion that, under all the circumstances, the Boers had got more than they could reasonably expect. Not so, however, the Boers themselves. On the 28th September the newly-elected Volksraad referred the Convention to a General Committee to report on, and on the 30th September the Report was presented. On the 3d October a telegram was despatched through the British Resident to "His Excellency W. E. Gladstone," in which the Volksraad states that the Convention is not acceptable—

(1.) Because it is in conflict with the Sand River Treaty of 1852.

(2.) Because it violates the peace agreement entered into with Sir Evelyn Wood, in confidence of which the Boers laid down their arms.

The Volksraad consequently declared that modifications were desirable, and that certain articles *must* be altered.

To begin with, they declare that the "conduct of foreign relations does not appertain to the Suzerain, only supervision," and that the articles bearing on these points must consequently be modified. They next attack the native question, stating that "the Suzerain has not the right to interfere with our Legislature," and state that they cannot agree to Article 3, which gives the Suzerain a right of veto on Legislation connected with the natives, to Article 13, by virtue of which natives are to be allowed to acquire land, and to the last part of Article 26, by which it is provided that whites of alien race living in the Transvaal shall not be taxed in excess of the taxes imposed on Transvaal citizens.

They further declare that it is "infra dignitatem" for the President of the Transvaal to be a member of a Commission. This refers to the Native Location Commission, on which he is, in the terms of the Convention, to sit, together with the British Resident, and a third person jointly appointed.

They next declare that the amount of the debt for which the Commission has made them liable should be modified. Considering that England had already made them a present of from 600,000 pounds to 800,000 pounds, this is a most barefaced demand. Finally, they state that "Articles 15, 16, 26, and 27, are superfluous, and only calculated to wound our sense of honour" (sic).

Article 15 enacts that no slavery or apprenticeship shall be tolerated.

Article 16 provides for religious toleration.

Article 26 provides for the free movement, trading, and residence of all persons, other than natives, conforming themselves to the laws of the Transvaal.

Article 27 gives to all the right of free access to the Courts of Justice.

Putting the "sense of honour" of the Transvaal Volksraad out of the question, past experience has but too plainly proved that these Articles are by no means superfluous.

In reply to this message, Sir Hercules Robinson telegraphs to the British Resident on the 21st October in the following words:—

"Having forwarded Volksraad Resolution of 15th to Earl of Kimberley, I am desired to instruct you in reply to repeat to the Triumvirate that Her Majesty's Government cannot entertain any proposals for a modification of the Convention *until after it has been ratified*, and the necessity for further concession proved by experience."

I wish to draw particular attention to the last part of this message, which is extremely typical of the line of policy adopted throughout in the Transvaal business. The English Government dared not make any further concession to the Boers, because they felt that they had already strained the temper of the country almost to breaking in the matter. On the other hand, they were afraid that if they did not do something, the Boers would tear up the Convention, and they would find themselves face to face with the old difficulty. Under these circumstances, they have fallen back upon their temporising and un-English policy, which leaves them a back-door to escape through, whatever turn things take. Should the Boers now suddenly turn round and declare, which is extremely probable, that they repudiate their debt to us, or that they are sick of the presence of a British Resident, the Government will be able to announce that "the necessity for further concession" has now been "proved by experience," and thus escape the difficulty. In short, this telegram has deprived the Convention of whatever finality it may have possessed, and made it, as a document, as worthless as it is as a practical settlement. That this is the view taken of it by the Boers themselves, is proved by the text of the Ratification which followed on the receipt of this telegram.

The tone of this document throughout is, in my opinion, considering from whom it came, and against whom it is directed, very insolent. And it amply confirms what I have previously said, that the Boers looked upon themselves as a victorious people making terms with those they have conquered. The Ratification leads off thus: "The Volksraad is not satisfied with this Convention, and considers that the members of the Triumvirate performed a fervent act of love for the Fatherland when they upon their own responsibility signed such an unsatisfactory state document." This is damning with faint praise indeed. It then goes on to recite the various points of object, stating that the answers from the English Government proved that they were well founded. "The English Government," it says, "acknowledges indirectly by this answer (the telegram of 21st October, quoted above) that the difficulties raised by the Volksraad are neither fictitious nor unfounded, inasmuch *as it desires from us the concession* that we, the Volksraad, shall submit it to a practical test." It will be observed that English is here represented as begging the favour of a trial of her conditions from the Volksraad of the Transvaal Boers. The Ratification is in these words: "Therefore it is that the Raad here unanimously resolves not to go into further discussion of the Convention, *and maintaining all objections to the Convention* as made before the Royal Commission or stated in the Raad, and for the purpose of showing to everybody that the love of peace and unity inspires us, *for the time and provisionally* submitting the articles of the Convention to a practical test, *hereby complying with the request of the English Government* contained in the telegram of the 13th October 1881, proceeds to ratify the Convention."

It would have been interesting to have seen how such a Ratification as this, which is no Ratification but an insult, would have been accepted by Lord Beaconsfield. I think that within twenty-four hours of its arrival in Downing Street, the Boer Volksraad would have received a startling answer. But Lord Beaconsfield is dead, and by his successor it was received with all due thankfulness and humility. His words, however, on this subject still remain to us, and even his great rival might have done well to listen to them. It was in the course of what was, I believe, the last speech he made in the House of Lords, that speaking about the Transvaal rising, he warned the Government that it was a very dangerous thing to make peace with rebellious subjects in arms against the authority of the Queen. The warning passed unheeded, and the peace was made in the way I have described.

As regards the Convention itself, it will be obvious to the reader that the Boers have not any intention of acting up to its provisions, mild as they are, if they can possibly avoid them, whilst, on the other hand, there is no force at hand to punish their disregard or breach. It is all very well to create a Resident with extensive powers; but how is he to enforce his decisions? What is he to do if his awards are laughed at and made a mockery of, as they are and will be? The position of Mr. Hudson at Pretoria is even worse than that of Mr. Osborn in Zululand. For instance, the Convention specifies in the first article that the Transvaal is to be known as the Transvaal State. The Boer Government have, however, thought fit to adopt the name of "South African Republic" in all public documents. Mr. Hudson was accordingly directed to remonstrate, which he did in a feeble way; his remonstrance was politely acknowledged, but the country is still officially called the South African Republic, the Convention and Mr. Hudson's remonstrations notwithstanding. Mr. Hudson, however, appears to be better suited to the position than would have been the case had an Englishman, pure and simple, been appointed, since it is evident that things that would have struck the latter as insults to the Queen he represented, and his country generally, are not so understood by him. In fact, he admirably represents his official superiors in his capacity of swallowing rebuffs, and when smitten on one cheek delightedly offering the other.

Thus we find him attending a Boer meeting of thanksgiving for the success that had waited on their arms and the recognition of their independence, where most people will consider he was out of place. To this meeting, thus graced by his presence, an address was presented by a branch of the Africander Bond, a powerful institution, having for its object the total uprootal of English rule and English customs in South Africa, to which he must have listened with pleasure. In it he, in common with other members of the meeting, is informed that "you took up the sword and struck the Briton with such force" that "the Britons through fear revived that sense of justice to which they could not be brought by petitions," and that the "day will soon come that we shall enter with you on one arena for the entire independence of South Africa," i.e., independence from English rule.

On the following day the Government gave a dinner, to which all those who had done good service during the late hostilities were invited, the British Resident being apparently the only Englishman asked. Amongst the other celebrities present I notice the name of Buskes. This man, who is an educated Hollander, was the moving spirit of the Potchefstroom atrocities; indeed, so dark is his reputation that the Royal Commission refused to transact business with him, or to admit him into their presence. Mr. Hudson was not so particular. And now comes the most extraordinary part of the episode. At the dinner it was necessary that the health of Her Majesty as Suzerain should be proposed, and with studied insolence this was done last of all the leading political toasts, and immediately after that of the Triumvirate. Notwithstanding this fact, and that the toast was couched by Mr. Joubert, who stated that "he would not attempt to explain what a Suzerain was," in what appear to be semi-ironical terms, we find that Mr. Hudson "begged to tender his thanks to the Honourable Mr. Joubert for the kind way in which he proposed the toast."

It may please Mr. Hudson to see the name of the Queen thus metaphorically dragged in triumph at the chariot wheels of the Triumvirate, but it is satisfactory to know that the spectacle is not appreciated in England: since, on a question in the House of Lords, by the Earl of Carnarvon, who characterised it as a deliberate insult, Lord Kimberley replied that the British Resident had been instructed that in future he was not to attend public demonstrations unless he had previously informed himself that the name of Her Majesty would be treated with proper respect. Let us hope that this official reprimand will have its effect, and that Mr. Hudson will learn therefrom that there is such a thing as *trop de zele*—even in a good cause.

The Convention is now a thing of the past, the appropriate rewards have been lavishly distributed to its framers, and President Brand has at last prevailed upon the Volksraad of the Orange Free State to allow him to become a Knight Grand Cross of Saint Michael and Saint George,—the same prize looked forward to by our most distinguished public servants at the close of the devotion of their life to the service of their country. But its results are yet to come—though it would be difficult to forecast the details of their development. One thing, however, is clear: the signing of that document signalised an entirely new departure in South African affairs, and brought us within a measurable distance of the abandonment, for the present at any rate, of the supremacy of English rule in South Africa.

This is the larger issue of the matter, and it is already bearing fruit. Emboldened by their success in the Transvaal, the Dutch party at the Cape are demanding, and the demand is to be granted, that the Dutch tongue be admitted *pari passu* with English, as the official language in the Law Courts and the House of Assembly. When a country thus consents to use a foreign tongue equally with its own, it is a sure sign that those who speak it are rising to power. But "the Party" looks higher than this, and openly aims at throwing off English rule altogether, and declaring South Africa a great Dutch republic. The course of events is favourable to their aspiration. Responsible Government is to be granted to Natal, which country not being strong enough to stand alone in the face of the many dangers that surround her, will be driven into the arms of the Dutch party to save herself from destruction. It will be useless for her to look for help from England, and any feelings of repugnance she may feel to Boer rule will soon be choked by necessity, and a mutual interest. It is, however, possible that some unforeseen event, such as the advent to power of a strong Conservative Ministry, may check the tide that now sets so strongly in favour of Dutch supremacy.

It seems to me, however, to be a question worthy of the consideration of those who at present direct the destinies of the Empire, whether it would not be wise, as they have gone so far, to go a little further and favour a scheme for the total abandonment of South Africa, retaining only Table Bay. If they do not, it is now quite within the bounds of sober possibility that they may one day have to face a fresh Transvaal rebellion, only on a ten times larger scale, and might find it difficult to retain even Table Bay. If, on the other hand, they do, I believe that all the White States in South Africa will confederate of their own free-will, under the pressure of the necessity for common action, and the Dutch element being preponderant, at once set to work to exterminate the natives on general principles, in much the same way, and from much the same motives that a cook exterminates black beetles, because she thinks them ugly, and to clear the kitchen.

I need hardly say that such a policy is not one that commands my sympathy, but Her Majesty's Government having put their hand to the plough, it is worth their while to consider it. It would at any rate be in perfect accordance with their declared sentiments, and command an enthusiastic support from their followers.

As regards the smaller and more immediate issue of the retrocession, namely, its effect on the Transvaal itself, it cannot be other than evil. The act is, I believe, quite without precedent in our history, and it is difficult to see, looking at it from those high grounds of national morality assumed by the Government, what greater arguments can be advanced in its favour, than could be found to support the abandonment of, — let us say, — Ireland. Indeed a certain parallel undoubtedly exists between the circumstances of the two countries. Ireland was, like the Transvaal, annexed, though a long time ago, and has continually agitated for its freedom. The Irish hate us, so did the Boers. In Ireland, Englishmen are being shot, and England is running the awful risk of bloodguiltiness, as it did in the Transvaal. In Ireland, smouldering revolution is being fanned into flame by Mr. Gladstone's speeches and acts, as it was in the Transvaal. In Ireland, as in the Transvaal, there exists a strong loyal class that receives insults instead of support from the Government, and whose property, as was the case there, is taken from them without compensation, to be flung as a sop to stop the mouths of the Queen's enemies. And so I might go on, finding many such similarities of circumstances, but my parallel, like most parallels, must break down at last. Thus — it mattered little to England whether or no she let the Transvaal go, but to let Ireland go would be more than even Mr. Gladstone dare attempt.

Somehow, if you follow these things far enough, you always come to vulgar first principles. The difference between the case of the Transvaal and that of Ireland is a difference not of justice but of cause, for both causes are equally unjust or just according as they are viewed, but of mere common expediency. Judging from the elevated standpoint of the national morality theory however, which, as we know, soars above such truisms as the foolish statement that force is a remedy, or that if you wish to retain your prestige you must not allow defeats to pass unavenged, I cannot see why, if it was righteous to abandon the Transvaal, it would not be equally righteous to abandon Ireland!

As for the Transvaal, that country is not to be congratulated on its success, for it has destroyed all its hopes of permanent peace, has ruined its trade and credit, and has driven away the most useful and productive class in the community. The Boers, elated by their success in arms, will be little likely to settle down to peaceable occupations, and still less likely to pay their taxes, which, indeed, I hear they are already refusing to do. They have learnt how easily even a powerful Government can be upset, and the lesson is not likely to be forgotten, for want of repetition to their own weak one.

Already the Transvaal Government hardly knows which way to turn for funds, and is, perhaps fortunately for itself, quite unable to borrow, through want of credit.

As regards the native question, I agree with Mr. H. Shepstone, who, in his Report on this subject, says that he does not believe that the natives will inaugurate any action against the Boers, so long as the latter do not try to collect taxes, or otherwise interfere with them. But if the Boer Government is to continue to exist, it will be bound to raise taxes from the natives, since it cannot collect much from its white subjects. The first general attempt of the sort will be the signal for active resistance on the part of the natives, whom, if they act without concert, the Boers will be able to crush in detail, though with considerable loss. If, on the other hand, they should have happened, during the last few years, to have learnt the advantages of combination, as is quite possible, perhaps they will crush the Boers.

The only thing that is at present certain about the matter is that there will be bloodshed, and that before long. For instance, the Montsoia difficulty in the Keate Award has in it the possibilities of a serious war, and there are plenty such difficulties ready to spring into life within and without the Transvaal.

In all human probability it will take but a small lapse of time for the Transvaal to find itself in the identical position from which we relieved it by the Annexation.

What course events will then take it is impossible to say. It may be found desirable to re-annex the country, though, in my opinion, that would be, after all that has passed, an unfortunate step; its inhabitants may be cut up piecemeal by a combined movement of native tribes, as they would have been, had they not been rescued by the English

Government in 1877, or it is possible that the Orange Free State may consent to take the Transvaal under its wing: who can say? There is only one thing that our recently abandoned possession can count on for certain, and that is trouble, both from its white subjects, and the natives, who hate the Boers with a bitter and a well-earned hatred.

The whole question, can, so far as its moral aspect is concerned, be summed up in a few words.

Whether or no the Annexation was a necessity at the moment of its execution,—which I certainly maintain it was—it received the unreserved sanction of the Home Authorities, and the relations of Sovereign and subject, with all the many and mutual obligations involved in that connection, were established between the Queen of England and every individual of the motley population of the Transvaal. Nor was this change an empty form, for, to the largest proportion of that population, this transfer of allegiance brought with it a priceless and a vital boon. To them it meant—freedom and justice—for where, on any portion of this globe over which the British ensign floats, does the law even wink at cruelty or wrong?

A few years passed away, and a small number of the Queen's subjects in the Transvaal rose in rebellion against Her authority, and inflicted some reverses on Her arms. Thereupon, in spite of the reiterated pledges given to the contrary—partly under stress of defeat, and partly in obedience to the pressure of "advanced views"—the country was abandoned, and the vast majority who had remained faithful to the Crown, was handed to the cruel despotism of the minority who had rebelled against it.

Such an act of treachery to those to whom we were bound with double chains—by the strong ties of a common citizenship, and by those claims to England's protection from violence and wrong which have hitherto been wont to command it, even where there was no duty to fulfil, and no authority to vindicate—stands—I believe—without parallel on our records, and marks a new departure in our history.

I cannot end these pages without expressing my admiration of the extremely able way in which the Boers managed their revolt, when once they felt that, having undertaken the thing, it was a question of life and death with them. It shows that they have good stuff in them somewhere, which, under the firm but just rule of Her Majesty, might have been much developed, and it makes it the more sad that they should have been led to throw off that rule, and have been allowed to do so by an English Government.

In conclusion, there is one point that I must touch on, and that is the effect of the retrocession on the native mind, which I can only describe as most disastrous. The danger alluded to in the Report of the Royal Commission has been most amply realised, and the prevailing belief in the steadfastness of our policy, and the inviolability of our plighted word, which has hitherto been the great secret of our hold on the Kafirs, has been rudely shaken. The motives that influenced, or are said to have influenced, the Government in their act, are naturally quite unintelligible to savages, however clever, who do believe that force is a remedy, and who have seen the inhabitants of a country ruled by England, defeat English soldiers and take possession of it, whilst those who remained loyal to England were driven out of it. It will not be wonderful if some of them, say the natives of Natal, deduce therefrom conclusions unfavourable to loyalty, and evince a desire to try the same experiment.

It is, however, unprofitable to speculate on the future, which must be left to unfold itself.

The curtain is, so far as this country is concerned, down for the moment on the South African stage; when it rises again, there is but too much reason to fear that it will reveal a state of confusion, which, unless it is more wisely and consistently dealt with in the future than it has been in the past, may develop into chaos.

APPENDIX

I. THE POTCHEFSTROOM ATROCITIES, &C.

There were more murders and acts of cruelty committed during the war at Potchefstroom, where the behaviour of the Boers was throughout both deceitful and savage, than at any other place.

When the fighting commenced a number of ladies and children, the wives and children of English residents, took refuge in the fort. Shortly after it had been invested they applied to be allowed to return to their homes in the town till the war was over. The request was refused by the Boer commander, who said that as they had gone there, they might stop and "perish" there. One poor lady, the wife of a gentleman well known in the Transvaal, was badly wounded by having the point of a stake, which had been cut in two by a bullet, driven into her side. She was at the time in a state of pregnancy, and died some days afterwards in great agony. Her little sister was shot through the throat, and several other women and children suffered from bullet wounds, and fever arising from their being obliged to live for months exposed to rain and heat, with insufficient food.

The moving spirit of all the Potchefstroom atrocities was a cruel wretch of the name of Buskes, a well-educated man, who, as an advocate of the High Court, had taken the oath of allegiance to the Queen.

One deponent swears that he saw this Buskes wearing Captain Fall's diamond ring, which he had taken from Sergeant Ritchie, to whom it was handed to be sent to England, and also that he had possessed himself of the carriages and other goods belonging to prisoners taken by the Boers.[*] Another deponent (whose name is omitted in the Blue Book for precautionary reasons) swears, "That on the next night the patrol again came to my house accompanied by one Buskes, who was secretary of the Boer Committee, and again asked

*

where my wife and daughter were. I replied, in bed; and Buskes then said, 'I must see for myself.' I refused to allow him, and he forced me, with a loaded gun held to my breast, to open the curtains of the bed, when he pulled the bedclothes half off my wife, and altogether off my daughter. I then told him if I had a gun I would shoot him. He placed a loaded gun at my breast, when my wife sprang out of bed and got between us."

[*] *Buskes was afterwards forced to deliver up the ring.*

I remember hearing at the time that this Buskes (who is a good musician) took one of his victims, who was on the way to execution, into the chapel and played the "Dead March in Saul," or some such piece, over him on the organ.

After the capture of the Court House a good many Englishmen fell into the hands of the Boers. Most of these were sentenced to hard labour and deprivation of "civil rights." The sentence was enforced by making them work in the trenches under a heavy fire from the fort. One poor fellow, F. W. Finlay by name, got his head blown off by a shell from his own friends in the fort, and several loyal Kafirs suffered the same fate. After these events the remaining prisoners refused to return to the trenches till they had been "tamed" by being thrashed with the butt end of guns, and by threats of receiving twenty-five lashes each.

But their fate, bad as it was, was not so awful as that suffered by Dr. Woite and J. Van der Linden.

Dr. Woite had attended the Boer meeting which was held before the outbreak, and written a letter from thence to Major Clarke, in which he had described the talk of the Boers as silly bluster. He was not a paid spy. This letter was, unfortunately for him, found in Major Clarke's pocket-book, and because of it he was put through a form of trial, taken out and shot dead, all on the same day. He left a wife and large family, who afterwards found their way to Natal in a destitute condition.

The case of Van der Linden is somewhat similar. He was one of Raaf's Volunteers, and as such had taken the oath of allegiance to the Queen. In the execution of his duty he made a report to his commanding officer about the Boer meeting, and which afterwards fell into the hands of the Boers. On this he was put through the form of trial, and, though in the service of the Queen, was found guilty of treason and condemned to death. One of his judges, a little less stony-hearted than the rest, pointed out that "when the prisoner committed the crime martial law had not yet been proclaimed, nor the State," but it availed him nothing. He was taken out and shot.

A Kafir named Carolus was also put through the form of trial and shot, for no crime at all that I can discover.

Ten unarmed Kafir drivers, who had been sent away from the fort, were shot down in cold blood by a party of Boers. Several witnesses depose to having seen their remains lying together close to Potchefstroom.

Various other Kafirs were shot. None of the perpetrators of these crimes were brought to justice. The Royal Commission comments on these acts as follows: —

"In regard to the deaths of Woite, Van de Linden, and Carolus, the Boer leaders do not deny the fact that those men had been executed, but sought to justify it. The majority of your Commissioners felt bound to record their opinion that the taking of the lives of these men was an act contrary to the rules of civilised warfare. Sir H. de Villiers was of opinion that the executions in these cases, having been ordered by properly constituted Court Martial of the Boers' forces after due trial, did not fall under the cognisance of your Commissioners.

"Upon the case of William Finlay the majority of your Commissioners felt bound to record the opinion that the sacrifice of Finlay's life, through forced labour under fire in the trenches, was an act contrary to the rules of civilised warfare. *Sir H. de Villiers did not feel justified by the facts of the case in joining in this expression of opinion* (sic). As to the case of the Kafir Andries, your Commissioners decided that, although the shooting of this man appeared to them, from the information laid before them, to be not in accordance with the rules of civilised warfare, under all the circumstances of the case, it was not desirable to insist upon a prosecution.

"The majority of your Commissioners, although feeling it a duty to record emphatically their disapproval of the acts that resulted in the deaths of Woite, Van der Linden, Finlay, and Carolus, yet found it impossible to bring to justice the persons guilty of these acts."

It will be observed that Sir H. de Villiers does not express any disapproval, emphatic or otherwise, of these wicked murders.

But Potchefstroom did not enjoy a monopoly of murder.

In December 1880, Captain Elliot, who was a survivor from the Bronker Spruit massacre, and Captain Lambart, who had been taken prisoner by the Boers whilst bringing remounts from the Free State, were released from Heidelberg on parole on condition that they left the country. An escort of two men brought them to a drift of the Vaal river, where they refused to cross, because they could not get their cart through, the river being in flood. The escort then returned to Heidelberg and reported that the officers would not cross. A civil note was then sent back to Captains Elliot and Lambart, signed by P. J. Joubert, telling them "to pass the Vaal river immediately by the road that will be shown to you." What secret orders, if any, were sent with this letter has never transpired; but I decline to believe that, either in this or in Barber's case, the Boer escort took upon themselves the responsibility of murdering their prisoners, without authority of some kind for the deed.

The men despatched from Heidelberg with the letter found Lambert and Elliot wandering about and trying to find the way to Standerton. They presented the letter, and took them towards a drift in the Vaal. Shortly before they got there the prisoners noticed that their escort had been reinforced. It would be interesting to know, if these extra men were not sent to assist in the murder, how and why they turned up as they did and joined themselves to the escort. The prisoners were taken to an old and disused drift of the Vaal river and told to cross. It was now dark, and the river was much swollen with rain; in fact, impassable for the cart and horses. Captains Elliot and Lambart begged to be allowed to outspan till the next morning, but were told that they must cross, which they accordingly attempted to do. A few yards from the bank the cart stuck on a rock, and whilst in this position the Boer escort poured a volley into it. Poor Elliot was instantly killed, one bullet fracturing his skull, another passing through the back, a third shattering the right thigh, and a fourth breaking the left wrist. The cart was also riddled, but, strange to say, Captain Lambert was untouched, and succeeded in swimming to the further bank, the Boers firing at him whenever the flashes of lightning revealed his whereabouts. After sticking some time in the mud of the bank he managed to effect his escape, and next day reached the house of an Englishman called Groom, living in the Free State, and from thence made his way to Natal.

Two of the murderers were put through a form of trial, after the conclusion of peace, and acquitted.

The case of the murder of Dr. Barber is of a somewhat similar character to that of Elliot, except that there is in this case a curious piece of indirect evidence that seems to connect the murder directly with Piet Joubert, one of the Triumvirate.

In the month of February 1881, two Englishmen came to the Boer laager at Lang's Nek to offer their services as doctors. Their names were Dr. Barber, who was well known to the Boers, and his assistant, Mr. Walter Dyas, and they came, not from Natal, but the Orange Free State. On arrival at the Boer camp they were at first well received, but after a little while seized, searched, and tied up all night to a disselboom (pole of a waggon). Next morning they were told to mount their horses, and started from the camp escorted by two men who were to take them over the Free State line.

When they reached the Free State line the Boers told them to get off their horses, which they were ordered to bring back to the camp. They did so, bade good-day to their escort, and started to walk on towards their destination. When they had gone about forty yards Dyas heard the report of a rifle, and Barber called out, "My God, I am shot!" and fell dead.

Dyas went down on his hands and knees and saw one of the escort deliberately aim at him. He then jumped up, and ran dodging from right to left, trying to avoid the bullet. Presently the man fired, and he felt himself struck through the thigh. He fell with his face to the men, and saw his would-be assassin put a fresh cartridge into his rifle and aim at him. Turning his face to the ground he awaited his death, but the bullet whizzed past his head. He then saw the men take the horses and go away, thinking they had finished him. After waiting a while he managed to get up, and struggled to a house not far off, where he was kindly treated and remained till he recovered.

Some time after this occurrence a Hottentot, named Allan Smith, made a statement at Newcastle, from which it appears that he had been taken prisoner by the Boers and made to work for them. One night he saw Barber and Dyas tied to the disselboom, and overheard the following, which I will give in his own words:—

"I went to a fire where some Boers were sitting; among them was a low-sized man, moderately stout, with a dark-brown full beard, apparently about thirty-five years of age. I do not know his name. *He was telling his comrades that he had brought an order from Piet Joubert to Viljoen, to take the two prisoners to the Free State line and shoot them there.* He said, in the course of conversation, 'Piet Joubert het gevraacht waarom was de mensche neet dood geschiet toen hulle bijde eerste laager gekom het.' ('Piet Joubert asked why were the men not shot when they came to the first laager.') They then saw me at the fire, and one of them said, 'You must not talk before that fellow; he understands what you say, and will tell everybody.'

"Next morning Viljoen told me to go away, and gave me a pass into the Free State. He said (in Dutch), 'you must not drive for any Englishmen again. If we catch you doing so we will shoot you, and if you do not go away quick, and we catch you hanging about when we bring the two men to the line, we will shoot you too.'"

Dyas, who escaped, made an affidavit with reference to this statement in which he says, "I have read the foregoing affidavit of Allan Smith, and I say that the person described in the third paragraph thereof as bringing orders from Piet Joubert to Viljoen, corresponds with one of the Boers who took Dr. Barber and myself to the Free State, and to the best of my belief he is the man who shot Dr. Barber."

The actual murderers were put on their trial in the Free State, and, of course, acquitted. In his examination at the trial, Allan Smith says, "It was a young man who said that Joubert had given orders that Barber had to be shot. . . . It was not at night, but in the morning early, when the young man spoke about Piet Joubert's order."

Most people will gather, from what I have quoted, that there exists a certain connection between the dastardly murder of Dr. Barber (and the attempted murder of Mr. Dyas), and Piet Joubert, one of that "able" Triumvirate of which Mr. Gladstone speaks so highly.

I shall only allude to one more murder, though more are reported to have occurred, amongst them—that of Mr. Malcolm, who was kicked to death by Boers,—and that is Mr. Green's.

Mr. Green was an English gold-digger, and was travelling along the main road to his home at Spitzcop. The road passed close by the military camp at Lydenburg, into which he was called. On coming out he went to a Boer patrol with a flag of truce, and whilst talking to them was shot dead. The Rev. J. Thorne, the English clergyman at Lydenburg, describes this murder in an affidavit in the following words:—

"That I was the clergyman who got together a party of Englishmen and brought down the body of Mr. Green who was murdered by the Boers and buried it. I have ascertained the circumstances of the murder, which were as follows:—Mr. Green was on his way to the gold-fields. As he was passing the fort, he was called in by the officers, and sent out again with a message to the Boer commandant. Immediately on leaving the camp, he went to the Boer guard opposite with a flag of truce in his hand; while parleying with the Boers, who proposed to make a prisoner of him, he was shot through the head."

No prosecution was instituted in this case. Mr. Green left a wife and children in a destitute condition.

II

PLEDGES GIVEN BY MR. GLADSTONE'S GOVERNMENT AS TO THE RETENTION OF THE TRANSVAAL AS A BRITISH COLONY

The following extracts from the speeches, despatches, and telegrams of members of the present Government, with reference to the proposed retrocession of the Transvaal, are not without interest:—

During the month of May 1880, Lord Kimberley despatched a telegram to Sir Bartle Frere, in which the following words occur: "*Under no circumstances can the Queen's authority in the Transvaal be relinquished.*"

In a despatch dated 20th May, and addressed to Sir Bartle Frere, Lord Kimberley says, "That the sovereignty of the Queen in the Transvaal could not be relinquished."

In a speech in the House of Lords on the 24th May 1880, Lord Kimberley said: —

"There was a still stronger reason than that for not receding; it was impossible to say what calamities such a step as receding might not cause. We had, at the cost of much blood and treasure, restored peace, and the effect of our now reversing our policy would be to leave the province in a state of anarchy, and possibly to cause an internecine war. For such a risk he could not make himself responsible. The number of the natives in the Transvaal was estimated at about 800,000, and that of the whites less than 50,0000. Difficulties with the Zulus and frontier tribes would again arise, and, looking as they must to South Africa as a whole, the Government, after a careful consideration of the question, came to the conclusion *that we could not relinquish the Transvaal*. Nothing could be more unfortunate than uncertainty in respect to such a matter."

On the 8th June 1880, Mr. Gladstone, in reply to a Boer memorial, wrote as follows: —

"It is undoubtedly a matter for much regret that it should, since the Annexation, have appeared that so large a number of the population of Dutch origin in the Transvaal are opposed to the annexation of that territory, but it is impossible now to consider that question as if it were presented for the first time. We have to do with a state of things which has existed for a considerable period, during which *obligations have been contracted, especially, though not exclusively, towards the native population, which cannot be set aside.* Looking to all the circumstances, both of the Transvaal and the rest of South Africa, and to the necessity of preventing a renewal of disorders, which might lead to disastrous consequences, not only to the Transvaal but to the whole of South Africa, *our judgment is that the Queen cannot be advised to relinquish the Transvaal.*"

Her Majesty's Speech, delivered in Parliament on the 6th January 1881, contains the following words: "A rising in the Transvaal has recently imposed upon me the duty of *vindicating my authority.*"

These extracts are rather curious reading in face of the policy adopted by the Government, after our troops had been defeated.

III. THE CASE OF INDABEZIMBI

This is a case which came under my own notice. The complainant is now a tenant of my own. When Indabezimbi appeared before Mr. Cochrane and myself, his appearance fully bore out his description of the assault made upon him. We did everything in our power to help him to recover his son and his property, but without effect. The matter was fully reported to Sir Hercules Robinson and Sir E. Wood, and a question was asked on the subject in the House of Commons. I append Mr. Courtney's answer. This case, which is perfectly authentic, will prove instructive reading, as showing the treatment the Kafir must expect at the hands of the Boer, now that he is no longer protected by us. It must be remembered that the vast majority of such incidents are never heard of. The Kafirs suffer, and are still. The assault and robbery of Indabezimbi took place in Natal territory.

Statement of Indabezimbi

"I used to work on Mr. Robson's son's place, and on his death I went to Meyer's (in the Utrecht district of the Transvaal) about a year ago. I took all my property with me. There lived on the farm old Isaac Meyer, Solomon Meyer, who died during the war, young Isaac Meyer, Jan Meyer, Martinus Meyer, also a man called Cornelius, a 'bijwooner,' who loved in Solomon's place after he died.

"According to custom, I sent my son to work for old Isaac Meyer, as I lived on his place. When the war began all the Meyer family moved further into the Transvaal, my son going with them as herd. I went up to Klip River with them as driver, where the river forms the boundary between the Free State and Transvaal. I returned at once, leaving my son with the Meyers. He was a small boy about twelve years of age. At the termination of the war the Meyers sent for me to drive them down. I met them a day's journey this side of Klip River. I asked them where my son was. Old Isaac Meyer told me he had sent him to look for horses; he did not return; and another boy was sent who brought the horses. The horses were found close by. No one went to look for my son. I asked old Isaac Meyer for leave to go and offer a reward amongst the Kafirs for my son. He refused, saying I must drive him home, and then he would give me a pass to come back and look for him. On our arrival at the farm I and my wife again applied to old Isaac Meyer to be allowed to go and see about my son. He refused, saying I must first shear the sheep. I replied that he well knew that I could not shear sheep. I said, 'How can I work when my heart is sore for my son?' Meyer said again that I must wait awhile as the rivers were full. I said how could that matter, seeing that both in coming and going with the waggons we crossed no rivers? As he refused me a pass, I started without one to seek my son. On arrival at Mavovo's kraal I met my brother, who told me that I must go no further, or the Boers would shoot me. Having no pass I returned. On my return my wives told me that the Meyers had come every morning to look for me with guns to shoot me, telling them that 'it was now no longer the days for sjamboking (flogging with hide whips) the natives, but the days for shooting them.' On hearing this I collected my goods, and by morning had everything on the Natal side of the Buffalo River—on Natal ground. About mid-day Martinus Meyer overtook us by Degaza's kraal and asked me what I was doing on the Natal side of the river. I told him I was leaving for Natal, because I found it altogether too hot for me in the Transvaal. He said that if I came back he would make everything comfortable. I refused. He then attacked me with a knobkerrie, and would have killed me had not one of my wives, seeing that I was badly hurt, knocked him down with a piece of iron. Martinus then mounted his horse and galloped off. I then got on my horse and fled. My wives hid themselves. In the afternoon there came to the waggon Jan Meyer, Martinus Meyer, young Isaac Meyer, and the man called Cornelius. They hunted all about for us with the object of shooting us, as they told Degaza's Kafirs. My wives then saw them inspan the waggon and take everything away. I had a waggon, twelve oxen, four cows, and a mare, also a box containing two hundred pounds in gold, a telescope, clothes, and other things. My wives found the box broken on the ground and all the contents gone. Forty sacks of grain belonging to me were also taken. I was robbed of everything I had, with the exception of the horse I escaped on. The waggon was one I hired from my brother (a relation); the oxen were my own brother's. Eighty pounds of the money I got from the Standard Bank in Newcastle for oxen sold to the owner of the store on the Ingagane Drift. The rest I had accumulated in fees from doctoring. I am a doctor amongst my own people. I come now to ask you to allow me to settle on your land as a refugee.

"(Signed) Indabezimbi, his X mark.

"This statement was made by Indabezimbi at Hilldrop, Newcastle, Natal, on the Seventeenth of August, Eighteen hundred and eighty-one, in the presence of the undersigned witnesses.

"(Signed) H. Rider Haggard. A. H. D. Cochrane. J. H. Gay Roberts.

"N.B.—The outrage of which Indabezimbi has here given an account occurred within a week of the present date, August 17th, 1881."

Statement of the woman Nongena, Wife of Indabezimbi

"My master's name is Isaac Meyer; he lives in the Transvaal, south of Utrecht. We have lived on the farm about a year. On the farm lived also Jan Meyer, Martinus Meyer, and young Isaac Meyer, sons of old Isaac Meyer. There was also another man on the farm, whose name I do not know. When the waggon went up with the Meyers' family to the centre of the Transvaal, when the late war broke out, my husband drove old Isaac Meyer's waggon, and my son Ungazaan also went to drive on stock. After my husband had driven the waggon to its destination in the Transvaal he returned to the kraal, leaving his son Ungazaan with the Meyers. After the war was over my husband was sent for by the Meyers to drive back the waggons. On arrival of the Meyers at the farm I found my husband had returned, but my son was left behind. I asked my master where my son was; my master replied, 'He did not know, he had sent to boy to bring up horses, but he had not brought them.' Another boy was sent who brought the horses. He said he had not seen the boy Ungazaan since he left to look for the horses, as they had left the place the morning after the boy was missing. My husband asked for a pass to go back and look for the boy; Meyer refused, and my husband went without one to look for Ungazaan, my son. He returned without the boy, owing, he said, to the want of a pass. My husband dared not go into the country without a pass. During my husband's absence, the three sons of old Isaac Meyer, namely, Martinus, Jan, and Isaac, came every morning to search for my husband, saying, 'We will kill him, he leaves our work to go without our leave for look for the boy.' They came once with sjamboks, but afterwards with guns, saying they would kill him if they found him. On hearing this my husband said, 'We cannot then stay here longer.' He then went at once and borrowed a waggon and twelve oxen, and during the night we packed the waggon three times, and took three loads across the Buffalo River to Degaza's kraal, which is on Natal ground, forty sacks of grain, 200 pounds in a box, with clothes and other things, also mats and skins, and four head of cattle and a horse. All these things were at Degaza's kraal before sunrise the next morning. The Induna Kabane, at the magistrate's office at Newcastle, knows of the money, and from whence it came. All the money is our money.

"About mid-day on the day after the night we moved, Martinus came on horseback to us at Degaza's kraal, and I saw him beating my husband with a kerrie; he hit him also in the mouth with his fist. He hit my husband on the head with a kerrie; he beat my husband on the foot when he was trying to creep away in a hut, and would have killed him had not one of his wives named Camgagaan hit Martinus on the head with a piece of iron. Martinus, on recovery, rode away; my husband also fled on a horse.

"I with the other wives fled, and hid ourselves close by in the grass and stones. Presently we saw from our own hiding-place three white men, armed with guns, seeking for us. Their names were Martinus Meyer, Jan Meyer, and Isaac Meyer, all three sons of old Isaac Meyer. They sought us in vain. From our hiding-place we heard the waggon driven away; and later, when we went back to Degaza's kraal, they told us that the Meyers had inspanned the waggon, and had returned with it to the Transvaal side of the Buffalo River. The names of those who saw the Boers go away with the waggon are Gangtovo, Capaches, Nomatonga, Nomamane, and others. The Boers took away on the waggon that night all the last load we had brought over from the Transvaal, together with all our clothes; and some of the sacks first brought over were loaded up, all our cattle were taken, and our box was broken, and the 200 pounds taken away. We found the pieces of the box on the ground when we came from our hiding-place. We then fled. The people at Degaza's kraal told us that the Boers had said that they would return, and take away that which they were forced to leave behind when they took the first load. We have since heard from Degaza that the Boers came back again and took what remained of our property at Degaza's kraal. Degaza saw the Boers take the things himself.

"This is all I know of the facts. The assaults and robbery took place, as near as I can say, about fourteen days ago."

(Signed) Nongena, her X mark.

Gagaoola, also wife of Indabezimbi, states: — "I have heard all that Nongena has told you. Her words are true; I was present when the assault and robbery took place."

(Signed) Gagaoola, her X mark.

These statements were made to us at Hilldrop, Newcastle, Natal, on the Twenty-second of August, Eighteen hundred and eighty-one.

A. H. D. Cochrane.

H. Rider Haggard.

(Signed) Ayah, her X mark, Interpreter.

Indabezimbi

"Mr. Alderman Fowler asked the Under Secretary of State for the Colonies, whether the British Resident at Pretoria had brought under the notice of the Transvaal Government the circumstances of an outrage committed in August last, by a party of Boers, on the person and property of a Kafir named Indabezimbi, who was at that time residing in Natal; and whether any steps had been taken by the authorities of the Transvaal either to institute a judicial inquiry into the matter, or to surrender the offenders to the Government of Natal.

"Mr. Courtney.—On the 13th of October the British Resident reported that, according to promise, the Government has caused an investigation to be made at Utrecht, and informed him that the result was somewhat to invalidate the statement of Indabezimbi; but that the documents connected with the investigation at Utrecht would speedily be forwarded to him with a view to correspondence through him with the Natal Government. No further communication has been received. It must be observed that, in the absence of any extradition convention, a judicial inquiry in this case is practically impossible, the outrage, whatever it was, having been committed in Natal, and the offenders being in the Transvaal. Her Majesty's Government are taking active steps to re-establish a system of extradition, in pursuance of Article 29, of the Convention. The despatches on this subject will be given to Parliament when the correspondence is completed."

IV. A BOER ADVERTISEMENT

It may be interesting to Englishmen to know what treatment is meted out to such of their fellow-countrymen as have been bold enough, or forced by necessity, to remain in the Transvaal since the retrocession. The following is a translation of an advertisement recently published in the "Volkstem," a Transvaal paper, and is a fair sample of what "loyalists" have to expect.

"WARNING

"We, the undersigned Burghers of the Ward Aapies river, hereby warn all loyal persons who have registered themselves with the British Resident, that they are not to come into our houses, or into our farms, and still less to offer to shake hands. They can greet us at a distance on the road *like Kafirs*, and those who act contrary to this notice can expect the result."

Presumably "the result" that the Englishman who takes the liberty to offer to shake hands with a Boer can expect, is to be beaten or murdered. This notice is signed by the Justice of the Peace or "Veld Cornet" of the district. Anybody who knows the estimation in which a Kafir is held by the Boers will understand its peculiar insolence.

V. "TRANSVAAL'S" LETTER TO THE "STANDARD"

The following letter appeared in the issue of the "Standard" of the 31st May 1882, and is dated Pretoria, 27th April. It is signed "Transvaal," probably because the author, were he to put his name at the foot of so candid a document, would find himself in much the same position as that occupied at the present moment by an Irish landlord who has outraged the susceptibilities of the Land League. He would be rigorously "boycotted," and might, in the event of any disturbance, be made into a target. The Transvaal Boers are very sensitive to criticism, especially where their native policy is concerned. I take the liberty to reprint the letter here, partly because I feel sure that I will be forwarding the wishes of the writer by assisting to give publicity to his facts, and partly on account of the striking and recent confirmation it affords, on every point, to my remarks on the same subject:—

"Sir,—In calling your attention to what is going on on the south-western border of the Transvaal, I may possibly tell you of some things which you may already have heard of, for in the present isolated condition of the country, without telegraphs, and with a very imperfect postal system, added to the jealousy of the Boer Government in keeping their actions secret from the outside world, it is not only very difficult to get at the truth of what is happening, but the people in one portion of the country are in many cases totally ignorant of what is going on in another. Nevertheless, I feel it incumbent on me to call the attention of the English people, through your widely circulating journal, to what has come under my observation with reference to the disgraceful native war which is, and has been, raging on the south-west border of this country.

"During the late Boer war, you may be aware of the fact that a very large number, if not all, of the natives, were strongly in favour of the English Government, and only awaited the signal from it to rush upon their old oppressors. But the natives, although forbidden by the English Government from joining with them against the Boers (it is hardly necessary to say that had it not been for this the war would have had a very different ending), nevertheless afforded an asylum and protection to the lives and property of refugee Englishmen and loyalists. Notable among these natives was a Chief named Montsiou, whose tribe is situated just outside the borders of the Transvaal to the south-west. This Chief and his people received numbers of refugees who fled to them for protection from the rapacity of the Boers, and watched over them and their property throughout the war. For this offence the Boers swore to be revenged on him, and hardly was the war finished when they commenced commandeering in the Potchefstroom district, under the pretence of protecting their borders, but with the ostensible purpose of inflicting chastisement on this loyal Chief; and, the better to effect their purpose, they allied themselves with a neighbouring Chief, who had some old grudge against him, and, by promises of assistance and hopes of plunder, induced him to commence a war, under cover of which they could join, and thus effect the purpose they had in view.

"The Chiefs whom the Boers had instigated to harass Montsiou got the worst of it, and the action of the Boers, who were actively commandeering in the Potchefstroom (district?), under Commandant

Cronge, was brought to the notice of the Royal Commission through complaints made by loyal Boers, and resulted in an inquiry into the subject, which showed that his opponent was the aggressor, and was acting under the advice of and assistance from the Boers. The Royal Commission managed to patch matters up, but no sooner were their labours over, and the country fairly handed over to the Boers, than Moshete and Masouw, instigated by the Boers, commenced again harassing Montsiou, with the avowed purpose of bringing on a war, and so far succeeded as to oblige Montsiou to take up arms in self-defence.

"From that time forward the war has gone on increasing in dimensions, until other Chiefs have been drawn into it, and the Boer volunteers fighting against Montsiou and Monkoroane are almost equal in numbers to the natives. The Boers, while doing all they can to crush Montsiou on account of the protection he afforded loyalists during the late war against the English Government, are careful not to do it in an official way, because that might cause trouble with England, whereas, by aiding and assisting it privately, they could do quite as much without incurring responsibility. You may naturally ask how I know all this, and what proofs I can advance in support of it. Some time after the Royal Commission had left the country, and the war had commenced again, Piet Joubert, who is Commandant-General, went down to the border with the object of putting an end to the war. This, I presume, he did for the sake of appearances, for it is well known that he entertains a strong hatred against those natives who in any way showed a partiality for British rule; and when it is remembered that Piet Joubert's journey did not result in a cessation of hostilities, but in an increase, and that ever since his journey the war has increased in area and in numbers, and that in no single instance has a Boer volunteer been prevented from crossing the border, or ammunition for use against Montsiou been stopped, the sincerity of his intentions may well be doubted.

"Then, again, officers in the Boer Jagers went about Pretoria endeavouring to obtain volunteers to fight against Montsiou, saying that they were to have some months' leave from the Government, and that subscriptions would be raised to assist those men who had no private means. This took place almost immediately after Piet Joubert's return from the border, and while he was in Pretoria, and the general opinion was that he was at the bottom of it; but as it became rather more public than was intended, the British Resident was obliged to take notice of it, and the result was that the Boers, though in general treating the British Resident with little consideration, thought it wisest to carry on their operations in a more private manner, more especially as their object could be attained quite as effectually in this way.

"While the Boers are assisting Moshete and Masouw by every means in their power, with the sole object of crushing Montsiou and Monkoroane, another loyal Chief, the Colonial Government, no doubt under instructions from home, are doing their best to prevent volunteers or ammunition reaching them, and have already rested men in Kimberley, who have been trying to raise volunteers to go to their assistance.

"The result of this is, that the loyal Chiefs are suffering under a double disadvantage; for while their enemies are receiving every assistance, they are blockaded on all sides, and, through the action of the English Government in preventing them obtaining assistance, are rapidly falling a prey to the Boers. Those only who know anything of the Boer method of warfare against natives will know what this means; and in spite of the Boer Government doing all they can to keep things secret, horrible tales of the cruelties perpetrated by them leak out occasionally.

"It seems to me a disgraceful thing, and a stain on the honour of England, that these loyal Chiefs and their tribes should be robbed, plundered, and shot down like dogs, simply because they afforded protection to the lives and property of Englishmen during the late war, and yet these things are going on and are being perpetrated on the border of England's Colonies. If England will not step in and insist on the Boers putting a stop to this murderous war, then in God's name let her not prevent these poor natives from obtaining ammunition and assistance to enable them to defend their country. They succoured our countrymen, and if we cannot succour them, the least we can do is not to interfere to prevent them from protecting themselves!

"Of course, it suits the Boer Government to make out that they have nothing to do with the war, and cannot prevent Boer Volunteers from fighting these Chiefs; and so long as the English Government rests satisfied with these answers, so long will this disgraceful state of things go on. Let the English Government be firm, however, and insist on the Boers taking no part in this war, and it will cease—a sure proof that the Boer Government have the power to stop it if they have the will.

"Not only are the Boers wreaking vengeance upon Montsiou and Monkoroane, but a friend of theirs, a Chief of the name of Kalafin, whose tribe is situated in the Zeerust district, Transvaal, has been robbed by them of everything he possessed. This Chief had English sympathies; and as he presumed to build a wall round his town he gave the Boers the excuse they wanted. He was ordered to take the wall down, which he did, at the same time proving that he only built it to prevent his cattle straying among the huts. He was then ordered to come to Pretoria, which he did accordingly. He was then ordered to pay a fine of three thousand cattle, which fine he paid. No sooner was this done than the Boers, bent on his ruin, raised the fine to ten thousand head. The poor Chief in vain pleaded his inability to pay. It was the old story of the wolf and the lamb. Because he couldn't pay, the Boers construed it into an act of disobedience, and at once ordered their men to go in and take everything he possessed. This tribe is small and weak, which the Boers well knew. Eye-witnesses of what followed say it was a heartrending sight. The women, with children in their arms, pleaded in vain to the Boers to leave them something or they would starve, but the latter only jeered at them. What these poor people will do God only knows, for the Boers stripped them of every living thing they possessed, and with the proceeds of this robbery the Boer Government intend to replenish their coffers.

"The British Resident, Mr. Hudson, it is believed, shuts his eyes to many things. No doubt his is a difficult position to fill; and doubtless he is aware that, if he reports everything to the English Government, the Boers have it in their power to make his position anything but a pleasant one. In any case, the English portion of the community here, while admitting his good qualities socially, have little confidence in him officially.

"My object in writing this letter, however, is not so much to show what a disgraceful state the Government is in, as to try and awaken sympathy in the breasts of my countrymen for the cause of these loyal Chiefs. While the Government are writing despatches to the British Resident, these Chiefs and their people are being ruined past remedying."

VI. A VISIT TO THE CHIEF SECOCOENI[*]

*[*] This paper was written just before the Annexation of the
Transvaal in 1877.*

Towards the end of March I had occasion to visit the Basuto chief
Secocoeni, in his native stronghold beyond the Loolu Berg, a range to
the north-east of Pretoria, about 250 miles away; and as this journey
was typical of travelling in the wilds of South Africa, an account of it
may prove interesting.

It is perhaps necessary to explain, for the benefit of those who
are not acquainted with South African politics, that Secocoeni is the
chieftain who has been at war with the late Transvaal Republic, who
drove back its forces, capturing some 7000 head of cattle. It is from
this raid that the present state of affairs has arisen; so that this obscure
chief, with his 9000 warriors, has materially affected the future
destinies of South Africa. Negotiations of peace had been set on foot,
and it was in connection with these delicate matters that the journey
was to be undertaken.

"Going to Secocoeni at this time of year! Ah!" said one gentleman.
"Well, look here. I sent five natives through that country in this same
month (March) last year; out of those five, three died of the fever,
and the other two just got through with their lives. I only tell you,
you know, that you may take precautions. This is a bad fever year."
However, fever or no fever, we had to go. As it was necessary to travel
rapidly, we could only take four riding-horses, three for ourselves
and the fourth for a Zulu named "Lankiboy," who also led a pack-
horse, and carried an enormous "knob-kerry," or shillelagh, stuck in
his button-hole, as though it were a wedding-bouquet.

Behind our saddles were fastened our saddle-bags, containing a
change of clothing, and in front we strapped a rug and a mackintosh.
Our commissariat consisted of four tins of potted ham, and our
medicine-chest of some quinine, Cockle's pills, and a roll of sticking-
plaster, which, with a revolver and a hunting-knife or two, completed
our equipment.

We knew little of our route save that our destination lay due
east, so due east we steered. After riding for about twenty miles,
and crossing the Mahaliesburg range, that stretches away north for

hundreds of miles, we came to a Boer's house, where we off-saddled to feed our horses. It must be understood that the Boers were the one certain difficulty, and one of the possible dangers, to be encountered on our road, for at no time are they are pleasant people to deal with, and just now they are remarkably unpleasant towards Englishmen.

For instance, at this first house, we managed to get some forage for our horses, before our scowling host found out who we were, but not a bit could we get to eat. "Have you no bread, myn Heer?" "We have no bread to spare." "Have you any eggs?" "We have no eggs." "Can you let us have some milk?" "Susan, have you got any milk to give these carles (fellows)?" Finally, we succeeded in buying three cups of milk for a shilling, "as a favour," and that is all we got from sunrise to sunset.

Riding, on empty stomachs, for another sixty miles over the plains, we came to a Boer's house where we had to sleep. Just before we reached the door, I noticed what I have often seen since, some graves in a row, with heaps of stones piled over them. It appears that these people do not care about bring buried in consecrated ground, their only anxiety being to be put in a coffin, and they are generally laid to rest near to their doors. There is neither railing nor headstone, and no trees or flowers, those green emblematic garments with which civilised people try to hide the ugliness of death. I remember once seeing several graves within two or three yards of the public road, so that in a year or so the waggons will be rumbling over the heads of those who lie beneath.

When you ride up to a Boer's house, the etiquette is to wait until some member of the family asks you to off-saddle, and then you must go in and shake hands with every one, a most disagreeable custom. None of the women—who are very plain—rise to meet one, they just hold out their hands. This house was a fair specimen of the sort of habitation indulged in by the ordinary Boer. The main room was about eighteen feet square, with that kind of door which allows the upper half to open whilst the lower remains shut, such as is used in stables in England. The flooring is made of cow-dung, into which peach stones are trodden at the threshold, in order to prevent its wearing away. The furniture consists of a deal table and some chairs, rather nearly made of strips of hide fastened to a wooden frame. There is no ceiling, but only beams, to which are fastened strips of "biltong," or game's flesh, dried in the sun. Out of this room open one or two more, in which the whole family sleep, without much attempt at privacy.

Sitting about the room were two or three young mothers, without stockings and nursing babies; in the corner, on a chair, made twice as large as any of the others, reposed the mother of the family, a woman of large size. The whole house was pervaded by a sickly odour, like that of a vault, whilst the grime and filth of it baffle description. And this was the place we had to eat and sleep in. However, there was no help for it; the only thing to do was to light one's pipe, and smoke. After an hour or so, supper was put upon the table, consisting of a bowl full of boiled bones, a small stack of mealie cobs, and, be it added, some good bread-and-butter. The eating arrangements of these people are certainly very trying. The other day we had to eat our dinner in a Boer's house, with a reeking ox-hide, just torn from the animal, lying on the floor beside us, together with portions of the poor beast's head whose flesh we were eating. However, on this occasion we were spared the ox-hide, and, being very hungry, managed to put up with the other discomforts. After a long grace our suppers were served out to us. I remember I got an enormous bone with but little flesh on it, which, if I may form an opinion from its great size and from a rapid anatomical survey, must have been the tibia of an ox. A young Boer sat opposite to me—a wonderful fellow. He got through several mealie cobs (and large ones too) whilst I was eating half a one. His method was peculiar, and shows what practice can do. He shoved a mealie cob into his mouth, gave it a bite and a wrench, just like one of those patent American threshing machines, brought the cob out perfectly clear of grain, and took another. After the supper was over, we had another long grace ending with: "voor spijze en drunk de Heer ik dank" (for food and drink the Lord I thank).

After supper we went outside in order to escape the feet-washing ceremony (all in the same water) which this "simple pastoral people" are said to indulge in, and which they might expect the "uitlander" (stranger) to enter into with enthusiasm. When we came back, we found that the women—who, by-the-by, do not eat till the men have finished—had done their meal, and gone to bed, having first made us up a luxurious couch on the floor, consisting of a filthy feather-bed, and an equally filthy blanket. My heart misgave me when I looked at that bed. It may have been fancy, but once or twice I thought it moved. However, there was no choice, unless we chose to sit up all night; so in we got, looking for all the world like three big sun-burned dolls put to bed by some little girl. I, as the youngest, blew out the light, and then!—from every side *they* came. Up one's arms, up one's legs, down one's back they scampered, till life became a burden. Sleep was impossible; one could only lie awake and calculate the bites per minute, and the quantity of blood one would lose before daybreak. Cold as it was, I would have turned out and slept in the veldt, only my rug was over my two companions as well as myself, so I could not take it. I have slept in a good many different places, and in very fairly uncomfortable places, but I never had such a night before.

At the first grey dawn of morning the old "frau" came stumbling out of the bedroom, and sat down without ceremony in her big chair. Waiting till she thought that we had reached a sufficiently advanced stage in our toilette—and her idea of what that was must have been a strange one—she shouted out to her daughters that they could "com," and in they all came. Very glad were we when we had paid our bill, which was a heavy one, and were in the saddle once more, riding through the cold morning mist that lay in masses on all the ridges of the hills like snow on mountains.

It was needful to start early, for we had more than sixty miles to cover, and our ponies had done a good journey the day before. The work that one can get out of these ponies is marvellous. There was my pony, "Mettle," who had my eleven stone to carry, to say nothing of the saddle, heavy saddle-bags, and a roll of rugs, who came in at the end of his journey as fresh as paint. We cantered easily over the great high-veldt prairies, now and then passing clumps of trees, outposts of the bush-veldt. These enormous plains, notwithstanding their dreary vastness, have a wild beauty of their own. The grass is what is called sour grass, and has a peculiar blue tinge, but stock do not like it so well as the low-veldt grass, which is sweeter, and fattens them more quickly, though it does not put them in such good fettle. The rock here is all white sandstone, and thinly overlaps an enormous bed of coal, cropping up from beneath the water-washed surface. At this time of year there are very few beasts or birds of any sort to be seen, though in the winter the veldt is one moving mass of "trek" or migratory game.

Our destination that day was Botsabelo, the most important mission-station, and one of the very few successful ones, in South-Eastern Africa. As we neared it, the country gradually broke into hills of peculiar and beautiful formation, which rendered the last two hours of our ride, in the dark, through an unknown country, rather a difficult job. However, we stumbled through streams, and over boulders, and about nine o'clock were lucky enough to come right upon the station, where we were most kindly received by Dr. Merensky. The station itself stands on the brow of a hill surrounded by gardens and orchards; beneath it lie slope and mountain, stream and valley, over which are dotted numbers of kraals, to say nothing of three or four substantial houses occupied by the assistant missionary and German artisans. Near Dr. Merensky's house stands the church, by far the best I have seen in the Transvaal, and there is also a store with some well-built workshops around it. All the neighbouring country belongs to the station, which is, in fact, like a small independent State, 40,000 acres in extent. On a hill-top overshadowing the station, are placed the fortifications, consisting of thick walls running in a circle with upstanding towers, in which stand one or two cannon; but it all reminds one more of an old Norman keep, with its village clustered in its protecting shadow, than of a modern mission establishment.

Dr. Merensky commenced his labours in Secocoeni's country, but was forced to fly from thence by night, with his wife and new-born baby, to escape being murdered by that Chief's orders, who, like most Kafir potentates, has an intense aversion to missionaries. Twelve years ago he established this station, and, gathering his scattered converts around him, defied Secocoeni to drive him thence. Twice that Chief has sent out a force to sweep him away, and murder his people, and twice they have come and looked, and, like false Sextus, turned back again. The Boers, too, have more than once threatened to destroy him, for it is unpleasant to them to have so intelligent a witness in their midst, but they have never dared to try. The place is really impregnable to Basutus and Boers; Zulus might carry it, with their grand steady rush, but it would be at a terrible sacrifice of life. In fact, Dr. Merensky has been forced, by the pressure of circumstances, to teach his men the use of a rifle, as well as the truths of Christianity; to trust in God, but also to "keep their powder dry." At a few minutes' notice he can turn out 200 well-armed natives, ready for offence or defence; and the existence of such a stronghold is of great advantage to the few English in the neighbourhood, for the Boers know well that should they attack them they might draw down the vengeance of Dr. Merensky's formidable body of Christian soldiers.

We only passed one night at Botsabelo, and next morning went on to Middelburg, or Nazareth, which is an hour's ride from the station. Here, too, we met with a warm welcome from the handful of English residents, but we were eager to push on as rapidly as possible, for our kind friends told us that it would be impossible to proceed to Secocoeni's on horseback, because of the deadly nature of the country for horses. So we had to hire an ox-waggon, which they provisioned for us, and, much to our disgust (as we were pressed for time), were obliged to fall back on that dilatory method of travelling.

We decided that we would take the three oldest and least valuable horses with us, in order to proceed with them from Fort Weeber, which was our next point, to Secocoeni's town, whither waggons could not reach. Few English readers are aware that there is a mysterious disease among horses in South Africa, peculiar to the country, called "horse-sickness." During the autumn season it carries off thousands of horses annually, though some are good and others bad years—a bad fever year being generally a bad horse-sickness year also, and *vice versa*. A curious feature about it is, that as the veldt gets "tamed," that is, fed off by domesticated animals, the sickness gradually disappears. No cure has yet been discovered for it, and very few horses pull through—perhaps, five per cent. These are called "salted horses," and are very valuable; as, although they are not proof against the disease, they are not so liable to take it. A salted horse may be known by the peculiar looseness and roughness of his skin, and also by a certain unmistakable air of depression, as though he felt that the responsibilities of life pressed very heavily upon him. He is like a man who has dearly bought his experience; he can never forget the terrible lesson taught in the buying.

On the fourth day from our start we left Middelburg, and, taking a north-east course from this outpost of civilisation, overtook the waggon, and camped, after a twenty miles' trek, just on the edge of the bush-veldt. We had two young Boers to drive our waggons—terrible louts. However, they understood how to drive a waggon, and whilst one of them drove, the other would sit for hours, with a vacant stare on his face, thinking. It is a solemn fact that, from the time we left Middelburg till the time we returned, neither of those fellows touched water, that is, to wash themselves. The only luxury in the shape of comforts of the toilette which they allowed themselves was a comb with a brass back, carefully tied to the roof of the waggon with two strips of ox-hide thick enough to have held a hundredweight of lead. I don't think they ever used it—it was too great a luxury for general use—but they would occasionally untie it and look at it. Our own outfit in the waggon was necessarily scanty, consisting of a few iron pots and plates, a kettle, some green blankets, a lantern, and an old anti-friction grease-can used for water, which gave it a fine flavour of waggon-wheels. We also had a "cartle," or wooden frame, across which were stretched strips of hide fitted into the waggon about two feet above the floor, and intended to sleep on; but the less said about that the better.

After we left the great high-veldt plains, over which the fresh breeze was sweeping, we dropped down into a beautiful bush-clad valley with mountains on either side. It was like making a sudden descent into the tropics. Not a breath of wind stirred the trees, and the sun shone with a steady burning heat. Scarcely a sound broke the silence, save the murmur of the river we crossed and recrossed, the occasional pipe of a bird, and the melancholy cry, half sigh, half bark, of an old baboon, who was swinging himself along, indignant at our presence.

If the sights and sounds were beautiful, the sun was hot, and the road fearful, and we were indeed glad when we reached "Whitehead's Cobalt Mine," and were most kindly received by the gentlemen who superintend the works. The house used to belong to some Boer, who had deserted the place, but left behind him a beautiful orchard of orange and peach trees. The place is very feverish and unhealthy, and the white ants so troublesome that everything has to be stood in sardine tins full of ashes.

On our way from the house we went to see the cobalt mine, which is on a hillside a mile away. It has only been established about three years, and has existed hitherto under the greatest difficulties as regards labour, transport, machinery, danger from surrounding native tribes, &c.; but it has already, the proprietor informed me, reduced the price of cobalt—the blue dye used to colour such things as the willow-pattern plates—by one-half in the English market, bringing it down from somewhere about 140 pounds to 80 pounds a ton. We were very much astonished to see the amount of work which had been done, as we expected to find a pit such as the Kafirs work for copper, but instead of that there was a large slanting shaft quite a hundred yards long, to say nothing of various openings out of it following branch leads of ore. There is also a vertical shaft one hundred feet deep, through which the ore comes up, and by which one can ascend and descend in a bucket. After we emerged from this awful hole, we went into another, a drive running straight into the mountain for more than three hundred feet, following a vein of black oxide of cobalt, which is much more valuable than the ore; and, though the vein is rarely more than a foot in thickness, pays very well. Leaving the mine, we rode on past some old Kafir copper-workings— circular pits—which must have been abandoned, to judge from their appearance, a hundred years ago, till we came to the banks of the great "Olifants'" or "Elephants'" river. This magnificent stream, though it is unnavigable owing to frequent rapids, has stretches miles long, down which a man-of-war could steam, and after its junction with the Elands' River it grows larger and larger till, pursuing a north-east course, it at length falls into the mighty Limpopo. It is a very majestic but somewhat sluggish stream, and its water is not very good. You cannot see the river till you are right upon it, owing to the great trees with which its steep banks are fringed, and in the early morning it is quite hidden from bank to bank by a dense mass of billows of white mist, indescribably strange to look upon.

But, beautiful as this country is, it is most unhealthy for man and beast. The close odour, the long creeping lines of mist, the rich rank vegetation, the steady heat of day and night, all say one word, "fever," and fever of the most virulent type. The traveller through this sort of country is conscious of a latent fear lest he should some day begin to feel hot when he ought to be cold, and cold when he ought to be hot, and so be stricken down, to rise prematurely old, or perhaps to die, and be buried in a lonely grave covered with stones to keep off the jackals. We were travelling in the very worst fever-month, March, when the summer vegetation is commencing to rot, and throw off its poisonous steam. What saved us here and afterwards, at Secocoeni's, was our temperate living, hard exercise, and plenty of quinine and tobacco-smoke.

All the country through which we were passing is good game-veldt, but we saw very little and killed nothing. This was chiefly owing to the fact that we did not dare go out of hearing of the waggon-wheels, for fear of getting lost in the bush, a thing very easily done. A few years back this veldt swarmed with big game, with elephants and giraffes, and they are even now occasionally seen. We managed now and again to get a glimpse of some of the beautiful "Impala" buck, or of a small lot of blue wilderbeestes vanishing between the trees, like a troop of wild horses. There are still plenty of lions about, but we did not hear any: whether it was that they had gone to the high-veldt after the cattle, or that they do not roar so much in summer, I do not know. Perhaps it is as well that we did not, for the roar of a lion is very generally followed by what the Dutch call a "skrech." After roaring once or twice to wake the cattle up, and make them generally uneasy, the lion stations himself about twenty yards to the windward of the waggon. The oxen get wind of him and promptly "skrech," that is, break their rims and run madly into the veldt. This is just what the lion wants, for now he can pick out a fat ox and quietly approach him from the other side till he is within springing distance. He then jumps upon him, crushes his neck with one bite, and eats him at his leisure.

And so we trekked on through the sunrise, through the burning mid-day and glowing sunsets, steering by the sun and making our own road; now through tambouki grass higher than the oxen, and now through dense bush, till at length, one day, we said good-bye to the Olifants' just where the Elands' River flows into it, and turned our faces eastward. This course soon brought us on to higher ground and away from the mimosa, which loves the low, hot valleys, into the region of the sugar bush, which thrives upon the hill-sides. This sugar bush is a very handsome and peculiar plant, with soft thick leaves, standing about twenty feet high. It bears a brush-like flower, each of which in the Cape Colony contains half a teaspoonful of delicious honey; but, curiously enough, though in other respects the tree is precisely similar, this is not the case in the Transvaal or Natal. At the proper season the Cape farmers go out with buckets and shake the flowers till they have collected sufficient honey to last them for the winter, a honey more fragrant than that made by bees.

After a long ride over the open, which must once have been thickly populated, to judge from the number of remains of kraals, we came at length to Fort Weeber. The fort is very badly situated in the hollow of a plain, and so surrounded by fine hills that it is entirely commanded. It consists of a single sod wall about two feet thick and five high, capped with loose stones, whilst at two of the corners stand, on raised platforms, a six-pounder and a three-pounder Whitworth gun. Inside the wall are built rows of mud huts, which are occupied by the garrison, leaving an open square, in the midst of which is placed the magazine. We found the garrison in a wretched condition. They have not received any pay except Government "good-fors" (promissory notes, generally known as "good-for-nothings"), so they are in a state of abject poverty; whilst they are rendered harmless as regards offensive operations, by the death, from horse-sickness, of eighty-two of the ninety horses they owned. However, the officers and garrison gave us a very grand reception. As we rode up, they fired a salute of twelve guns, and then, after we had dismounted and been received by the officers, we were taken through a lane made by the garrison drawn up in a double line, and, just as we got to the middle, "bang" went the eighty rifles over our heads. Then an address was read (the volunteers are great people for addresses), but a more practical welcome soon followed in the shape of a good dinner.

Next morning we started, a party of seven, including the interpreter, to ride over the Loolu Berg to Secocoeni's, a distance of about thirty-eight miles.

For the first five miles we passed through the most curious granite formation, a succession of small hills entirely composed of rounded boulders of granite, weighing from five to 1000 tons, and looking exactly like piles of gigantic snow-balls hurled together by some mighty hand. The granite formation prevails in all this part of the country, and individual boulders sometimes take very curious shapes; for instance, in the bush-veldt we passed a great column towering high above the trees, composed of six boulders getting smaller and smaller from the base up, and each accurately balanced on the one beneath it. Then we crossed the range of hills which overlooks the fort, and passing Secocoeni's old kraal where he used to live before he retreated to his fastnesses, we arrived at a great alluvial valley nine miles broad, on the other side of which rises the Loolu. It was on this plain that the only real fight between the volunteers and Secocoeni's men took place, when the former managed to get between the Basutus and the hills, and shot them down like game, killing over 200 men. Leaving the battle-field, where the skeletons still lie, a little to our right, we crossed the plain and came to the foot of the Loolu, all along the base of which stand neat villages inhabited by Secocoeni's people. Some of these villages have been burnt by the volunteers, and the remainder are entirely deserted, their inhabitants having built fresh huts among the rocks in almost inaccessible places. The appearance of these white huts peeping out all over the black rocks was very curious, and reminded one of the Swiss chalets.

By the stream that runs along past the villages we off-saddled, as both ourselves and our horses were nearly exhausted by the burning heat; but as there was not much time to lose, after a short rest we started off again, and rode on over a bed of magnetic iron lying on the ground in great lumps of almost pure metal, until we came to a stretch of what looked remarkably like gold-bearing quartz, and then to a limestone formation. The whole country is evidently rich beyond measure in minerals. All this time we were passing through scenery inexpressibly wild and grand, and when we had arrived at the highest spot of the pass, it reached a climax of savage beauty. About forty miles in front of us towered up another magnificent range of blue-tinged mountains known as the Blue Berg, whilst all around us rose great bush-clad hills, opening away in every direction towards gorgeous-coloured valleys. The scene was so grand and solemn that I do not think it lies in the power of words to describe it.

Here we had to dismount to descend a most fearful precipitous path consisting of boulders piled together in the wildest confusion, from one to another of which we had to jump, driving the horses before us. Half-way down we off-saddled to rest ourselves, and as we did so we noticed that the gall was running from one of the horses' noses. We knew too well what was the matter, and so left him there to die during the night. This horse was by far the finest we had with us, and his owner used to boast that the poor beast had often carried him, a heavy man, from his house to Pretoria, a distance of nearly ninety miles, in one day. He was also a "salted" horse. It is a curious thing that the sickness generally kills the best horses first.

After a short rest we started on again, and at the end of another hour reached the bottom of the pass. From thence we rode along a gulley, that alternately narrowed and widened, till at length it brought us right on to Secocoeni's beautiful, fever-stricken home.

All three of us had seen a good deal of scenery in different parts of the world, and one of the party was intimately acquainted with the finest spots in South Africa, but we were forced to admit that we had never seen anything half so lovely as Secocoeni's valley. We had seen grander views, indeed the scene from the top of the pass was grander, but never anything that so nearly approached perfection in detail. Beautiful it was, beautiful beyond measure, but it was the sort of beauty under whose veil are hidden fever and death. And so we pushed on, through the still hot eventide, till at length we came to the gates of the town, where we found "Makurupiji," Secocoeni's "mouth" or prime minister, who had evidently been informed of our coming by his spies waiting to receive us.[*]

[*] Makurupiji committed suicide after the town had been stormed, preferring death to imprisonment.

Conducted by this grandee, we went on past the Chief's kraals, down to the town, whence flocked men, women, and children, to look on the white lords; all in a primitive state of dress, consisting of a strip of skin tied round the middle, and the women with their hair powdered with some preparation of iron, which gave it a metallic blue tinge.

At length we stopped just opposite a beautiful fortified kopje[*] perforated by secret caves where the ammunition of the tribe is hidden. No stranger is allowed to enter these caves, or even to ascend the kopje, though they do not object to one's inspecting some of the other fortifications. Dismounting from our wearied horses, we passed through a cattle kraal and came into the presence of "Swasi," Secocoeni's uncle, a fat old fellow who was busily engaged in braying a skin. Nearly every male Basutu one meets, be he high or low, is braying a hide of some sort, either by rubbing or by masticating it. It is a curious sight to come across some twenty of these fellows, every one of them twisting or chewing away.

[*] Afterwards stormed in the attack on Secocoeni's town by Sir Garnet Wolseley.

Swasi was a sort of master of the household; his duty it was to receive strangers and see that they were properly looked after; so, after shaking hands with us furiously (he was a wonderful fellow to shake hands), he conducted us to our hut. It stood in a good-sized courtyard beautifully paved with a sort of concrete of limestone which looked very clean and white, and surrounded by a hedge of reeds and sticks tightly tied together, inside which ran a slightly raised bench, also made of limestone. The hut itself was neatly thatched, the thatch projecting several feet, so as to form a covering to a narrow verandah that ran all round it. Inside it was commodious, and ornamented after the Egyptian style with straight and spiral lines, painted on with some kind of red ochre, and floored with a polished substance. Certainly these huts are as much superior to those of the Zulus as those who dwell in them are inferior to that fine race. What the Basutus gain in art and handiness they lose in manliness and gentlemanly feeling.

We had just laid ourselves down on the grass mats in the courtyard—for it was too hot to go into the hut—thoroughly exhausted with our day's work and the heat, when in came two men, each of them dragging a fine indigenous sheep. They were accompanied by Makurupiji, who brought us a message from Secocoeni to the effect that he, the Chief, sent to greet us, the great Chiefs; that he sent us also a morsel to eat, lest we should be hungry in his house. It was but a morsel—it should have been an ox, for great Chiefs should eat much meat—but he himself was pinched with hunger, his belt was drawn very tight by the Boers. He was poor, and so his gift was poor; still, he would see if to-morrow he could find a beast that had something besides the skin on its bones, that he might offer it to us. After this magniloquent address the poor animals were trundled out by the other gate to have their throats cut.

After getting some supper and taking our quinine, we turned in and slept that night in the best way that the heat would let us, rising next morning with the vain hope of getting a bathe. Of all the discomforts we experienced at Secocoeni's, the scarcity and badness of the water was the worst. Bad water, when you are in a hotbed of fever, is a terrible privation. And so we had to go unwashed, with the exception of having a little water poured over our hands out of gourds. We must have presented a curious sight at breakfast that morning. Before us knelt a sturdy Kafir, holding a stick in each hand, on which were respectively speared a leg and a side of mutton, from which we cut off great hunks with our hunting-knives, and, taking them in our fingers, devoured them like beasts of prey. If we got a bit we did not like, our mode of dispensing of it was simple and effective. We threw it to one of the natives standing round us, among whom was the heir-apparent, who promptly gobbled it up.

Breakfast finished, a message came from Secocoeni asking for spirits to drink. But we were not to be taken in in this way, for we knew well that if we sent the Chief spirits we should get no business done that day, and we did not care to run the risk of fever by stopping longer than we could help; so we sent back a message to the effect that business must come first and spirits afterwards. The head men, who brought this message, said that they could perfectly understand our objection, as far as Secocoeni and ourselves were concerned, since we had to talk, but as they had only to sit still and listen there could be no possible objection to their having something to drink. This argument was ingenious, but we did not see the force of it, as our stock of spirits, which we had brought more for medicine than anything else, was very limited. Still, we were obliged to promise them a "tot" after the talking was over, in order to keep them civil.

Our message had the desired effect, for presently Secocoeni sent to say that it was now time to talk, and that his head men would lead us to him. So we started up, accompanied by "Makurupiji," "Swasi," and "Galook," the general of his forces, a fat fellow with a face exactly like a pig. The sun beat down with such tremendous force that, though we had only three-quarters of a mile to walk, we felt quite tired by the time we reached the Chief's kraals. Passing through several cattle kraals, we came to a shed under which sat the heir-apparent dressed in a gorgeous blanket with his court around him. Leaving him, we entered an inner cattle kraal, where, in one corner, stood a large, roughly-built shed, under the shade of which squatted over a hundred of the head men of the tribe, gathered together by Secocoeni to "witness."[*]

[*] *As each chief came up to the meeting-place he would pass before the enclosure where Secocoeni was sitting and salute him, by softly striking the hands together, and saying something that sounded like "Marema."*

Opening out of this kraal was the chief's private enclosure, where stood his huts. As we drew near, Secocoeni, who had inspired such terror into the bold Burghers of the Republic, the chief of nine thousand warriors, the husband of sixty-four wives, the father of a hundred children, rose from the ox-hide on which he was seated, under the shade of a tree, and came to the gate to meet us. And a queer sight this potentate was as he stood there shaking hands through the gate. Of middle age, about forty-five years of age, rather fat, with a flat nose, and small, twinkling, black eyes, he presented an entirely hideous and semi-repulsive appearance. His dress consisted of a cotton blanket over which was thrown a tiger-skin kaross, and on his head was stuck an enormous old white felt hat, such as the Boers wear, and known as a "wilderbeeste chaser."

After we had been duly introduced, he retreated to his ox-hide, and we went and squatted down among the head men. Secocoeni took no active part in the proceedings that followed; he sat in his enclosure and occasionally shouted out some instructions to Makurupiji, who was literally his "mouth," speaking for him and making use of the pronoun "I." During the four hours or so that we were there Secocoeni never stopped chewing an intoxicating green leaf, very much resembling that of the pomegranate, of which he occasionally sent us some.

After the business of the Commission had come to an end, and some of our party started on their homeward journey, we were detained by Secocoeni, who wished to see us privately. He sent for us to his private enclosure, and we sat down on his ox-hide with him and one or two head men. It was very curious to see this wily old savage shoving a handful of leaves into his mouth, and giving his head a shake, and then making some shrewd remark which went straight to the bottom of whatever question was in hand. At length we bade Secocoeni good-bye, having promised to deliver all his respectful messages to our chief, and, thoroughly wearied, arrived at our own hut. Tired as we were, we thought it would be better to start for the fort at once, rather than risk the fever for another night. So we made up our minds to a long moonlight ride, and, saddling up, got out of Secocoeni's town about 3.30 P.M., having looked our last upon this beautiful fever-trap, which only wants water scenery to make it absolutely perfect. Half-way up, we saw the poor horse we had left sick the day before, lying dead, with dry foam all round his mouth, and half his skin taken off by some passing Basutu. A couple of hundred yards farther on we found another dying, left by the party who had started before us. It was in truth a valley of the shadow of death. Luckily our horses lasted us back to the fort, but one died there, and the other two are dead since.

Beautiful as was the scene by day, in the light of the full moon it was yet more surpassingly lovely. It was solemn, weird. Every valley became a mysterious deep, and every hill, stone, and tree shone with that cold pale lustre which the moon alone can throw. Silence reigned, the silence of the dead, broken only once or twice by the wild whistling challenge of one of Secocoeni's warriors as he came bounding down the rocks, to see who we were that passed. The effect of the fires by the huts, perched among the rocks at the entrance to the pass, was very strange and beautiful, reminding one of the midnight fires of the Gnomes in the fairy tales.

And so we rode on, hour after hour, through the night, till we well-nigh fell asleep in our saddles, and at length, about two o'clock in the morning, we reached the waggons to find the young Boers fast asleep in our bed. We kicked them out, and, after swallowing some biscuits, tumbled in ourselves for the few hours' rest which we so sadly needed.

On the following morning, Thursday, two of the party bade farewell to our hosts at the fort and started on one of the quickest possible treks, leaving our companion to proceed across country to the fort established by President Burgers, or "Porocororo," as the Basutus call him, at Steelport.

We returned to Middelburg by an entirely different route from that by which we came. Leaving the valley of the Olifants to our right, we trekked along the high-veldt, and thus avoided all the fever country. Roughly speaking, we had about 120 miles of country to get over to reach Middelburg, and we determined to do this in three days and two nights, so as to get in on the Saturday night, as we were much pressed for time. Now, according to English ideas, it is no great thing to travel 120 miles in three days; but it is six days' journey in an ox-waggon over bad country, and we were going to do it in half that time by doubling the speed.

Of course, to do this we had to trek night and day. For instance, on the first day we inspanned at 10.30 A.M. and trekked till within an hour of sundown; at sundown we inspanned, and with one outspan trekked till sunrise; outspanned for two hours, and on again, being seventeen and a half hours under the yoke out of the twenty-four, and covering fifty-five miles. Of course, one cannot do this sort of travelling for more than two or three days without killing the oxen; as it was, towards the end, as soon as the yokes were lifted off, the poor beasts dropped down as though they were shot, and most of them went lame. Another great disadvantage is that one suffers very much from want of sleep. The jolting of the springless machine, as it lumbered over rocks a foot high and through deep spruits or streams, brought our heads down with such a fearful jar on the saddle-bags that we used for pillows, that all sleep was soon knocked out of them; or, even if we were lucky enough to be crossing a stretch of tolerably smooth ground, there was a swaying motion that rubbed one's face up and down till the skin was nearly worn through, polishing the saddle-bags to such an extent that we might almost have used them for looking-glasses as well as pillows.

At Secocoeni's kraal we had engaged two boys to carry our packs as far as the fort, who, on their arrival, were so well satisfied with the way in which we treated them that they requested to be allowed to proceed with us. These young barbarians, who went respectively by the names of "Nojoke" and "Scowl," as being the nearest approach in English to their Sisutu names, were the greatest possible source of amusement to us, with their curious ways.[*] I never saw such fellows to sleep; it is a positive fact that Nojoke used frequently to take his rest coiled up like a boa constrictor in a box at the end of the waggon, in which box stood three iron pots with their sharp legs sticking up. On those legs he peacefully slumbered when the waggon was going over ground that prohibited our even stopping in it. "Scowl" was not a nice boy to look at, for his naked back was simply cut to pieces and covered with huge weals, of which everybody, doubtless, thought we were the cause. On inquiring how he came to get such a tremendous thrashing, it turned out that these Basutus have a custom of sending young men of a certain age[+] out in couples, each armed with a good "sjambok" (a whip cut from the hide of a sea-cow), to thrash one another till one gives in, and that it was in one of these encounters that the intelligent Scowl got so lacerated; but, as he remarked with a grin, "My back is nothing, the chiefs should see that of the other boy."

[*] *Of these two lads, Nojoke subsequently turned out worthless, and went to the Diamond Fields, whilst Scowl became an excellent servant, until he took to wearing a black coat, and turned Christian, when he shortly afterwards developed into a drunkard and a thief.*

[+] *The age of puberty.*

We spent one night at Middelburg, and next morning, bidding adieu to our kind English friends, started for Pretoria, taking care to end our first day's journey at a house where an Englishman lived, so as to ensure a clean shakedown. Here we discovered that the horse I was riding (the sole survivor of the five we had started with) had got the sickness, and so we had to leave him and hire another. This horse, by the by, recovered, which is the only instance of an animal's conquering the disease which has yet come under my observation. We hired the new horse from a Boer, who charged us exactly three times its proper price, and then preached us a sermon quite a quarter of an hour long on his hospitality, his kindness of heart, and his willingness to help strangers. I must tell you that, just as we were going to sleep the night before, a stranger had come and asked for a shakedown, which was given to him in the same room. We had risen before daybreak, and my companion was expatiating to me, in clear and forcible language, on the hypocrisy and scoundrelism of this Boer, when suddenly a sleepy voice out of the darkness murmured thickly, "I say, stranger, guess you shouldn't lose your temper; guess that 'ere Boer is acting after the manner of human natur'." And then the owner of the voice turned over and went to sleep again.

We had over sixty miles to ride that day, and it must have been about eight o'clock at night, on the sixteenth day of our journey, when we reached Pretoria and rode straight up to our camp, where we were heartily greeted. I am sure that some of our friends must have felt a little disappointed at seeing us arrive healthy and fat, without a sign of fever, after all their melancholy predictions. It would not have been "human natur'" if they had not. When we got to the camp, I called out to Masooku, my Zulu servant, to come and take the horses. Next moment I heard a rush and a scuttle in the tent like the scrimmage in a rabbit-burrow when one puts in the ferrets, and Masooku shouted out in Zulu, "He has come back! by Chaka's head, I swear it! It is his voice, his own voice, that calls me; my father's, my chief's!"

And so ended one of the hardest and most interesting journeys imaginable—a journey in which the risk only added to the pleasure. Still, I should not care to make it again at the same time of year.

VII. A ZULU WAR-DANCE

In all that world-wide empire which the spirit of the English colonisation has conquered from out of the realms of the distant and unknown, and added year by year to the English dominions, it is doubtful whether there be any one spot of corresponding area, presenting so many large questions, social and political, as the colony of Natal. Wrested some thirty years ago from the patriarchal Boers, and peopled by a few scattered scores of adventurous emigrants, Natal has with hard toil gained for itself a precarious foothold hardly yet to be called an existence. Known chiefly to the outside world as the sudden birthplace of those tremendous polemical missiles which battered so fiercely, some few years ago, against the walls of the English Church, it is now attracting attention to the shape and proportion of that unsolved riddle of the future, the Native Question. In those former days of rude and hand-to-mouth legislation, when the certain evil of the day had to be met and dealt with before the possible evil of the morrow, the seeds of great political trouble were planted in the young colony, seeds whose fruit is fast ripening before our eyes.

When the strong aggressive hand of England has grasped some fresh portion of the earth's surface, there is yet a spirit of justice in her heart and head which prompts the question, among the first of such demands, as to how best and most fairly to deal by the natives of the newly-acquired land. In earlier times, when steam was not, and telegraphs and special correspondents were equally unknown agencies for getting at the truth of things, this question was more easily answered across a width of dividing ocean or continent. Then distant action might be prompt and sharp on emergency, and no one would be the wiser. But of late years, owing to these results of civilisation, harsh measures have, by the mere pressure of public opinion, and without consideration of their necessity in the eyes of the colonists, been set aside as impracticable and inhuman. In the case of Natal, most of the early questions of possession and right were settled, sword in hand, by the pioneer Dutch, who, after a space of terrible warfare, drove back the Zulus over the Tugela, and finally took possession of the land. But they did not hold it long. The same hateful invading Englishman, with his new ideas and his higher forms of civilisation, who had caused them to quit the "Old Colony," the land of their birth, came and drove them, *vi et armis*, from the land of their adoption. And it was not long before these same English became lords of this red African soil, from the coast up to the Drakensberg. Still there were difficulties; for although the new-comers might be lords of the soil, there remained yet a remnant, and a very troublesome remnant, of its original and natural masters: shattered fragments of the Zulu power in Natal, men who had once swept over the country in the army of Chaka the Terrible, Chaka of the Short Spear, but who had remained behind in the fair new land, when Chaka's raids had been checked by the white man and his deadly weapons. Remnants, too, of conquered aboriginal tribes, who had found even Chaka's rule easier than that of their own chieftains, swelled the amount to a total of some 100,000 souls.

One of the first acts of the English Government, when it took up the reins, was to allot to each of these constituent fragments a large portion of the land. This might perhaps have been short-sighted legislation, but it arose from the necessity of the moment. According to even the then received ideas of colonisation and its duties, it was hardly possible—danger apart—to drive all the natives over the frontier, so they were allowed to stay and share the rights and privileges of British subjects. But the evil did not stop there. Ere long some political refugees, defeated in battle, fled before the avenging hand of the conqueror, and craved place and protection from the Government of Natal. It was granted; and the principle once established, body after body of men poured in: for, in stepping over the boundary line, they left the regions of ruin and terrible death, and entered those of peace, security, and plenty.

Thus it is that the native population of Natal, fed from within and without, has in thirty years increased enormously in number. Secluded from the outside world in his location, the native has lived in peace and watched his cattle grow upon a thousand hills. His wealth has become great and his wives many. He no longer dreads swift "death by order of the king," or by word of the witch-doctor. No "impi," or native regiment, can now sweep down on him and "eat him up," that is, carry off his cattle, put his kraal to the flames, and himself, his people, his wives, and children to the assegai. For the first time in the story of the great Kafir race, he can, when he rises in the morning, be sure that he will not sleep that night, stiff, in a bloody grave. He has tasted the blessings of peace and security, and what is the consequence? He has increased and multiplied until his numbers are as grains of sand on the sea-shore. Overlapping the borders of his location, he squats on private lands, he advances like a great tidal wave, he cries aloud for room, more room. This is the trouble which stares us in the face, looming larger and more distinct year by year; the great over-growing problem which thoughtful men fear must one day find a sudden and violent solution. Thus it comes to pass that there hangs low on the horizon of South Africa the dark cloud of the Native Question. How and when it will burst no man can pretend to say, but some time and in some way burst it must, unless means of dispersing it can be found.

There is now at work among the Kafir population the same motive power which has raised in turn all white nations, and, having built them up to a certain height, has then set to work to sap them until they have fallen—the power of civilisation. Hand in hand the missionary and the trader have penetrated the locations. The efforts of the teacher have met with but a partial success. "A Christian may be a good man in his way, but he is a Zulu spoiled," said Cetywayo, King of the Zulus, when arguing the question of Christianity with the Secretary for Native Affairs; and such is, not altogether wrongly, the general feeling of the natives. With the traders it has been different. Some have dealt honestly—and more, it is to be feared, dishonestly— not only with those with whom they have had dealings, but with their fellow-subjects and their Government. It is these men chiefly who have, in defiance of the law, supplied the natives with those two great modern elements of danger and destruction, the gin-bottle and the rifle. The first is as yet injurious only to the recipients, but it will surely react on those who have taught them its use; the danger of possessing the rifle may come home to us any day and at any moment.

Civilisation, it would seem, when applied to black races, produces effects diametrically opposite to those we are accustomed to observe in white nations: it debases before it can elevate; and as regards the Kafirs it is doubtful, and remains to be proved, whether it has much power to elevate them at all. Take the average Zulu warrior, and it will be found that, in his natural state, his vices are largely counter-balanced by his good qualities. In times of peace he is a simple, pastoral man, leading a good-humoured easy life with his wives and his cattle, perfectly indolent and perfectly happy. He is a kind husband and a kinder father; he never disowns his poor relations; his hospitality is extended alike to white and black; he is open in his dealings and faithful to his word, and his honesty is a proverb in the land. True, if war breaks out and the thirst for slaughter comes upon him, he turns into a different man. When the fierce savage spirit is once aroused, blood alone will cool it. But even then he has virtues. If he is cruel, he is brave in the battle; if he is reckless of the lives of others, he regards not his own; and when death comes, he meets it without fear, and goes to the spirits of his fathers boldly, as a warrior should. And now reverse the picture, and see him in the dawning light of that civilisation which, by intellect and by nature, he is some five centuries behind. See him, ignoring its hidden virtues, eagerly seize and graft its most prominent vices on to his own besetting sins. Behold him by degrees adding cunning to his cruelty, avarice to his love of possession, replacing his bravery by coarse bombast and insolence, and his truth by lies. Behold him inflaming all his passions with the maddening drink of the white man, and then follow him through many degrees of degradation until he falls into crime and ends in a jail. Such are, in only too many instances, the consequences of this partial civilisation, and they are not even counterbalanced, except in individual cases, by the attempt to learn the truths of a creed which he cannot, does not, pretend to understand. And if this be the result in the comparatively few individuals who have been brought under these influences, it may be fair to argue that it will differ only in degree, not in kind, when the same influences are brought to bear on the same material in corresponding proportions. Whatever may or may not be the effects of our partial civilisation when imperfectly and spasmodically applied to the vast native population of South Africa, one thing must, in course of time, result from it. The old customs, the old forms, the old feelings, must each in turn die away. The outer expression of these will die first, and it will not be long before the very memory of them will fade out of the barbaric heart. The rifle must replace, and, indeed, actually has replaced, the assegai and the shield, and portions of the cast-off uniforms of all the armies of Europe are to be seen where, until lately, the bronze-like form of the Kafir warrior went naked as on the day he was born. But so long as native customs and ceremonies still linger in some of the more distant locations, so long will they exercise a certain attraction for dwellers amid tamer scenes. It is therefore from a belief in the magnetism of contrast that the highly-civilised reader is invited to come to where he can still meet the barbarian face to face and witness that wild ceremony, half jest, half grim earnest—a Zulu war dance.

It was the good fortune of the writer of this sketch to find himself, some years ago, travelling through the up-country districts of Natal, in the company of certain high officials of the English Government. The journey dragged slowly enough by waggon, and some monotonous weeks had passed before we pitched our camp, one drizzling gusty night, on a high plateau, surrounded by still loftier hills. A wild and dismal place it looked in the growing dusk of an autumn evening, nor was it more suggestively cheerful when we rode away from it next morning in the sunshine, leaving the waggons to follow slowly. Our faces were set towards a great mountain, towering high above its fellows, called Pagadi's Kop—Pagadi being a powerful chief who had fled from the Zulus in the early days of the colony, and had ever since dwelt loyally and peacefully here in this wild place, beneath the protection of the Crown. Messengers had been duly sent to inform him that he was to receive the honour of a visit, for your true savage never likes to be taken by surprise. Other swift-footed runners had come back with the present of a goat, and the respectful answer, so Oriental in its phraseology, that "Pagadi was old, he was infirm, yet he would arise and come to greet his lords." Every mile or so of our slow progress a fresh messenger would spring up before us suddenly, as though he had started out of the earth at our feet, and prefixing his greeting with the royal salute, given with up-raised arm, "Bayete! Bayete!"—a salutation only accorded to Zulu royalty, to the governors of the different provinces, and to Sir T. Shepstone, the Secretary for Native Affairs—he would deliver his message or his news and fall into the rear. Presently came one saying, "Pagadi is very old and weak; Pagadi is weary; let his lords forgive him if he meet them not this day. To-morrow, when the sun is high, he will come to their place of encampment and greet his lords and hold festival before them. But let his lords, the white lords of all the land from the Great Mountain to the Black Water, go up to his kraal, and let them take the biggest hut and drink of the strongest beer. There his son, the chief that is to be, and all his wives, shall greet them; let his lords be honoured by Pagadi, through them." An acknowledgment was sent, and we still rode on, beginning the ascent of the formidable stronghold, on the flat top of which was placed the chief's kraal. A hard and stiff climb it was, up a bridle path with far more resemblance to a staircase than a road. But if the road was bad, the scenery and the vegetation were wild and beautiful in the extreme. Now we came to a deep "kloof" or cleft in the steep mountain-side, at the bottom of which, half hidden by the masses of ferns and rich rank greenery, trickled a little stream; now to an open space of rough ground, covered only with huge, weather-washed boulders. A little further on lay a Kafir mealie-garden, where the tall green stalks were fairly bent to the ground by the weight of the corn-laden heads, and beyond that, again, a park-like slope of grassy veldt. And ever, when we looked behind us, the vast undulating plain over which we had come stretched away in its mysterious silence, till it blended at length with the soft blue horizon.

At last, after much hard and steady climbing, we reached the top and stood upon a perfectly level space ten or twelve acres in extent, exactly in the centre of which was placed the chief's kraal. Before we dismounted we rode to the extreme western edge of the plateau, to look at one of the most perfectly lovely views it is possible to imagine. It was like coming face to face with great primeval Nature, not Nature as we civilised people know her, smiling in corn-fields, waving in well-ordered woods, but Nature as she was on the morrow of the Creation. There, to our left, cold and grey and grand, rose the great peak, flinging its dark shadow far beyond its base. Two thousand feet and more beneath us lay the valley of the Mooi river, with the broad tranquil stream flashing silver through its midst. Over against us rose another range of towering hills, with sudden openings in their blue depths through which could be seen the splendid distances of a champaign country. Immediately at our feet, and seeming to girdle the great gaunt peak, lay a deep valley, through which the Little Bushman's River forced its shining way. All around rose the great bush-clad hills, so green, so bright in the glorious streaming sunlight, and yet so awfully devoid of life, so solemnly silent. It was indeed a sight never to be forgotten, this wide panoramic out-look, with its towering hills, its smiling valleys, its flashing streams, its all-pervading sunlight, and its deep sad silence. But it was not always so lifeless and so still. Some few years ago those hills, those plains, those rivers were teeming each with their various creatures. But a short time since, and standing here at eventide, the traveller could have seen herds of elephants cooling themselves yonder after their day's travel, whilst the black-headed white-tusked sea-cow rose and plunged in the pool below. That bush-clad hill was the favourite haunt of droves of buffaloes and elands, and on that plain swarmed thousands upon thousands of springbok and of quagga, of hartebeest and of oribi. All alien life must cease before the white man, and so these wild denizens of forest, stream, and plain have passed away never to return.

Turning at length from the contemplation of a scene so new and so surprising, we entered the stockade of the kraal. These kraals consist of a stout outer palisade, and then, at some distance from the first, a second enclosure, between which the cattle are driven at night, or in case of danger. At the outer entrance we were met by the chief's eldest son, a finely-built man, who greeted us with much respect and conducted us through rows of huts to the dwelling-places of the chief's family, fenced off from the rest by a hedge of Tambouki grass. In the centre of these stood Pagadi's hut, which was larger and more finely woven and thatched than the rest. It is impossible to describe these huts better than by saying that they resemble enormous straw beehives of the old-fashioned pattern. In front of the hut were grouped a dozen or so of women clad in that airiest of costumes, a string of beads. They were Pagadi's wives, and ranged from the first shrivelled-up wife of his youth to the plump young damsel bought last month. The spokeswoman of the party, however, was not one of the wives, but a daughter of Pagadi's, a handsome girl, tall, and splendidly formed, with a finely-cut face. This prepossessing young lady entreated her lords to enter, which they did, in a very unlordly way, on their hands and knees. So soon as the eye became accustomed to the cool darkness of the hut, it was sufficiently interesting to notice the rude attempts at comfort with which it was set forth. The flooring, of a mixture of clay and cow-dung, looked exactly like black marble, so smooth and polished had it been made, and on its shining, level surface couches of buckskin and gay blankets were spread in an orderly fashion. Some little three-legged wooden sleeping-pillows and a few cooking-pots made up its sole furniture besides. In one corner rested a bundle of assegais and war-shields, and opposite the door were ranged several large calabashes full of "twala" or native beer. The chief's son and all the women followed us into the hut. The ladies sat themselves down demurely in a double row opposite to us, but the young chieftain crouched in a distant corner apart and played with his assegais. We partook of the beer and exchanged compliments, almost Oriental in their dignified courtesy, in the soft and liquid Zulu language, but not for long, for we still had far to ride. The stars were shining in southern glory before we reached the place of our night's encampment, and supper and bed were even more than usually welcome. There is a pleasure in the canvas-sheltered meal, in the after-pipe and evening talk of the things of the day that has been and those of the day to come, here, amid these wild surroundings, which is unfelt and unknown in scenes of greater comfort and higher civilisation. There is a sense of freshness and freedom in the wind-swept waggon-bed that is not to be exchanged for the softest couch in the most luxurious chamber. And when at length the morning comes, sweet in the scent of flowers, and glad in the voice of birds, it finds us ready to greet it, not hiding it from us with canopy and blind, as is the way of cities.

The scene of the coming spectacle of this bright new day lies spread before us, and certainly no spot could have been better chosen for dramatic effect. In front of the waggons is a large, flat, open space, backed by bold rising ground with jutting crags and dotted clumps of luxuriant vegetation. All around spreads the dense thorn-bush, allowing but of one way of approach, from the left. During the morning we could hear snatches of distant chants growing louder and louder as time wore on, and could catch glimpses of wild figures threading the thorns, warriors hastening to the meeting-place. All through the past night the farmers for miles around had been aroused by the loud insistent cries of the chief's messengers as they flitted far and wide, stopping but a moment wherever one of their tribe sojourned, and bidding him come, and bring plume and shield, for

Pagadi had need of him. This day, we may be sure, the herds are left untended, the mealie-heads ungathered, for the herdsmen and the reapers have come hither to answer to the summons of their chief. Little reck they whether it be for festival or war; he needs them, and has called them, and that is enough. Higher and higher rose the fitful distant chant, but no one could be seen. Suddenly there stood before us a creature, a woman, who, save for the colour of her skin, might have been the original of any one of Macbeth's "weird sisters." Little, withered, and bent nearly double by age, her activity was yet past comprehension. Clad in a strange jumble of snake-skins, feathers, furs, and bones, a forked wand in her outstretched hand, she rushed to and fro before the little group of white men. Her eyes gleamed like those of a hawk through her matted hair, and the genuineness of her frantic excitement was evident by the quivering flesh and working face, and the wild, spasmodic words she spoke. The spirit at least of her rapid utterances may thus be rendered:—

"Ou, ou, ou, ai, ai, ai. Oh, ye warriors that shall dance before the great ones of the earth, come! Oh, ye dyers of spears, ye plumed suckers of blood, come! I, the Isanusi, I, the witch-finder, I, the wise woman, I, the seer of strange sights, I, the reader of dark thoughts, call ye! Come, ye fierce ones; come, ye brave ones, come, and do honour to the white lords! Ah, I hear ye! Ah, I smell ye! Ah, I see ye; ye come, ye come!"

Hardly had her invocation trailed off into the "Ou, ou, ou, ai, ai, ai," with which it had opened, when there rushed over the edge of the hill, hard by, another figure scarcely less wild, but not so repulsive in appearance. This last was a finely-built warrior arrayed in the full panoply of savage war. With his right hand he grasped his spears, and on his left hung his large black ox-hide shield, lined on its inner side with spare assegais. From the "man's" ring round his head arose a single tall grey plume, robbed from the Kafir crane. His broad shoulders were bare, and beneath the arm-pits was fastened a short garment of strips of skin, intermixed with ox-tails of different colours. From his waist hung a rude kilt made chiefly of goat's hair, whilst round the calf of the right leg was fixed a short fringe of black ox-tails. As he stood before us with lifted weapon and outstretched shield, his plume bending to the breeze, and his savage aspect made more savage still by the graceful, statuesque pose, the dilated eye and warlike mould of the set features, as he stood there, an emblem and a type of the times and the things which are passing away, his feet resting on ground which he held on sufferance, and his hands grasping weapons impotent as a child's toy against those of the white man,—he who was the rightful lord of all,—what reflections did he not induce, what a moral did he not teach!

The warrior left us little time, however, for either reflections or deductions, for, striking his shield with his assegai, he rapidly poured forth this salutation:—

"Bayete, Bayete, O chief from the olden times, O lords and chief of chiefs! Pagadi, the son of Masingorano, the great chief, the leader of brave ones, the son of Ulubako, greets you. Pagadi is humble before you; he comes with warrior and with shield, but he comes to lay them at your feet. O father of chiefs, son of the great Queen over the water, is it permitted that Pagad' approach you? Ou, I see it is, your face is pleasant; Bayete, Bayete!"

He ends, and, saluting again, springs forward, and, flying hither and thither, chants the praises of his chief. "Pagadi," he says, "Pagad', chief and father of the Amocuna, is coming. Pagad', the brave in battle, the wise in council, the slayer of warriors; Pagad' who slew the tiger in the night time; Pagadi, the rich in cattle, the husband of many wives, the father of many children. Pagad' is coming, but not alone; he comes surrounded with his children, his warriors. He comes like a king at the head of his brave children. Pagadi's soldiers are coming; his soldiers who know well how to fight; his soldiers and his captains who make the hearts of brave men to sink down; his shakers of spears; his quaffers of blood. Pagad' and his soldiers are coming; tremble all ye, ou, ou, ou!"

As the last words die on his lips the air is filled with a deep, murmuring sound like distant thunder; it swells and rolls, and finally passes away to give place to the noise of the rushing of many feet. Over the brow of the hill dashes a compact body of warriors, running swiftly in lines of four, with their captain at their head, all clad in the same wild garb as the herald. Each bears a snow-white shield carried on the slant, and above each warrior's head rises a grey heron's plume. These are the advance-guard, formed of the "greys" or veteran troops. As they come into full view the shields heave and fall, and then from every throat bursts the war-song of the Zulus. Passing us swiftly, they take up their position in a double line on our right, and stand there solemnly chanting all the while. Another rush of feet, and another company flits over the hill towards us, but they bear coal-black shields, and the drooping plumes are black as night; they fall into position next the firstcomers, and take up the chant. Now they come faster and faster, but all through the same gap in the bush. The red shields, the dun shields, the mottled shields, the yellow shields, follow each other in quick but regular succession, till at length there stands before us a body of some five hundred men, presenting, in their savage dress, their various shields and flashing spears, as wild a spectacle as it is possible to conceive.

But it is not our eyes only that are astonished, for from each of those five hundred throats there swells a chant never to be forgotten. From company to company it passes, that wild, characteristic song, so touching in its simple grandeur, so expressive in its deep, pathetic volume. The white men who listened had heard the song of choirs ringing down resounding aisles, they had been thrilled by the roll of oratorios pealing in melody, beautiful and complex, through the grandest of man's theatres, but never till now had they heard music of voices so weird, so soft and yet so savage, so simple and yet so all-expressive of the fiercest passions known to the human heart. Hark! now it dies; lower and lower it sinks, it grows faint, despairing: "Why does he not come, our chief, our lord? Why does he not welcome his singers? Ah! see, they come, the heralds of our lord! our chief is coming to cheer his praisers, our chief is coming to lead his warriors." Again it rises and swells louder and louder, a song of victory and triumph. It rolls against the mountains, it beats against the ground: "He is coming, he is here, attended by his chosen. Now we shall go forth to slay; now shall we taste of the battle." Higher yet and higher, till at length the chief, Pagadi, swathed in war-garments of splendid furs, preceded by runners and accompanied by picked warriors, creeps slowly up. He is old and tottering, and of an unwieldy bulk. Two attendants support him, whilst a third bears his shield, and a fourth (oh bathos!) a cane-bottomed chair. One moment the old man stands and surveys his warriors and listens to the familiar war-cry. As he stands, his face is lit with the light of battle, the light of remembered days. The tottering figure straightens itself, the feeble hand becomes strong once more. With a shout, the old man shakes off his supporters and grasps his shield, and then, forgetting his weakness and his years, he rushes to his chieftain's place in the centre of his men. And as he comes the chant grows yet louder, the time yet faster, till it rises, and rings, and rolls, no longer a chant, but a war-cry, a paean of power. Pagadi stops and raises his hand, and the place is filled with a silence that may be felt. But not for long. The next moment five hundred shields are tossed aloft, five hundred spears flash in the sunshine, and with a sudden roar, forth springs the royal salute, "Bayete!"

The chief draws back and gives directions to his *indunas*, his thinkers, his wise ones, men distinguished from their fellows by the absence of shield and plume; the *indunas* pass on the orders to the captains, and at once the so-called dance begins. First they manoeuvre a little in absolute silence, and changing their position with wonderful precision and rapidity; but as their blood warms there comes a sound as of the hissing of ten thousand snakes, and they charge and charge again. A pause, and the company of "greys" on our right, throwing itself into open order, flits past us like so many vultures to precipitate itself with a wild, whistling cry on an opposing body which rushed to meet it. They join issue, they grapple; on them swoops another company, then another and another, until nothing is to be distinguished except a mass of wild faces heaving; of changing forms rolling and writhing, twisting and turning, and, to all appearances, killing and being killed, whilst the whole air is pervaded with a shrill, savage sibillation. It is not always the same cry; now it is the snorting of a troop of buffaloes, now the shriek of the eagle as he seizes his prey, anon the terrible cry of the "night-prowler," the lion, and now—more thrilling than all— the piercing wail of a woman. But whatever the cry, the cadence rises and falls in perfect time and unanimity; no two mix with one another so as to mar the effect of each.

Again the combatants draw back and pause, and then forth from the ranks springs a chosen warrior, and hurls himself on an imaginary foe. He darts hither and thither with wild activity, he bounds five feet into the air like a panther, he twists through the grass like a snake, and, finally, making a tremendous effort, he seems to slay his airy opponent, and sinks exhausted to the ground. The onlookers mark their approval or disapproval of the dancer's feats by the rising and falling of the strange whistling noise which, without the slightest apparent movement of face or lip, issues from each mouth. Warrior after warrior comes forth in turn from the ranks and does battle with his invisible foe, and receives his meed of applause. The last warrior to spring forward with a wild yell is the future chief, Pagadi's son and successor, our friend of yesterday. He stands, with his shield in one hand and his lifted battle-axe—borne by him alone—in the other, looking proudly around, and rattling his lion-claw necklets, whilst from every side bursts forth a storm of sibillating applause, not from the soldiers only, but from the old men, women, and children. Through all his fierce pantomimic dance it continues, and when he has ended it redoubles, then dies away, but only to burst out again and again with unquenchable enthusiasm.

In order, probably, to give the warriors a brief breathing space, another song is now set up, and it is marvellous the accuracy and knowledge of melody with which the parts are sung, like a glee of catch, the time being kept by a conductor, who rushes from rank to rank beating time with a wand. Yet it is hardly like chanting, rather like a weird, sobbing melody, with tones in it which range from the deepest bass to the shrillest treble. It ends in a long sigh, and then follows a scene, a tumult, a melee, which hardly admits of a description in words. The warriors engage in a mimic combat, once more they charge, retreat, conquer, and are defeated, all in turns. In front of them, exciting them to new exertions, with word and gesture, undulate in a graceful dance of their own the "intombis," the young beauties of the tribe, with green branches in their hands, and all their store of savage finery glittering on their shapely limbs. Some of these maidens are really handsome, and round them again dance the children, armed with mimic spears and shields. Wild as seems the confusion, through it all, even the moments of highest excitement, some sort of rough order is maintained; more, it would seem, by mutual sounds than by word of command or sense of discipline.

Even a Zulu warrior must, sooner or later, grow weary, and at length the signal is given for the dance to end. The companies are drawn up in order again, and receive the praise and thanks of those in whose honour they had been called together. To these compliments they reply in a novel and imposing fashion. At a given signal each man begins to softly tap his ox-hide shield with the handle of his spear, producing a sound somewhat resembling the murmur of the distant sea. By slow degrees it grows louder and louder, till at length it rolls and re-echoes from the hills like thunder, and comes to its conclusion with a fierce, quick rattle. This is the royal war-salute of the Zulus, and is but rarely to be heard. One more sonorous salute with voice and hand, and then the warriors disappear as they came, dropping swiftly and silently over the brow of the hill in companies. In a few moments no sign or vestige of dance or dancers remained, save, before our eyes, the well-trodden ground, a few lingering girls laden with large calabashes of beer, and in our ears some distant dying snatches of chants. The singers were on their joyful way to slay and devour the oxen provided as a stimulus and reward for them by their chief's liberality.

When the last dusky figure had topped the rising ground over which the homeward path lay, and had stood out for an instant against the flaming background of the western sun, and then dropped, as it were, back into its native darkness beyond those gates of fire, the old chief drew near. He had divested himself of his heavy war-dress, and sat down amicably amongst us.

"Ah," he said, taking the hand of Sir Theophilus Shepstone, and addressing him by his native name, "Ah! t'Sompseu, t'Sompseu, the seasons are many since first I held this your hand. Then we two were young, and life lay bright before us, and now you have grown great, and are growing grey, and I have grown very old! I have eaten the corn of my time, till only the cob is left for me to suck, and, *ow*, it is bitter. But it is well that I should grasp this your hand once more, oh, holder of the Spirit of Chaka,[*] before I sit down and sleep with my fathers. *Ow*, I am glad."

> [*] *The reader must bear in mind that the Zulu warrior is buried sitting and in full war-dress. Chaka, or T'chaka, was the founder of the Zulu power.*

Imposing as was this old-time war-dance, it is not difficult to imagine the heights to which its savage grandeur must have swelled when it was held—as was the custom at each new year—at the kraal of Cetywayo, King of the Zulus. Then 30,000 warriors took part in it, and a tragic interest was added to the fierce spectacle by the slaughter of many men. It was, in fact, a great political opportunity for getting rid of the "irreconcilable" element from council and field. Then, in the moment of wildest enthusiasm, the witch-finder darted forward and lightly touched with a switch some doomed man, sitting, it may be, quietly among the spectators, or capering with his fellow-soldiers. Instantly he was led away, and his place knew him no more.

Throughout the whole performance there was one remarkable and genuine feature, the strong personal attachment of each member of the tribe to its chief—not only to the fine old chief, Pagadi, their leader in former years, but to the head and leader for the years to come.

It must be remembered that this system of chieftainship and its attendant law is, to all the social bearings of South African native life, what the tree is to its branches; it has grown through long, long ages amid a people slow to forget old traditions, and equally slow to receive new ideas; dependent on it are all the native's customs, all his keen ideas of right and justice; in it lies embodied his history of the past, and from it springs his hope for the future. Surely even the most uncompromising of those marching under the banner of civilisation must hesitate before they condemn this deep-rooted system to instant uprootal.[*] The various influences of the white man have eaten into the native system as rust into iron, and their action will never cease till all be destroyed. The bulwarks of barbarism, its minor customs and minor laws, are gone, or exist only in name; but its two great principles, polygamy and chieftainship, yet flourish and are strong. Time will undo his work, and find for these also a place among forgotten things. And it is the undoubted duty of us English, who absorb people and territories in the high name of civilisation, to be true to our principles and our aim, and aid the great destroyer by any and every safe and justifiable means. But between the legitimate means and the rash, miscalculating uprootal of customs and principles, which are not the less venerable and good in their way because they do not accord with our own present ideas, there is a great gulf fixed. Such an uprootal might precipitate an outburst of the very evils it aims at destroying.

[*] *I do not wish the remarks in this paper, which was written some years ago, to be taken as representing my present views on the Natal native question, formed after a longer and more intimate acquaintance with its peculiarities, for which I beg to refer the reader to the chapter on Natal. – Author.*

What the ultimate effect of our policy will be, when the leaven has leavened the whole, when the floodgates are lifted, and this vast native population (which, contrary to all ordinary precedent, does *not* melt away before the sun of the white man's power) is let loose in its indolent thousands, unrestrained, save by the bonds of civilised law, who can presume to say? But this is not for present consideration. Subject to due precautions, the path of progress must of necessity be followed, and the results of such following left in the balancing hands of Fate and the future.